D0742918

COA

The World of

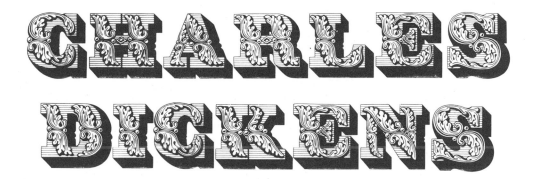
CHARLES
DICKENS

Angus Wilson

Martin Secker & Warburg

PR
4581
W52

This book was designed and produced by

George Rainbird Limited,
Marble Arch House,
44 Edgware Road,
London, W.2

First published in England 1970 by

Martin Secker & Warburg Limited,
14 Carlisle Street,
Soho Square,
London, W1V 6NN

First printing March 1970
Second printing November 1970

Colour originated and printed by
Westerham Press, Westerham, Kent, England
Text filmset in Century by
Jolly & Barber, Rugby, Warwickshire, England
Book printed and bound by
Butler & Tanner, Frome, Somerset, England

House editor: Caroline Lightburn
Designer: Pauline Harrison
Indexer: H. V. Molesworth Roberts

SBN: 436 57513 2

© Angus Wilson 1970

All rights reserved
No part of this publication may be
reproduced, stored in a retrieval system
or transmitted, in any form or by any means,
electronic, mechanical, photocopying, recording
or otherwise, without the prior permission of
Martin Secker & Warburg Limited

For
Betty, Charles and Neville Blackburn

Acknowledgments

It is quite impossible adequately to express my gratitude to my friends Madeline House, editor of the Pilgrim Edition of *The Letters of Charles Dickens*, and Michael Slater, editor of *The Dickensian*, for reading the typescript of this book at very short notice and making very many most valuable suggestions for its improvement – all the faults, of course, are mine. To Sir Francis Meynell I am very grateful for lending me his copy of the Nonesuch Edition of the *Letters*, on which, for events after 1839, I have heavily relied. For events before that date I have made use of the splendid first volume of the Pilgrim Edition. Anyone outlining Dickens's life must depend greatly, as I have, upon Forster's *Life*, which I have consulted in the two-volume Dent edition of 1966, and on Edgar Johnson's two-volume *Life* of 1953. Professor Fielding's 1960 edition of Dickens's *Speeches* has been invaluable to me. The vast and ever-increasing mass of literature both biographical and critical is impossible to detail here; I can only hope that my familiarity with it will be apparent in the following pages. For an extraordinarily comprehensive survey of all this literature down to 1960, with splendidly lucid comment, readers are referred to Professor Ada Nisbet's contribution on Dickens in *Victorian Fiction: A Guide to Research*, 1964, edited by Lionel Stevenson. I shall make mention of only one detailed work here, Professor Collins's *Dickens and Education*, 1963; and that not only because of the intrinsic fascination which it shares with other works not mentioned here, but because its comprehensive nature made me feel free to omit all but a brief reference to this central interest of Dickens's social concerns. For absorbing study of Dickens's methods of composition the reader is referred to *Dickens at Work* by John Butt and Kathleen Tillotson, 1957. To my friend John Lehmann I am most grateful for his permission to quote from his grandfather's letter in *Ancestors and Friends*.

Some of the critical ideas in this book have come to me as a result of stimulating discussion in seminars at the University of East Anglia. And finally, of course, the pages of *The Dickensian* over its long years of publication are an extraordinary mine of the unexpected and the relevant.

Angus Wilson

Contents

Colour Plates

Preface

CHARLES DICKENS was born on 7 February 1812 in a small lower-middle-class terrace house in Portsmouth, a busy seaport situated almost in the centre of England's southern coast. He died a hundred years ago on 9 June 1870 near the cathedral town of Rochester, Kent, some thirty miles south-east of London, at his small country house, Gad's Hill Place, a property which, like most properties belonging to the well-to-do professional upper middle class, he had much and at some cost improved.

He was social critic, active philanthropist, literary editor, journalist, public speaker, talented actor, keen traveller, long-distance walker – by day with boon companions, often, as the years went by, at night alone – amateur but serious criminologist, amateur but less serious conjurer, hypnotist, devoted organizer of convivial social occasions and boisterous participant in them when the guests were children or old friends, particularly at Christmas time and, above all, on Twelfth Night. His deep vein of benevolence was only slightly seamed both publicly and privately by a capacity for occasional relentless quarrelling pursued with a masterful implacability. He stood to a vast section of the Victorian public both at home and abroad as a symbol for household happiness. Many circumstances that mar this domestic picture for us were not generally known during his lifetime nor indeed until more than fifty years after his death; but even in his own day the image was sadly although not deeply tarnished for some of his friends and readers by his public separation from his wife in 1858 after twenty-two years of marriage. The strange contrast between the penury and distress of his late childhood and the prosperity and outwardly high-spirited success of his adult life was only revealed to the public after his death by the friend in whom he had confided his history. The intense ardours and desperate miseries of his relationships with the women he fell in love with were, of course, not generally known until long after his death, indeed will probably never be known enough to put an end to romantic conjecture. He was a dutiful, strongly critical son to insufficient parents, and a loving, dutiful and sometimes harshly critical parent to children he found largely unsatisfactory as they grew up. Above all, he was a devout and practising Christian, however much sectarians of all denominations raised and still raise their eyebrows at his kind of Christianity.

In his Public Life, (so wide in scope and reputation that it can only be spelled with capitals) and in his private life, he engaged with a formidable energy that aged him prematurely; by temperament he was given both to hilarious gaiety and to long, brooding, even occasionally desperate depressions. He both worked and played harder than his body could afford.

Such a life, with the contradictions and strangenesses it inevitably involved, makes Dickens a very interesting man. But there have been and are innumerable highly successful men with hidden private lives, unstable temperaments, abnormal energies and complex, contradictory views about life's meaning. What distinguishes Dickens from them is his literary genius and his lifelong devotion to his art. What matters about his public and private life is the way in which they both fed his great novels; what matters about his opinions is their relation to, sometimes their conflict with, the meaning of his fiction. The world we have inherited is the imaginative world of Charles Dickens. His novels were great works of art and entertainment – Dickens would not have separated the two and nor need we. Each novel exists as a world of its own, to be judged separately. But also, however purist critics may object, as with all great artists the life of these individual works blends and fuses into a complete whole – the World of Charles Dickens. It is as a guide to exploring this Dickens imaginative system — both the various novels which are its planets and the whole marvellous group as it revolves around him – that this account of his life has been written.

Chapter I
Childhood 1812–22

 I know it's coming! O! the Mask! To hear such a cry from a young child awaking from a nightmare would disturb any fond parents; it would probably as much surprise them. But then the child that spoke these unusual words was a very unusual child.

Toys are the first food on which our fancy is nourished. Dickens was much interested in the growth of his own imagination, and in 1850, when he was thirty-eight, he wrote a detailed account of his memories of his own first toys, in the form of a vision of a Christmas Tree.

I look into my youngest Christmas recollections! All toys at first, I find. Up yonder, among the green holly and red berries, is the Tumbler with his hands in his pockets who wouldn't lie down, but whenever he was put upon the floor, persisted in rolling his fat body about, until he rolled himself still, and brought those lobster eyes of his to bear upon me – when I affected to laugh very much, but in my heart of hearts was extremely doubtful of him. Close beside him is that infernal snuff-box, out of which there sprang a demoniacal Counsellor in a black gown, with an obnoxious head of hair, and a red cloth mouth, wide open, who was not to be endured on any terms, but could not be put away either; for he used suddenly, in a highly magnified state, to fly out of Mammoth Snuff-Boxes in dreams, when least expected. Nor is the frog with cobbler's wax on his tail, far off; for there was no knowing where he wouldn't jump; and when he flew over the candle, and came upon one's hand with that spotted back – red on a green ground – he was horrible. The cardboard lady . . . was milder and was beautiful; but I can't say as much for the larger cardboard man, who used to be hung against the wall and pulled by a string; there was a sinister expression in that nose of his; and when he got his legs round his neck (which he very often did), he was ghastly, and not a creature to be alone with.

When did that dreadful Mask first look at me? Who put it on, and why was I so frightened that the sight of it is an era in my life? It is not a hideous visage in itself; it is even meant to be droll; why then were its stolid features so intolerable? Surely not because it hid the wearer's face. An apron would have done as much; and though I should have preferred even the apron away; it would not have been absolutely insupportable, like the Mask. Was it the immovability of the Mask? . . . Perhaps that fixed and set change coming over a real face, infused into my quickened heart some remote suggestion and dread of the universal change that is to come on every face, and make it still? Nothing reconciled me to it . . . . Nor was it any satisfaction to be shown the Mask, and see that it was made of paper, and to have it locked up and be assured that no one wore it. The mere recollection of that fixed face, the mere knowledge of its existence anywhere, was sufficient to awaken me in the night all perspiration and horror, with, 'O! I know it's coming! O! the Mask!'

Memory is selective; and so it is not surprising that these childhood toys which Charles Dickens recalls when he was nearing forty should have so close a link with some of the adult obsessions of his books. The Tumbler ushers in his many circus and showground folk and the demoniacal Counsellor prepares us for those sinister figures – Fagin, the merry old gentleman; the playful demon, Quilp, breathing fire and brimstone; the Mephistolean murderer and self-styled gentleman, Rigaud, of *Little Dorrit* – who carry out the Devil's work in Dickens's world with cruel glee and dressed quite openly in three different traditional guises of their Master. As to the cardboard gentleman whose appearance with his legs round his neck was so ghastly, I don't think it fanciful to suggest that he was the first of those men hung by the neck until they were dead – murderers and suicides – whose dreadful end so much obsessed Dickens both in his life and in his novels. The Mask above all, though it speaks for the theatre and theatre people, who were at the centre of much of Dickens's delight in life from his nursery years until his death, also speaks for the self-deception, the deception of others, the hypocrisy, the play-acting both hilarious and sinister that so often makes Dickens's imaginative world a place fraught with anxiety, since so many

THE HUMORS OF A COUNTRY FAIR

An early nineteenth-century fair, showing the touring actors and side-shows including Ham Shoo, 'who vill eat a Hogshead of Burning Pitch'.

of those in it, those indeed who dominate the scene, are not what they appear.

Excessive symbol-seeking is the vice of many otherwise valuable modern critics of Dickens's novels, understandably carried away by the closeness of the author himself to the primitive sources of story-telling, to legend and to myth. Nevertheless it does not seem unreasonable to say that if one had to choose a single symbol to represent the rich, varied life of Dickens's novels, there would not be a better one than the Mask. Indeed, all the toys I have detailed relate so closely to central themes of his life and work, that I am happy to concede to the sceptical the frog, whose only appearance in the works is as the Expiring Frog to which Mrs Leo Hunter addressed her famous ode in *Pickwick Papers*.

What also strikes the reader of the passage I have quoted is the degree to which the remembered toys are associated with uncertainty and fear. This mixture of play and terror – cliché perhaps to the modern parent, who is learned in child psychology, but not to the Victorians – is central to the whole of Dickens's world of fancy; indeed, for me it makes insoluble, even pointless, the constant controversy between those critics and readers who champion Dickens the laughter-maker, those (so numerous in our day) who espouse the cause of Dickens the spine-chiller, and those (so few today, so many in the days of Little Nell) who give their allegiance to Dickens the tear-jerker. Dickens is all of these, and all of them with genius, and, what is more, very often at least two of them at the same time. Above all, his world is never quite out of the shadow of Death; indeed some of its brightest, funniest scenes get their humour and their pathos from a constant sense of mortality. Not that the shadow (as

Herman Bras, a Prussian youth weighing over 500 lb. and (right) Simon Paap, the celebrated Dutch Dwarf.

befits a Christian author) is by any means always seen as a grim thing. That he should speculate upon whether his childhood alarm at the stillness of the Mask may have been some premonition of the nature of Death is absolutely characteristic of the creator of Little Nell, Paul Dombey, Tiny Tim and Jo, the crossing-sweeping boy. Indeed the passage contains in little the essence of Dickens's world – its delight charged with terror (and – for this reversible quality is one of the secrets of his world – the terror charged with delight): its reality threatened by deception; its childhood ringed by mortality; its absurd, hilarious fancies proposed with gravity.

But the manner as well as the content of this small passage may also offer a useful clue to much that seems to me to be misunderstood both about his life and his work. The passage I have quoted appears in *The Christmas Tree*, his Christmas article for 1850 in the magazine *Household Words*, which he edited.

The cardboard man: 'When he got his legs round his neck he was ghastly.'

The Christmas articles and stories, successors of the Christmas Books of which the first had been the famous *Christmas Carol* of 1843, were a yearly high point in Dickens's relations with his tens of thousands of readers – and it would hardly be too much to say that Dickens's relations with his readers were for him the high point of his life – what Mrs Tillotson has called 'the most interesting love-affair of his life'. Here in these Christmas articles and stories he communicated with his wider family, seated before their thousand festive logs, digesting their thousand turkeys and plum puddings. Christmas in his own home, with his own family, was a peak celebration of high spirits and good will for Dickens; but the wider family of his readers had an ideal meaning for him that was absent from flesh and blood – from a father given to petty borrowing, from children given to making the house noisy when he was at work – dutiful and loving son and father though he was.

Opposite. Through his special stories Christmas became the annual high point in Dickens's relations with his readers.

George Cruikshank

'When did that dreadful Mask first look at me? Who put it on, and why was I so frightened?'

The tone, then, of these Christmas articles could be completely intimate and personal, as here. It tells of a father's Christmas delights when he was a child and confesses that the father had also been weak, that he had been afraid. But it tells of his childhood fears with a calm, rational concern for their cause – was it the stillness of the Mask that was frightening? Did that fear come from some childish intuition of the nature of Death? It is concerned to be serious about a child's fears, but it is also concerned to get them into proportion, to use exaggeration to ridicule them a little. There is a kind of tender mockery of his childhood self in the parodied Gothic 'O! I know it's coming! O! the Mask!' This is not just the tiny child in bed afraid; it is also Dickens, who has known ham stage melodrama, laughing a little. No child ever awoke from a sweaty nightmare with exactly those stylized words outside of the boards of the popular Early Victorian theatre. But Dickens is only laughing a little, he was always a moralist, and never more so than at Christmas. His favourite moral was that in an increasingly utilitarian, industrial world we needed to cultivate the imagination, the fancy of childhood; this was a great part of his interpretation of 'Except ye . . . become as little children', a text like all Christ's words of great importance to him. So here he is communicating with the children of all ages among this readers, who know what fear means. At the same time he is giving support to the parents, the adults of all ages among his readers, who are concerned to reason away those childish fears. But, above all, he is concerned to wake up, to bring to life the child *in* the parents so that his adult readers may once again recapture their own first toy times.

This is the tone of much of Dickens's writing – intuitive at one level, rational and didactic at the next, but finally imparting the lesson, that only the intuitive life can make a deadened, materialistic world flower again. His ordinary readers no doubt responded to it directly and unconsciously in his lifetime. It is not easy for us to do so. We do not expect such a mixture of artistry, clowning and propaganda, such a web of sharp observations, shrewd comment, uncontrolled hamming and profound insight. It is hard for us to accept it, harder perhaps for the trained literary critic and the scholar, who necessarily seek clear shapes and patterns, than it is for the general reader who is less disturbed by being asked for a mixed response. With the discovery by the highly educated in the last thirty years that Dickens, with his extraordinary intuition, leaps the century and speaks to our fears, our violence, our trust in the absurd, more than any other English Victorian writer, there has been a flood of fascinating new interpretation of his work, sometimes wilfully and exaggeratedly Freudian, Jungian or Marxist, more often valuably discerning. But the rediscovery of this intuitive Dickens, this laughing, crying child inside the bearded public man in a frock coat, has inevitably been one-sided. Now that the intellectuals have had their say in giving us the frenzied, prophetic Dickens, the more patient scholars have begun to point out that Dickens was neither a divine half-wit nor a dancing dervish; and he was not an inspired seer. Histrionic he was, excitable enough at various times for public rumour to declare him mad; but he held the madman with a will of iron. As these scholars have shown by quotation from his public speeches, his journalism, his letters, he was a man with a high sense of public responsibility, impatient of checks, it is true, but always a radical liberal seeking constantly to humanize the social progress in which, despite all the doubts and setbacks, he resolutely tried to be a hopeful believer. 'Manly', 'frank', 'earnest', were the Victorian adjectives of praise in which Dickens believed, and he always tried to practise these virtues.

Surely both intellectuals and scholars are right – the perpetual child with a strange, sensitive, ludicrous apprehension of life co-existed with the parent, active, impatient, competent, witty, compassionate reformer and man of the world. Throughout his life the balance proved often very hard to maintain. The exceptional tension evidenced in the passage about the fearful Mask and the ghastly cardboard man is what immediately strikes the reader – although we should remember that the Victorians did not make our demand (surely an innately absurd demand) for a nursery without any tensions. What were the circumstances of Dickens's childhood, as far as we know them, that made for this unusual morbid tension so fruitful in his future work?

Family

Charles Dickens's father, John, was a clerk in the Navy Pay Office. He was about twenty-six when his son was born. He had been married in 1809 to the eighteen-year-old Elizabeth Barrow, whose father, Charles Barrow, was Chief Conductor of Moneys in the Navy Pay Office, a position of considerable financial responsibility. Detailed genealogies of both the Dickens and the Barrow families have been compiled, but the ancestors remain mere names, and no picture of heredity could possibly be assembled from them. Charles Dickens would surely have been glad of this; although in his early middle age he bitterly attacked the coarse pretensions of self-made men like Mr Bounderby of *Hard Times,* his own life was a supreme example of the Victorian success story, above all of the Victorian virtue of self-reliance. The whole of the first chapter of *Martin Chuzzlewit* indeed is given up to mockery of concern with ancestors and family trees. A man, for Dickens, is himself and himself alone.

Yet, however little he liked status derived from forbears, as an English Victorian middle-class man he could not altogether escape concern for class and gentility. The Regency period in which he grew up saw the last public

Elizabeth and John Dickens.

flauntings of aristocratic contempt for the middle classes. The days of the previous century when the middle-class heroines of Samuel Richardson – Clarissa Harlowe and Harriet Byron, or the later heroines of Fanny Burney's novels, Evelina and Cecilia – had reason to fear not only insulting overtures but abduction by aristocratic rakes, were gone forever; Jane Austen's Elizabeth Bennet had already demonstrated to aristocratic arrogance in the person of Lady Catherine de Bourgh that times were changing and that patronage was no longer sufferable; but when Dickens was young, as his early novels and sketches show, the flashier part of the aristocracy had still not given up the marauding, aggressive public manners of the eighteenth-century rakes and dandies. As Miss Petowker in *Nicholas Nickleby* says: 'There's something in his appearance quite . . . dear, dear what's that word again? . . . What do you call it when lords break off door knockers and beat policemen, and play at coaches with other people's money, and all that sort of thing? . . . Ah! aristocratic.'

Kate Nickleby, resisting with womanly pride Sir Mulberry Hawk's drunken passes, her brother Nicholas, challenging with manly courage his sister's would-be seducer, are striking a blow for the middle classes of gentle birth against the last, clumsy assaults of aristocratic insolence. The melodramatic language of the scenes suggests that they come more from the stage than from life; nevertheless for the reader of *Nicholas Nickleby*, published in 1839, they obviously still had a contemporary truth. As time went by this concern for class status diminished, although Dickens was never wholly immune from the English vice of snobbery – there was talk of his father's Staffordshire ancestors and the sad use in later life of a sham crest for a book-plate. But when he became a fully established world-wide public figure he could follow his own inclination and claim status for himself that was entirely his own, the result of his own manly independence.

As a rising young man, however, the need for assertion of gentility is still

The aristocracy had still not given up marauding, aggressive public manners.

with him both in his letters and in his novels (Mr Pickwick is nothing if not an independent gentleman of means; Kate and Nicholas Nickleby are to command our sympathy from being newly poor gentlefolk; Oliver Twist is of gentle birth). This emphasis on gentility was surely what he carried from his home, and the class-consciousness would have been the more acute because the Dickens family only just qualified for this status. In this social respect Charles Dickens was born on the outer edge of the world he wished to belong to. We may believe an early acquaintance of the Dickens family, who speaks of 'more than a ghost of gentility hovering in their company'.

The financial ups and downs of his expansive, impecunious father, even before the inevitable crash, must have made the assertions of gentility more strident. Such an atmosphere of social tightrope acrobatics would be sufficient in itself to have produced the nervous tension we have noted in these earliest memories of his toys: the terror of the Mask. Children respond to financial anxiety as they do to marital bickering long before they can comprehend its meaning. But there was more reason for uncertainty about the family social status than the wavering financial fortunes of Mr and Mrs John Dickens. On both sides of the family there were skeletons in the cupboards, although they were skeletons of very different kinds.

In the first place there lived in retirement in Oxford Street in London his grandmother Dickens, a respectable old lady with a sufficient income from savings. But, though respectable, she was a retired domestic servant. Admittedly her service had been with the highest in the land – originally a maid at the London house of the Marquis of Blandford, and, before her honourable retirement, housekeeper to the great Marquis of Crewe. Dickens's grandfather, indeed, dead long before his birth, had been the Crewe butler. It is true, no doubt, that if one had asked a member of the great Crewe family about the Dickenses, they would have spoken with high regard for the old lady who had been in their service and laughed at the social pretensions of the butler's son, more especially since John Dickens was known to them as a black sheep who had pestered his old mother for loans. But that was not at all likely to be how John Dickens saw it, although it had been the Crewe interest that had procured him his post at the Navy Pay Office. Domestic service and government service were not easily announced together, even though they each depended upon the same patronage. Now, in addition, he was married to the daughter of the Head of the Moneys Section of his own department; his wife's family had many genteel connections, her brothers were rising young professional gentlemen. The below-stairs Dickens ancestry seems to have been conveniently soft-pedalled – and this is significant, when we are considering the childhood atmosphere of Dickens's home, for it must have involved at least some very conscious suppression of his father's childhood memories, since he had passed that childhood below stairs.

No doubt much of this was done with an eye to the Barrow genteel connections, yet, in fact, Mrs Dickens had a more disturbing skeleton in her cupboard. Charles Barrow, her father, the honoured, the impressive Head of the Moneys Section, who had risen so rapidly (some said through illegitimate connection with the aristocracy), was found to have been systematically falsifying his accounts for nine years. During this period he had embezzled nearly £6,000. This scandalous discovery was made two years before Charles Dickens was born. Threatened with legal proceedings Charles Barrow fled abroad, eventually dying in the Isle of Man (outside English legal jurisdiction) in 1826, when Dickens was fourteen years old. It seems hard to believe that this outlaw beyond the seas did not trouble the social status of the Dickens household, although one is glad to note, to the credit of the English public service, that it did not affect John Dickens's position in the Navy Office nor that of his brother-in-law Thomas, the fugitive's son; nor, however the disgrace may have embarrassed them, did it prevent the young parents from naming Charles after his errant grandfather.

Nevertheless, just as social status demanded some suppression of his paternal grandmother, legal outlawry surely must have produced some

The below-stairs Dickens ancestry seems to have been conveniently soft-pedalled.

cloaked, mysterious references to his absent maternal grandfather. At the least where a young couple were naturally so sociable as Charles Dickens's parents, there must have been an acceptance of white lies: 'my country child-hood on the Crewe estate', 'my father who lives abroad'. Mystery and false-seeming are so often thought to be mere melodramatic apparatus in Dickens's novels, but they must have been accepted social facts of his childhood.

Loyalty of domestic service, of course, is a staple virtue in Dickens's novels, from Sam Weller onwards (and, indeed, he valued it greatly in his private life). But domestic servants in his novels seldom cross the class barrier. An impor-tant exception is the marriage of the well-to-do young man about town, Mr Toots, with Susan Nipper, Florence Dombey's Cockney maid. True, Susan is the Susanna, the comic soubrette of *Dombey and Son*, and Mr Toots is the divine idiot; nevertheless they are both transparently on the side of the angels, and Susan Nipper is intended to be, in every sense that honour demands, what her husband calls her, 'a very remarkable woman'. But this insistence that character, honesty and loyalty may suffice to unlock the green baize door that leads from the servants' hall into the drawing room is, like the rest of the resolution of *Dombey and Son*, half in the world of fairy story, where Susan Toots can be the accepted social equal and the friend of her former mistress, Mrs Gay (née Florence Dombey), and also still remain in some undetermined sense (at any rate in that most important of all Dickensian senses – at heart) her own darling Miss Floy's loyal maid, Nipper.

As to his grandfather beyond the seas, I cannot but think that the tension of the scandal hanging around his childhood home must have been felt by the sensitive child. Flight overseas for suspected felons, bankrupts and, indeed, any persons visited with moral or social disgrace, was a commonplace of Victorian life and fiction (Calais, Boulogne, Cherbourg must have teemed with these involuntary exiles). Too much stress, therefore, need not be laid upon the number of characters in Dickens's novels who escape overseas; these are largely plot mechanisms, although it is notable that the device diminished as Dickens grew older and his grandfather's disgrace vanished into the past. More important, I think, are two situations which are always charged with heightened atmosphere in his novels. The first is the menace that forever surrounds the lives of the respectable from the very existence of a criminal friend or relative at large – this is the fate of Mrs Rudge, the dark secret of David Copperfield's aunt, Betsy Trotwood, the strange tension of Mrs Clen-nam's tomblike home in *Little Dorrit*, the central situation of *Great Expecta-tions*. The other is the extraordinary vividness of two fictional scenes – early and late in his career – of foiled attempts by criminals to get away from England's shores. The first is the brilliant 'Anwerks package' scene in *Martin Chuzzlewit* (1843) when Jonas Chuzzlewit, the murderer, is turned back as he boards ship for the Low Countries by a note from Nadgett, the relentless detective. The other is the climax of *Great Expectations* (1860), the dramatic police interception of the illegally returned transported convict Magwitch's attempt to get to the Continent and, at long last, to liberty. Both these scenes have a detail of circumstance, a power of apprehension, and, particularly with

Jonas Chuzzlewit's foiled escape, a sort of hopeless *déjà vu* quality that suggests to me the feeding of fiction by an often-told story.

If it is argued that all these fictional incidents – Rudge, Miss Trotwood's skeleton husband, Flintwitch's mysterious twin brother, the foiled murderer, Jonas, the foiled convict, Magwitch – are too melodramatic to connect with life, I think that this is to fail to understand how heightened and dramatic the often-rehearsed stories of family events become. And the Dickens household must surely have been an intensely histrionic one. The chief features of Dickens's parents as they are transformed into his fiction is self-dramatization. What little we know of Dickens's parents in life backs up this fictional picture. John Dickens is recalled so often by his orotund, stagey phrases; one of Dickens's own references to Elizabeth Dickens in her senile old age speaks of her desire to be got up in sables 'like a female Hamlet'. They were a lively couple and had equally lively children. Dickens himself had high spirits that, as we shall see, strayed on occasions into hysteria. His favourite brother, Fred, was famous for his imitations. Together on holiday at Broadstairs in 1842 Charles and Fred are recorded as maintaining a continuous, mock technical exchange when sailing – 'Brail up your capstan-bar', 'Sheepshank your mizzen', etc. Fred and the youngest brother, Augustus, took prominent parts in the amateur theatrical productions which were Dickens's delight. Dickens's elder sister, Fanny, was his companion when as children they entertained the company with duets and recitations. As to melodrama, the subsequent careers of Dickens's brothers, Fred and Augustus, mixtures of financial disaster and marital storms, must have given full opportunity for the continuation of the Micawber tradition set by the parents. The Crummles family with their treatment of the smallest daily domestic incident as though it was part of their stage performance – did not Mrs Crummles introduce dinner with: 'Let the mutton and onion sauce appear!'? – surely reflects something of the Dickens family in the matter of home dramatics. Indeed it is tempting to see in Mr Crummles's eulogies upon the genius of his daughter, the Infant Phenomenon, something of what no doubt were John Dickens's boasts of his son when fame had made him the Inimitable Boz. Enough perhaps has been said to suggest that the tensions, the terrors, the high spirits and the dramatic facility were with Charles Dickens from a very early age; or that, if they were not, he certainly looked back at thirty-seven and thought that they had been.

Dickens was only seven months old when financial pressures forced his parents to leave their better home, where he was born, for something cheaper – a pattern of change that was always to mark his life under his parents' many roofs. It is possible that the toys belong, some of them, to Portsmouth, which he afterwards claimed faintly to remember. But in 1814, some months after his second birthday, his father was appointed to a London post. It is ironical that Dickens, who has celebrated London eternally, as Balzac Paris, or Dostoevsky St Petersburg, could later remember nothing specifically of this London interlude, which lasted until he was four years old. Then in 1816 John Dickens was appointed to one of the principal naval dockyards in Chatham at the mouth of the river Medway in Kent, thirty miles south-east of London. Here Dickens lived first at No. 2 Ordnance Terrace, one of a pleasant row of middle-class houses. Then from 1821, probably owing to his father's financial improvidence, at a less genteel address nearer to the dockyards, St Mary's Place. The pattern was indeed a repeat of the Portsmouth years. Nevertheless, Charles Dickens enjoyed these Chatham times and looked back to them as the happiest period of his life.

'The deep sea, and the fish that are in it.'

Here emerges that once essential figure of all middle-class homes, his nurse; here he was introduced to the nursery legend; here he did his first lessons at home, and from here he attended his first school; here he invented his first imaginative games in his own head and in play with other children; from here he visited his first theatres; here he read his first story books and played them out for himself in a toy theatre; here he first heard from a young playmate 'of a terrible banditti called "The Radicals" whose principles were that the Prince Regent wore stays, and that nobody had any right to any salary, and that the Army and Navy ought to be put down – horrors at which I trembled in my bed after supplicating that The Radicals might be speedily taken and hanged' – his own strong radicalism of later years was always to be subject to such bouts of respectable bourgeois fears.

The toy-world, animistic, infant environment of moving objects, and of faces in inanimate things, was to remain, however, the most pervasive element of his novels, in which houses, furniture and all everyday objects have a mysterious life and people participate in the 'thingness' of their surroundings.

Now to this toy world was to be added the world of legend, of invented stories and of almost mythic people: 'Little Red Riding Hood was my first love. I felt that if I could have married Little Red Riding Hood, I should have known perfect bliss.' This nursery story that he chiefly recalls contains the benevolent grandmother who is really the wolf. *Robin Hood, Valentine and Orson, The Yellow Dwarf* and *Mother Bunch* were other nursery stories that he many times details in 'The Christmas Tree' and the last three, at any rate, crop up in both his articles and his novels. *Robin Hood*, available in a number of editions, verse and prose, must have early strengthened his radicalism:

> But wicked lords and slothful priests
> Bishops and monks I spite,
> And those that give their minds to live
> On other people's right.

These words of Robin Hood lie very close to Dickens's heart in his frequent 'defender of the people' role.

Mother Bunch, a popular collection of children's tales, is, like Dickens himself, an extraordinary mixture. Many of the stories, including *The Yellow Dwarf*, are crude fairy stories in which miraculous events and astonishing deeds overtake one another like the incidents in any child's own made-up stories:

'Little Red Riding Hood was my first love.'

'The King boldly advanced, and, meeting with two terrible sphinxes, laid them dead at his feet with the sword. Next he attacked six dragons that opposed him, and dispatched them also. Then he met with four and twenty nymphs,' and so on; or even more childish: 'the air was darkened with showers of biscuits, tarts, cheesecakes and all manner of sweetmeats'. Others again, like *Little George*, are of a simple moralising kind; an infant version of what Dickens complained of in the then popular *Sandford and Merton,* or the sort of moral story that Mrs Pardiggle left at the houses of the poor brickmaker: 'No, I 'ain't read the little book wot you left. There 'ain't nobody here as knows how to read it; and if there was, it wouldn't be suitable to me. It's a book fit for a babby and I'm not a babby.' Little George is given a 'little catechism bound in silver; a pocket Bible with ruby clasps' – it is a ritzy version of what the adult Dickens was to dislike in the Ragged Schools. In later days Dickens's hatred of any attempt to introduce moralism into children's fantasy was always fierce. The crude satire of his early *Mudfog Papers* (1837) illustrates this when a member of the learned association strongly deprecating all nursery tales suggests that 'Jack and Jill' may be exempted from the general censure inasmuch as the hero and heroine 'were depicted as going up a hill to fetch a pail of water, which was a laborious and useful occupation'. As late as 1853 Dickens attacked his old friend, the artist George Cruikshank, for adapting the old nursery tales for temperance propaganda.

His chief emphasis in his account of this early nursery world, however, is upon *The Arabian Nights Entertainments*. It is the book that, after the New Testament and Shakespeare's works, he quotes or alludes to most often in his novels; it appears again and again in his letters. As a whole *The Arabian Nights* are so familiar to him that the reference may be upon any or all occasions. It was a standby in public speeches; examples from *The Arabian Nights* make their appearance in his first speech in the U.S.A. (Boston 1842), and in Washington, and a few days later in Richmond, Virginia: 'Like the genie in the story', or 'like the princess in *The Arabian Nights* who . . . ' are little more to Dickens than the familiar Cockney mythic world to Sam Weller when he says 'as the charity boy said ven he got to the end of the alphabet', or 'this is rayther too rich as the young lady said to the pastrycook'. *The Arabian Nights,* indeed, is a sort of exotic original Mrs Harris, as useful as an authority in all cases where imagination is at work as that mythical lady was a general aid to Mrs Gamp when her rich fancy needed substantial support.

But there is a more particular way in which *The Arabian Nights* remained important to Charles Dickens – the manner of his story-telling. *The Arabian Nights Entertainments* are constructed on the basis of the Sultana Scheherezade's nocturnal narrations which are, in the most literal sense, compulsive, for by leaving the Sultan each dawn in suspense she postpones the carrying out of his death sentence upon her. David Copperfield's dormitory stories are only told under fear of losing the patronage of his hero, Steerforth. The whole development of Charles Dickens as an artist is from a compulsive story-teller to a constructor of elaborate stories that make their point on many levels. The reasons that led him into publishing his novels in monthly or occasionally in weekly episodes are usually partly practical, occasionally fortuitous. But I should say that the pattern of Scheherezade's narration, so familiar to him from childhood, must have inclined him towards acceptance of this periodical, direct relationship with his readers which gave him such great satisfaction. The printer's boy at the door, waiting for the next instalment, was a sort of threatening executioner.

So we may say that he depended always upon a relation to his audience as direct as the poor threatened Sultana's – tell us another or else. . . . His early novels grew out of journalistic occasional writing and passed through the picaresque or wanderer's novel like *Pickwick Papers* or *Nicholas Nickleby* in which some character may at any moment interrupt the narrative to tell a story. Yet Dickens, I think, always hankered after a means of telling his fiction more directly even than this – like the Eastern story-teller of *The Arabian Nights Entertainments*, or, indeed, of those Eastern stories, greatest to him of all stories, the parables of Jesus. Before he evolved the novel narrative in the complex and sustained form that we find in his mature work he made one attempt to present himself as a story-teller of exactly this kind. In 1840, when

'The King upon his throne can't write his acts of Parliament in print without having begun when he were a unpromoted prince with the alphabet.' Joe in *Great Expectations*.

A a

A—was an Archer,
And shot at a Frog.

B b

B—was a Butcher,
And kept a great Dog.

Y y

Y—was a Youth,
Who did not love School.

Z z

Z—was a Zany,
And looked like a Fool.

The Wreck — **Building a Hut** — **The Man Friday** — **Making the Boat** — **The Savages**

My Bible
by WILLIAM JOLLY.

What taught me in my Youthful days,
Ever to walk in wisdom's ways,
And every day my God to Praise?
MY BIBLE.

What bade me have an upright heart,
To act through life an honest part,
Nor have recourse to guile or art?
MY BIBLE.

What told me I should not profane
The Sabbath day, but love the same,
And e'er revere its sacred name?
MY BIBLE.

What told me I should learn to shun,
Whatever was by Sinners done,
And from the Paths of vice to run?
MY BIBLE.

What told me ne'er to turn mine eye,
From Widow's tears, or Orphan's cry,
But Pity feel, for mis'ry's sigh?
MY BIBLE.

What taught me love and peace to bear,
To all Mankind, to act sincere,
As though the eye of God were near?
MY BIBLE.

What made me shun each evil way,
What made me love at home to stay,
And night and morn, my Prayers to say?
MY BIBLE.

Then thro' my life may I revere
The sacred Page, still hold it dear,
For 'tis a source of Comfort here.
MY BIBLE.

Through this were taught, whene'er goodness sprung
In whose just praise the vallies rung,
"O! let me have" cried every tongue,
A BIBLE!

What told me I should ever love,
Almighty God who reigns above,
Nor fail each day the same to prove?
MY BIBLE.

May ignorance no longer reign,
Henceforth the Heathen shall proclaim
His Makers love—and bless the name of
BIBLE!

And, when old Age shall weaken me,
My constant care on earth shall be,
To live with God, and often see
MY BIBLE.

London Published July 9th 1812 by William Darton Jun. 58 Holborn Hill.

the first gush of his imaginative spring seemed momentarily spent, he devised the idea of Master Humphrey, a typical Dickensian character of the weaker kind that so frequently makes its appearance in the Christmas stories or other journalistic pieces when his imaginative powers are working at half cock – a rambling, whimsical, eccentric, old bachelor – but, as it seemed, a perfect mouthpiece for the sort of personal, erratic story-telling that Dickens wanted to create in relation to his readers. In fact, Master Humphrey as the Scheherezade narrator proved a failure with the public, but the first story that the old man told, *The Old Curiosity Shop*, was a magnificent success which, Dickens believed, did more than any other work to bring him into direct emotional relationship with his readers. The story, he saw, was all; the teller an unnecessary intervention. He resumed *Barnaby Rudge*, the first really organized novel that he wrote, and dropped Master Humphrey, his clock and all the other narrative link devices, never to revive the attempt again, save to wind up the series. The public readings of his last years can perhaps be seen as his final attempt at this primitive, direct, oriental-style story-telling.

The general sense of wonder that came not only from his beloved *Arabian Nights,* but from all the nursery stories of his childhood, remained with Dickens for his whole life. Most good novelists have their roots among such legends, but none so persistently and deeply as he. From those roots there grew a natural jungle of images – comic, sad, frightening   that invades most of his prose, giving it a peculiar and personal poetry, which defies the hideously job-lot garden ornaments (the Victorian equivalents of stone gnomes and toadstools) that he so often chose when he consciously set out to embellish his work with beautiful language. This exceptional sense of wonder, of the world beneath the surface, was married to a very exact journalist's eye and ear for the surface world around him. The offspring of such a marriage are the monstrous, captivating creatures of Dickens's world, a world in which we can never be quite sure, until we have learnt his own special grammar, if his words are going to take us to the exactitude of closely imitated speech, which will suddenly spiral off into a strange, decorated version of itself as a character turns into a humour; or to the invocation of a fairyland or ogreland, which ends fairly and squarely situated in an exactly described area of London. Yet he was deeply concerned with the reality of happening or of motive in his novels as we may see in his many letters to his friend, John Forster, with whom he discussed his books in some detail as he wrote them. He intended what he wrote to convince the reader as real, that that was how he saw it.

Apart from two exceptions – the necessity to sustain a central hopeful chord in the human heart and some concern for contemporary sexual conventions – where Dickens errs in realism it would be a mistake to attribute this to any direct disregard. The strangeness of his world is largely that Dickens's reality had a greater intermixture of the wondrous and the grotesque than most men's.

He would be astonished, no doubt, at the complex patterns detected in his novels by many modern university critics, but about the praise given to him for his hold on the mythic qualities of story-telling he would, for all his concern

'More solitary than Robinson Crusoe, who had nobody to look at him, and see that he was solitary.' *David Copperfield.*

with 'reality', be delighted and not really surprised. For Dickens never ceased to know, as he shows in *Dombey and Son*, that it is not the learned of this world, the Dr Blimbers crammed with factual knowledge, who matter; but Glubb, 'the old, crab-faced man, in a suit of battered oilskin, who drew Paul Dombey's invalid chair' – 'he knows all about the deep sea, and the fish that are in it, and the great monsters that come and lie on the rocks in the sun, and dive into the water again when they're startled, blowing and splashing so that they can be heard for miles'. Dickens's novels bear lasting testimony to these monsters. He is always against the Blimber Academy which, in Miss Blimber's prim words, 'is not the place for Glubbs of any kind'.

The hold that Old Glubb's wonders of the deep had upon the imagination of little Paul Dombey reminds us that, in myth and legend, the made-up story heard from the mouth of a mother or of a nurse is as powerful, more so probably, than the traditional fairy story. It was in those first happy years in Ordnance Terrace, Chatham, that Dickens's nurse, Mary Weller, makes her appearance. It is not surprising that the nurse of a child then so obscure should herself remain rather dimly seen. What is more typical of the whole Dickens story is that the incidents associated with her are in some ways so contradictory, that, if it were not for lack of evidence, it would seem almost that there must have been two nurses (the one kind and loving, the other more sinister – once again, the expected Dickens antithesis).

Whatever she may have contributed to his happiness was well rewarded afterwards by his blessed use of her name – especially when one remembers that Sam Weller's bride, 'the very smart and pretty-faced servant girl' at Mr Magistrate Nupkins's, was also called Mary. And if his nurse had but half the loving warmth of David Copperfield's nurse, Peggotty, she must have been a paragon among nurses. Yet as she is recalled in 'Nurses' Stories', an essay that appeared in *All the Year Round* in 1860, and as she is probably also recalled in *The Holly Tree*, the Christmas story for 1855, she appears in a different light. In these we read: 'The Young Woman had a fiendish enjoyment of my terrors', and 'her name was Mercy, though she had none on me'. She is described as a 'sallow woman with a fishy eye, an aquiline nose, and a green gown' – very far from Sam Weller's bride. 'May she have been repaid my debt of obligation to her in the matter of nightmares and perspiration,' he adds. Her stories, like many servants' tales to their charges, have a macabre ring or, at any rate, struck a sinister, if relished note in Dickens's memory when he recalled them. Indeed he prefaces his account of these tales by saying: 'I suspect we should find our nurses responsible for most of the dark corners we are forced to go back to against our wills.'

The dark corners to which he returns in this article are tritely ghoulish enough to be laughable, or rather, Dickens in the father role of narrator we have already seen him assume in talking of his toys, makes them ridiculous. There is 'Captain Murderer' who renders his wives into meat pies (could Mary Weller have adapted Blue Beard to the English scene?). Once again, as with his toys, it seems almost too good that Charles Dickens, whose work is obsessed with the special, the almost ritual part played in human life by murder, should have had 'Captain Murderer' for his nursery horror-hero. But we are dealing again with memory, whose recall is partial. This story and many other hauntings and horrible crimes the young Dickens tried to evade as fiction, but Mary Weller (if it were she) always entrapped him by the simple device of adding that they happened to her sister-in-law, to her brother-in-law, or some other relative. She seems even to have chosen to play the part of heroine herself in one story:

> a brave and lovely servant-maid married to the landlord of a country Inn; which landlord had this remarkable characteristic, that he always wore a silk nightcap, and never would on any consideration take it off. At last, one night, when he was fast asleep, the brave and lovely woman lifted up his silk nightcap on the right side, and found that he had no ear there; upon which she sagaciously perceived that he was the clipped housebreaker [a notorious burglar who had lost an ear in commission of his brutal crimes], who had married her with the intention of putting her to death. She immediately heated the poker and terminated his career, for which she was taken to King George upon his throne and received the compliments of royalty on her great discretion and valour.

Dickens, in this re-telling, uses many of his most loved ironic phrases – in particular 'had this remarkable characteristic' and 'never would on any consideration', wordings that he always employed to describe the perverse means by which some improbable plot or event was brought about in the theatre or in popular fiction. That he hugely enjoys the absurd improbability of his nurse's tales is evident; the same relish seems to attach to his own telling of some of the more extravagant sinister events in his novels. But he is also evidently delighted by the sheer accumulation of gory detail in these remembered nurse's stories. His reference to his nurse's 'fiendish enjoyment' is a strange compound of admiration, accusation and complicity in the infliction of terror upon his childhood self. He would not, he must have known, have wished to have been without those nightmares, which were to prove so fruitful to him. And then again he, like Mary Weller, could say with the fat boy, Joe, 'I wants to make your flesh creep'. His delight in the invention of the horrific becomes less evident as he grows older, but in the early work, when Squeers is bullying the boys at Dotheboys Hall, or Quilp is teasing his wife or his mother-in-law, it would be hard to say which is most gleefully tormenting – the fictional characters or their author. Even in the last decade of his life he praised the sense of humour of a Kent audience at one of his readings because they laughed so loudly at Squeers and the boys. This is not to say that there was any pronounced sadistic quality in Dickens's writing, only a certain fiendish enjoyment like his nurse's in the effects he knows that he can produce; that, and in emulation no doubt of the success of the story 'Captain Murderer', an extraordinary, almost childishly delighted surprise at the badness of his own villains. From the time in 1838 that he wrote to Forster about Fagin, 'not yet having disposed of the Jew who is such an out-and-outer that I don't know what to make of him', Dickens retained a sort of comic, admiring amazement at the black horrors he could draw out of 'the dark corners' of his mind that is much like his shocked but laughing attitude to his flesh-creeping nurse.

Mary Weller (or her Mr Hyde) did not limit herself to story-telling. She took Charles, and, no doubt, his brothers and sisters for walks and, when out walking, she called upon her friends as nurses will. We know how, despite all Mr Dombey's cutting off Mrs Toodle from her family by naming her Richards when he appointed her to the high honour of nurse to his heir, she still was tempted to return to her low origins and suffered dismissal for it. John Dickens's household was less grand and more easy-going than Mr Dombey's awful, glacial home. Even so, with Mary Weller, Dickens recalls:

> In my very young days I was taken to so many lyings-in that I wonder I escaped becoming a professional martyr to them in after-life. I suppose I had a very sympathetic nurse, with a large circle of married acquaintance . . . . I remember to have waited on a lady who had four children (I am afraid to write five, though I fully believe it was five) at a birth. This meritorious woman held quite a reception in her room on the morning when I was introduced there . . . the four (five) deceased young people lay, side by side, on a clean cloth on a chest of drawers; reminding me by a homely association, which I suspect their complexion to have assisted, of pigs' feet as they are usually displayed at a neat tripe-shop.

The whole grotesque, almost to our ears facetious, account of child mortality, in particular its association with childbirth, and what no doubt must have been the talk between nurse Weller and the bereaved mother, have surely a foretaste of what is to be the wondrous-hideous world of Mrs Gamp.

More striking, probably, to the modern reader is the notion that a child should be taken into a stranger's death chamber. The event would have seemed less peculiar to the Victorians. What seems an obsessive interest in death is in part only a reflection of a general familiarity, which is no longer so intelligible to us in an age when illness and in particular what we now prefer to call in hospital language 'terminal illness' seldom takes place at home. The incidence of child mortality, too, was so high as to make it a commonplace. That a child should be familiar with what daily threatened was both inevitable because it was so commonplace, and, to certain religious views of the awful, a valuable lesson in the need to be prepared, to be in a right frame of mind for death. There may, possibly, have been some element of this pious motive in this visit of his nurse, for Dickens tells us of the occasion that:

> Hot caudle was handed round . . . and a subscription was entered into among the company, which became extremely alarming to my consciousness of having pocket-money on my person. This fact being known to my conductress, whoever she was, I was earnestly exhorted to contribute, but resolutely declined: therein disgusting the company, who gave me to understand that I must dismiss all expectations of going to Heaven.

The ambiguous picture that he gives here of his nurse is reflected in the manner by which in so short a story we are told first, 'a very sympathetic Nurse' and then, 'my conductress, whoever she was'. Whether it was Mary Weller or not who drew this religious morality from the visit, she certainly claimed many years later, when interviewed after her famous charge's death, that it was she who always sang to him the evening hymn – a memory that came to him when he was forty-five and wrote to his friend Forster: 'Somebody (who I wonder, and which way did *she* go when she died?) [it could not have been his mother, for she did not die until 1863] hummed the Evening Hymn to me and I cried on the pillow.'

Whoever this religious mentor and whatever her teaching, if she was responsible for introducing the young Charles to Chapel Christianity with its hellfire sermons she set up a lifelong aversion in him. This hostility must surely have been born when he was a boy at Chatham. Next door to his parents' house was a Baptist chapel which is said to have been in the charge of the Reverend William Giles, the minister of the more important Zion Baptist Chapel in Chatham. Although the Dickens parents became friendly with this minister and may have on occasion attended his chapel, nothing that we know about them would suggest that they ever adopted more than the ordinary church-going Church of England convention of their time – certainly it is hard to imagine either the expansive boon companion, John Dickens, or his wife with

'I look up the inside of his outstretched coatsleeve . . . and I hate him.'

her addiction to pleasure being for a moment devotees of long-sermoned, temperance-tract Nonconformity. Nor is there, as far as I know, anything to associate Mr Giles the minister with the Stiggins-Chadband variety of religion – quite to the contrary if we consider what is known of his son, William junior, Dickens's first school teacher. Yet there is no doubt that it was at this time that Dickens acquired his horror of long sermons:

> On summer evenings, when every flower, and tree, and bird, might have better addressed my soft young heart, I have in my day been caught in the palm of a female hand by the crown, have been violently scrubbed from the neck to the roots of the hair as a purification for the Temple, and then have been carried off highly charged with saponaceous electricity, to be steamed like a potato in the unventilated breath of the powerful Boanerges Boiler and his congregation, until what small mind I had, was quite steamed out of me. In which pitiable plight I have been haled out of the place of the meeting, at the conclusion of the exercises, and catechized respecting Boanerges Boiler, his fifthly, his sixthly, and his seventhly, until I have regarded that revered person in the light of a most dismal and oppressive Charade. Time was, when I was carried off to platform assemblages at which no human child, whether of wrath or grace, could possibly keep its eyes open, and when I felt the fatal step stealing, stealing over me, and when I gradually heard the orator in possession, spinning and humming like a great top, until he rolled, collapsed, and tumbled over, and I discovered, to my burning shame and fear, that as to that last stage it was not he, but I. I have sat under Boanerges when he has specifically addressed himself to us – us the infants – and at this present writing I hear his lumbering jocularity (which never amused us, though we basely pretended that it did) and I behold his big round face, and I look up the inside of his outstretched coatsleeve, as if it were a telescope with the stopper on, and I hate him with an unwholesome hatred for two hours.

This is not just a boyish, Tom Sawyer-like hostility to Sunday clothes and washing. From it was to ripen not only the mockery and distaste for Mr Stiggins, who got his desserts from Tony Weller, for the Little Bethel that Kit Nubbles hated so, for the Reverend Melchisedech Howler, who plagued poor Bunsby, and above all for the odious, oily Mr Chadband, but also the fierce hatred for the much more sinister atmosphere that surrounds the Murdstones and Mrs Clennam – an oppressive air of sadism, of sexual frustration and of death in life. There is no evidence after the happy Chatham days for Dickens's involvement with a Calvinist world; yet there does seem to me to be a more potent influence here than an occasional visit to Chapel, the occasional boredom of a long-winded sermon with parents or nurse. Was there another more pious servant who sometimes had charge of Master Charles?

Long sermons, Calvinist teaching, is one of his chief childhood terrors as he recalls it in memoirs and in his novels. In the novels it is associated with the terrors of mental arithmetic – of Mr Murdstone asking: 'If I go into a cheesemonger's shop, and buy five thousand Double Gloucester cheeses at fourpence-halfpenny each, present payment', or Uncle Pumblechook's running sum that lasted all through breakfast: 'Seven? And four? And eight? And six? And two?' This, I think, is a good example of how Dickens establishes in a few short humorous sentences the close tie between Evangelical piety and hard-headed business, which has been the subject of many lengthy historical theses. But ironically he seems to have been susceptible to Double Gloucester cheeses himself with children: Wilfred Meynell, in a private memoir telling of Dickens's relation to his wife Alice's family, says that '"Nine times nine?" in his demanding voice still resounded in the grown-up Alice's ears.'

Mary Weller (or Mrs Gibson as she had then become) certainly showed no dark, Calvinist, forbidding side when after the novelist's death she was interviewed by the Dickensian, Robert Langton. On the contrary she recalls affectionately two of the profane occupations of the small boy which were to have a most lasting influence in his life: 'Little Charles was a terrible boy to read,' she said; and again: 'Sometimes Charles would come downstairs and say to me, "Now Mary, clear the kitchen, we are going to have such a game", and then George Stroughill would come in with his Magic Lantern, and they would sing, recite and perform parts of plays.'

In the young Charles Dickens's reading after the days of nursery tales we have in some ways the very core of his novels.

'It was in a little room upstairs to which I had access (for it adjoined my

'Little Charles was a terrible boy to read.' Illustrations from *Don Quixote* and *The Citizen of the World*.

The magic lantern for which Mary Weller cleared the table.

own)'; we learn in *David Copperfield* how the young Charles came upon the great picaresque novels of the eighteenth century – *Roderick Random, Peregrine Pickle, Humphrey Clinker, Tom Jones, The Vicar of Wakefield*, their French counterpart *Gil Blas* and their great predecessor *Don Quixote. Tristram Shandy,* if not immediately among them, was later to become an equal favourite. Most of Dickens's early novels are still set in the loose, wandering mould of Fielding and Smollett. The heroes, Nicholas Nickleby and Martin Chuzzlewit above all, with their unheroic faults of pride and sarcasm, of egotism and selfishness, are in the proper unheroic, 'black sheep with golden hearts' tradition of Tom Jones himself or of Roderick Random, although the early Victorian sexual reticence of Dickens gives his young heroes a curiously empty, sexless quality beside the strapping, wenching, near-rogue heroes of the eighteenth century. So strong is the likeness that one can well believe Dickens when he tells us: 'I have been Tom Jones (a child's Tom Jones, a harmless creature) for a week together. I have sustained my own idea of Roderick Random for a month at a stretch.' In his novels he went on with this impersonation until he was over thirty, perhaps until the character of David Copperfield (in whose person he here speaks) had shown that author, author's past self and author's hero figure could after a fashion be combined into one without resort to picaresque models from boyhood reading.

His earliest toy theatres, background to his first shared imaginative games.

More important, however, than the young heroes, the 'walking gentlemen' that Fielding and Smollett bequeathed to Charles Dickens, are two other sets of characters that appear in many of his early novels. The one – Don Quixote himself – requires little explanation. His connection with Mr Pickwick, as Dostoevsky saw, is basic. Hardly less important in the same vein of simplicity is Sterne's Uncle Toby, another blessed fool, from whom Captain Cuttle surely descends. Indeed the idea of what Dostoevsky was later to paint as the divine idiot is as powerful a part of Dickens's interpretation of Christ's beatitudes as it is of Dostoevsky's; and the existence of divine simpletons in Dickens's works is perhaps one of the chief reasons why Dostoevsky admired them so much. With Don Quixote, of course, goes Sancho Panza, who, with the reinforcement of the faithful, shrewd, worldly servants of the young heroes Tom Jones, Peregrine Pickle, Roderick Random and the rest, goes to make up Sam Weller, Joe Willett, Mark Tapley and, surely, Job Trotter. It is not for nothing that Dickens recalls himself as a boy with his head 'full of Partridge, Strap, Tom Piper and Sancho Panza'. If we add Corporal Trim, Uncle Toby's levelheaded batman, we have all the ingredients, save only the dialogue, for Sam Weller – the earthy, faithful clown, who teaches his innocent gentlemen master the ways of the world. About this boyhood reading, however, it can in general be said that because 'Charles was a terrible boy to read', he had models ready

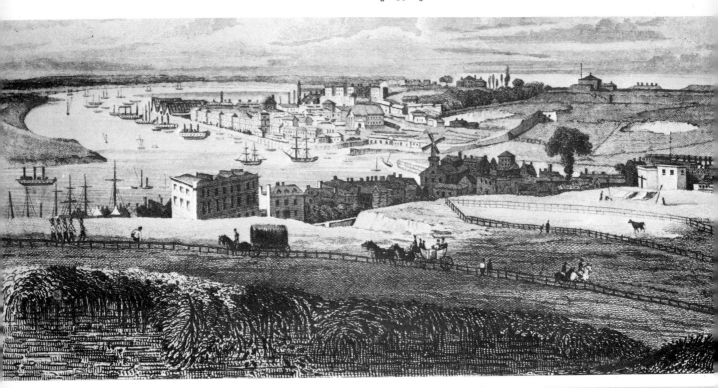

Dickens and his father took long walks in Chatham and Rochester and through the surrounding countryside.

to hand when his first incredible success made him a popular novelist over-night; and also that the first ten years of his writing life were spent in enlarging those remembered boyhood models to suit a new century and to express an imagination that sought to bring fictional unity to the richly individualist and eccentric Victorian world he lived in.

The novelists Cervantes, Le Sage, Fielding, Smollett and Sterne had much to offer Dickens that was to mould his genius, but they cannot at all account for the extra dimension of drama that marks his novels at their highest and at their lowest. Here no doubt we must go back to the magic lantern for which Mary Weller cleared the table, to his earliest toy theatres, to those juvenile dramatic works based upon plays of the period that were the background to his first shared imaginative games – games which were soon fed by the real theatre.

Life at Chatham

Pantomime he had known from his almost infant pre-Chatham days. From the preface to the *Life of Grimaldi* (a hack editing job he carried out with his father's aid in the overworked days following the success of *Pickwick Papers*) we learn that when he was only eight years old he had seen that great clown at Chatham.

But the Theatre Royal (although the great stars of the day did visit there)

Cobham Park, Dickens's first sight of the aristocratic, feudal world.

was to give him not only a delight in the play but also (almost more important to his writing) that comic delight in the great gulf between the play and what the poor players make of it (particularly of Shakespeare) which is a staple of his humour both directly and in metaphor from *Sketches by Boz* and Sam Weller down to Mr Wopsle's Hamlet in *Great Expectations*. At the Theatre Royal, Chatham, he tells us that he first learned 'how that wicked king (Richard III) slept in war-time on a sofa much too short for him, and how fearfully his conscience troubled his boots', and 'that the witches in *Macbeth* have an awful resemblance to the Thanes and other proper inhabitants of Scotland; and that the Good King Duncan couldn't rest in his grave, but was constantly coming out of it and calling himself somebody else'. Here were not only the shortcomings of contemporary Shakespearean touring productions but all the clichés of bad contemporary theatre which were to be one of his staple comic devices for expressing the gap in life between the ideal and its absurd realization. But, however he mocks this melodramatic dialogue and action throughout his novels (though diminishingly in the later works), they were to prove an unfortunate standby when his imagination failed to keep pace with the complications of his plots and narratives. Above all, as he was to say years later when he was over fifty, the theatre was for him a constant haven from a real world that he often found hideous: 'having for an hour or two quite forgotten the real world, and . . . coming out into the street with a kind of wonder that it should be so wet, and dark, and cold, and full of jostling people and irreconcilable cabs.'

Before the Chatham years were over, before he had reached eleven years, his theatre-going had become an independent activity. Lodging with the Dickens family, who in the latters years at St Mary's Place were having to pull in their financial reins, was a young man, recently down from Sandhurst, awaiting a commission, James Lamert, step-son of Mrs Dickens's sister. He was an ardent producer of amateur theatricals, and also often took the small boy Charles to the Theatre Royal. Surely to see the play with a lively young man, an *aficionado*, one not really yet an adult and only marginally a member of the family is the start of true theatre-going and not the childish though enjoyable activity of family parties at the theatre. It is certainly a difference of pleasure that Dickens himself registers – compare, for example, the family party that visits Miss Snevellici's benefit night in *Nicholas Nickleby* with any of the many young gents who haunt the theatres in *Sketches by Boz*.

Other aspects of Chatham were to mark the end of Eden, the end of certainties which for most middle-class children would last on into their adolescence, but which for Charles Dickens were never to recur. Most importantly, he was never after Chatham to be able to love his mother so completely, nor to trust either of his parents so fully. As he was to say in the character of the Haunted Man: 'My parents at the best were of that sort whose care soon ends.'

Mrs Dickens, according to Mary Weller, was 'a dear, good mother and a fine woman'. With her sister, she taught her many children, including Charles, in their early years. According to his great friend and biographer, John Forster,

---

'"He's the wictim of connubiality," as Bluebeard's domestic chaplain said ven he buried him.' Sam Weller in *Pickwick Papers*.

Overleaf. 'She played Juliet, and Helen Macgregor, and did the skipping rope hornpipe between the pieces.' Mr Crummles in *Nicholas Nickleby*.

WEBB'S CHARACTERS IN BLUE BEARD.   Plate 9

Foot Combat.

Horse Combat

London. Pub. by W. WEBB, 146, Old Street, St. Luke's

SKELT'S COMBAT IN THE FORTY THIEVES.

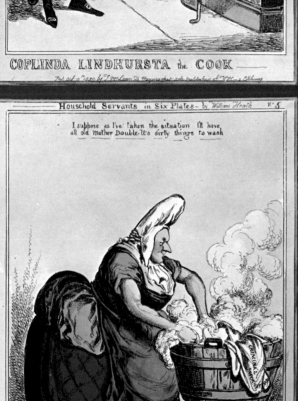

Dickens frequently said that: 'his first desire for knowledge and his earliest passion for reading were awakened by his mother, from whom he learned the rudiments not only of English, but also, a little later, of Latin. She taught him regularly every day for a long time, and taught him, he was convinced, thoroughly well.' The future novelist, for whom education was always a first priority, could hardly pay a greater tribute. But it was the last tribute he was to pay to his mother. If he was to find his father's weakness intolerable in later years, he was to find his mother's ineffectual, genteel attempts at firmness more unforgiveable.

From his father in these happy Chatham days he seems rather to have received companionship. John Dickens, as he was later recalled by one who knew him in Devonshire, was 'a chatty, pleasant companion, possessing a varied fund of anecdote and a genuine vein of humour', an ideal friend for an imaginative, lively boy. Together they took long walks in Chatham and Rochester, and through the surrounding countryside. It was with his father that he made awed note of the house Gad's Hill, which was later to be the crown of his success as an established gentleman – a status to which his father never ceased to aspire. It was with his father that he first knew the English countryside, which was to remain in a curious, Cockney sort of way a symbol to him of English happiness, of hospitality and good old customs, of innocent cheer – indeed it was through Dingley Dell and Muggleton, the very centres of Pickwickian innocence, that he and his father walked. With his father, too, perhaps accompanying him in the course of his duty into the dockyard or on sailing trips up the River Medway, he must have first seen the convicts who worked at unloading, and the marshes at Cooling, north-east of Chatham, off which the galley ships lay, and from these arose eventually the story of his second and more chastened fictional self, Pip. With his father he explored the grounds of Cobham Park, his first sight of the aristocratic, feudal world, to which in his later fame he was to adjust himself so levelheadedly, a place appropriately associated with the most Dickensian of all Shakespearean characters, Falstaff. Above all he must soon have seen that his father shared with him a quality that he came later to prize as the foundation of all virtues – energy. Then, in fact, was formed the deep affection for his father that survived nearly thirty years of John Dickens's financial Micawberism.

For the rest, Chatham gave him his only really satisfactory schooldays, at the newly formed establishment of the young William Giles, son of the Baptist Minister. Long years later – twelve years after Dickens's death – Giles's sister recalled the schoolboy as very handsome, with long curly hair of a light colour and of a very amiable, agreeable disposition. Certainly he seems to have received much encouragement and special coaching from his headmaster. When in 1822 John Dickens was transferred to London, Charles remained at Chatham for a few more happy months, boarding at the school. On his final parting, William Giles gave Dickens a copy of Goldsmith's *Bee*; but years later he gave him something far more lasting, when after the success of *Pickwick Papers* he sent his former pupil a snuff box inscribed to the Inimitable Boz –

'I have never used any other armorial bearings than my Father's crest.' Dickens in a letter, 1869.

a title that Dickens with careful, precautionary self-mocking loved most to use, for no other so completely expressed his great certainty that he was somebody quite exceptional and apart.

When, around Christmas 1822, a small boy not yet eleven years old, he departed unaccompanied on the coach from Chatham to join his parents in London, he happily did not know how close the events of the next year would come to sucking down this exceptional and apart boy into the vast pond life of London's hopeless, swarming poor. Was it then with hindsight that he recalled his long journey? 'Through all the years that have since passed, have I ever lost the smell of damp straw in which I was packed – like game – and forwarded, carriage paid, to the Cross Keys, Wood Street, Cheapside, London? There was no other inside passenger, and I consumed my sandwiches in solitude and dreariness, and it rained hard all the way, and I thought life sloppier than I had expected to find it.'

Chapter II
Youth 1822–36

amden Town, where Dickens's parents had now established themselves at 16 Bayham Street, was a near-suburb, separated from London proper by half built-up areas and by intervening patches of wasteland or scrub. Dickens himself gives a brilliant description in *Dombey and Son* of this very district after 1835 (over a decade later) when the railway was relentlessly driving a thunderous void through the property and lives of an incredulous population, half artisan, half small bourgeois, all living in that intensely isolated, almost village community that is the mark of the metropolises of nineteenth-century fiction – of Raskolnikov's Petersburg, of Gervaise Coupeau's Paris, and of Sampson Brass's London alike a smallness of range that has not yet wholly faded from the life of many great cities.

Stagg's Gardens . . . was a little row of houses, with little squalid patches of ground before them, fenced off with old doors, barrel staves, scraps of tarpaulin, and dead bushes; with bottomless tin kettles and exhausted iron fenders thrust into the gaps. Here the Stagg's Gardeners trained scarlet beans, kept fowls and rabbits, erected rotten summer-houses (one was an old boat), dried clothes, and smoked pipes . . . . Stagg's Gardens was regarded by its population as a sacred grove not to be withered by railroads; and so confident were they generally of its long outliving any such ridiculous inventions that the master chimney-sweeper at the corner, who was understood to take the lead in the local politics of the Gardens, had publicly declared that on the occasion of the Railroad opening, if it ever did open, two of his boys should ascend the flues of his dwelling, with instructions to hail the future with derisive jeers from the chimney-pots.

Bayham Street was altogether a cut above this – terraces of two-storeyed houses built only ten years before; but there must have been many Stagg's Gardens around the corner for Charles to wander in during the coming months of enforced idleness. And Bayham Street itself was a mixed community where the Dickens family lived cheek by jowl with those small tradesmen, minor professional men, who like themselves laid claim to gentility, but also with those respectable artisans, who were not at all their social equals. They hung now rather precariously upon a lower social peg than at St Mary's Terrace, Chatham, as St Mary's Terrace itself had been a decline from the happy carefree days of Ordnance Terrace. Mary Weller in her old age recollected some lessening hospitality and conviviality in the move from one Chatham house to another. Now they had no Mary Weller; married to a shipwright in the Chatham dockyard she had remained behind when the family moved to London. Now there was only 'The Orfling', a young orphan maid of all work brought from Chatham Workhouse, a member of the lowest stratum of the great Victorian servant class. Even she must have been fitted with difficulty into some remote recess as The Marchioness was at Sally Brass's in *The Old Curiosity Shop*, for beside Mr and Mrs Dickens and their six children they still had the lodger, young James Lamert – all in four rooms. Well, they needed to save; and no doubt like many indigent, genteel people they welcomed London's greater anonymity to disguise their embarrassment and attempts at

'Stagg's Gardens was regarded by its population as a sacred grove not to be withered by railroads.'

retrenchment. If John Dickens is at all fairly pictured in Wilkins Micawber, he no doubt always believed that something would turn up before ruin 'stared them in the face'. But ruin, like the railway, could not be staved off by incredulity.

It is hard not to feel touched by the Dickens parents in their plight. They were obviously so much nicer when small prosperity allowed them to be so – he so much less shifty, she no doubt less maddeningly silly, less frightenedly hard. The years of conviviality and hospitality were so few and their scale so modest that it seems cruel they should pay for them so dearly. But their creditors thought otherwise – financial rectitude, proper housekeeping, were their watchwords, and they pressed for belated payment for the few years of fat. And after this experience of 1823 and 1824 Charles Dickens was to acquire, for all his life, a high rectitude about financial matters and a primness about exact household management that would have done credit to the most respectable of bourgeois traders.

'London going out of Town or The March of Bricks and Mortar!'

Early Victorian society was a cruel jungle for people who clung with difficulty to the ornamental edge of gentility.

London

Early Victorian society was a cruel jungle – most cruel for the plain poor, who could fall no lower, but cruel enough for people like the Dickens parents, who clung with difficulty to the ornamental edge of gentility. These are the strange creatures that fill the pages of Dickens and of Dostoevsky; small government servants, half-pay captains, minor professional men – music teachers, art and dancing masters, clergymen (one thinks not only of the dirty chaplain in Mr Pickwick's Fleet Prison, but of Thackeray's elegant Charles Honeyman), engineers and inventors, small tradesmen; it is they who make up the population of the debtors' prisons, the Fleet and the Marshalsea, as shown us in *Pickwick Papers* and in *Little Dorrit*. With their childish egotism, their childish high spirits, their plausibility, their shabby gentility, their boastful dreams of status and achievement, their shifty, sudden flashes of scared anger, their more embarrassing moments of scared ingratiating, their dirty linen, pomaded whiskers and lounging lives, they present – these Marmeladovs, Ivolgins and Lebedevs, these Micawbers, Jingles, Dorrits and Chevy Slymes – some of the weirdest, the most 'improbable' of the blown-up monsters in the nineteenth-century fictional zoo. But, of course, they stand out – naked, oversized, repulsive, comic and a little pathetic – for they are the cumbrous grasshoppers among the thrifty ants, trying hard to convince themselves even in the winter days by their over life-size character acts that the Victorian world owed them a living. The ants never thought so. There were hundreds among these (often the more socially humble) who came there not by gamblers' bad luck but by real bad luck – a common occurrence in a jungle society. Dickens recognized these and gave them special compassion, as, for example, to the cobbler, whose room Sam Weller shares in the Fleet. But the Dickens parents were not among these guiltless, however much their son might dream in later fictions that it was so.

John and Elizabeth Dickens were of those who wanted a jolly Dickensian Christmas every day. Not that John Dickens shrank from hard work; far from it, his industry was one of the things that made his son love him. But he got the proportion between working and playing wrong – a fatal thing in Victorian society unless you were a rich man.

When the eleven-year-old Charles arrived at Bayham Street the grasshoppers' summer days were nearly at an end. Chatham creditors pressed; London tradesmen grew insulting. There was one compensation that must have flattered the parents' gentility despite the low neighbourhood and the low demands for money; and, let it be said, that must have pleased their constant pride for their children. Their eldest daughter, Fanny, Charles's closest companion in the family, was accepted as a pupil boarder at the Royal Academy of Music. Talent, Art, Deportment and Status all in one. But for Charles his favourite sister's happy success, although it too was to be interrupted by the vagaries of family fortune, must have been a bitter pill to swallow.

They had sung duets together, and been acclaimed by the neighbours, and his comic songs and imitations – heralds, after all, of one of the world's greatest comic geniuses – had seemed more applauded than her talents. But now she was chosen to be trained to become a concert singer and he was left in the alleys and streets of London to survive as best he could.

He, Charles, so lately the proud and happy recipient of Mr Giles's encouragement and congratulations, had no genteel niche available. Indeed, in the press of penury he seems to have been entirely forgotten. No school was mentioned for him. John Dickens, enveloped in a whirl of activity to keep the wolf from the door (often the best drug to enable one to forget its presence) was glad to have the bright, lively boy to run 'important' errands. 'What would I have given,' Dickens said years later, 'if I had had anything to give, to have been sent back to any other school, to have been taught something anywhere?'

In his immediate reaction to the changed circumstances the boy suffered once again and badly from an old physical foe, the kidney spasms that had attacked him more than once in earlier childhood. But no physical illness could alter facts; when he recovered he returned to the bewildered sense of being displaced, of losing in the to-do of his parents' concern for their financial safety the happy, developing, awakening personality that he had found in Giles's school. Bewilderment and a bitter sense of abandonment were bottled up in him, and were never released until, in his late twenties, he found a friend in whom he felt a complete assurance and trust, John Forster. The most traumatic events of that horrible time – his father's imprisonment, his own menial employment at a blacking factory – were only given in confidence to

Forster over twenty years later, in 1847, as a result of a chance remark. When indeed Forster made them part of his published biography of his friend in 1872, only Dickens's wife, Catherine, of all his family and friends, had ever heard of them. It is, however, of the greatest importance that Charley Dickens, his eldest son, in his preface to the Macmillan edition of *David Copperfield*, tells us that his mother had authorised him to reveal that Dickens had read the suppressed autobiographical fragment to her. She had, she told her son, urged her husband not to publish it because of its harsh tone towards his father and even more towards his mother. This story has not been enough emphasized by biographers in estimating the closeness of Dickens's relation to his wife. Incidentally it adds Catherine Dickens as a witness to my suggestion that Dickens was peculiarly unfair to his mother.

The suppression of these memories, however, fed his novels, even after he had felt able to confide them to his friend, provided, indeed, one of the most vital images of his fictional world – the contrast of the warm, happy, family fireside within and the desolate streets and wastelands outside. Upon that contrast he rung in the course of his novels many marvellous changes.

From these days come the many lost children, poor and abandoned. From these days come also a certain righteousness, a certain hardness in Dickens's life, that he acquired to save himself from the pit he had nearly fallen into, and, I think, as an over-compensation, some part of the indulgent sentimentalism with which he often spoils the picture of innocence so essential to the Gospel ethic he wanted to preach.

Although the story has been told so many times, no words of others have described his experience more dramatically than his own confessions to Forster or the autobiographical fragment which he composed in 1845 or 1846 and later gave to his friend in confidence, when chance unstopped the dam of his secrecy:

> I know my father to be as kindhearted and generous a man as ever lived in the world. Everything that I can remember of his conduct to his wife, or children, or friends, in sickness or affliction, is beyond all praise. By me, as a sick child, he has watched night and day, unweariedly and patiently, many nights and days . . . .
> He was proud of me, in his way, and had a great admiration of the comic singing. But in the ease of his temper, and the straitness of his means, he appeared to have utterly lost at this time the idea of educating me at all, and to have utterly put from him the notion that I had any claim upon him in that regard, whatever. So I degenerated into cleaning his boots of a morning, and my own; and making myself useful in the work of the little house; and looking after my younger brothers and sisters (we were now six in all); and going on such poor errands as arose out of our poor way of living.

Both the idolatry of his father and the cruel fall of the idol from his pedestal are completely alive still in this sketch given to Forster some twenty years later.

He found in London at first some echoes of the old Chatham happiness – visits to his godfather Huffam at Limehouse where his comic singing was in delighted demand, visits to a Barrow uncle in Soho where there were new books to explore, even at home in Bayham Street James Lamert – still, one supposes, awaiting a commission – came to his rescue again and helped him to make a toy theatre.

But soon the parental demands for errands were doubled, for Mrs Dickens decided that it was up to her to save the situation. Always, like Mrs Micawber, like Mrs Nickleby, obsessed with 'connections' as the means of escape from penury, she decided that the trading interests with India of Mr Huffam, Charles's godfather, were a sure means of securing boarding pupils from parents who were forced to send their children home from that intemperate climate. To accommodate such socially superior children a decent house in a decent neighbourhood would be required; and this would bring the incidental advantages that the Dickens family could move from the unsalubrious area of Bayham Street. Something of this kind must have been her thinking if Dickens's portrait of Mrs Nickleby was as accurate a portrait of his mother as by inference he later suggested.

Finding a suitable and nearby district proved not too difficult. Bloomsbury, as we can see in Dickens's first published book, *Sketches by Boz*, was then a lower-middle-class world with pretensions, a neighbourhood where, however ends were stretched to make them meet, there were no common 'poor' among the neighbours to disgrace one. A great step up from Bayham Street.

Here, in Bloomsbury, at Gower Street North, Mrs Dickens found just the right house, put up a brass plate, had circulars printed, and dispatched the small Charles to deliver them. All, alas, to no end – except an increased rent. Dickens writes contemptuously more than bitterly of her efforts: 'Nobody ever came to school, nor do I recollect that anybody ever proposed to come, or that the least preparation was made to receive anybody. But I know that we got on very badly with the butcher and baker; that very often we had not too much for dinner; and that at the last my father was arrested.' The details of this attack upon his mother's ill-thought-out scheme deserve careful attention, for he directly connects it to the failure of household management (which is only partly logical) and to the imprisonment of his father (which is quite illogical). And Mrs Dickens was to blot her copybook in the eyes of her son more finally before she was done.

The blacking factory

Before his father's arrest and imprisonment, which Dickens notes as the end result of his mother's foolish daydream of being practical, something very momentous happened to Charles himself. He was set to work 'with common men and boys, a shabby child'. He found himself an abandoned small boy, ill-lodged, underfed, often aimlessly wandering the streets – 'no advice, no counsel, no encouragement, no consolation, no support, from anyone that I can call to mind, so help me God'. And it all seemed to happen in a horrible flash of time. James Lamert, despairing perhaps of the army commission, had accepted a managerial post in a newly-founded shoe-blacking factory, capital-ized by a relative. This factory – Warren's – was a new and comparatively

small affair off the Strand, but it had the publicity advantage of the same name
and almost the same address as the well-established, well-known and much-
advertised firm of Robert Warren. The new enterprise did not hesitate to make
use of the coincidence. No one knew the Dickens's financial circumstances better
than Lamert, although with their move to Gower Street he no longer lodged
with them. He had always been a friend to Charles, and now he suggested that
the boy should work at the factory, labelling bottles for six or seven shillings
a week. At last a useful connection had paid off! Mr and Mrs Dickens, Charles
remembered, accepted with alacrity.

Shortly after this his father was removed to Marshalsea debtors' prison,
and here, a little later, as was common with the families of debtor prisoners,
Mrs Dickens, torn out of genteel Bloomsbury and dreams of high-class boarding
schools, with her four youngest children and the little maid of all work, joined
her husband. Events, in fact, had come together about as badly for Charles
Dickens as they could.

James Lamert, in putting forward his suggestion for Charles's employment,
had not been forgetful either of Charles's promising talents or of the Dickens's
gentility. He proposed to give the dinner hour each working day to assisting
Charles in continuing his education; but in the busy affairs of a new business,
where young Lamert was on his mettle to improve his relatives' invested
capital, this soon proved too demanding of time. At first Charles was separated
in his work from the 'common men and boys', but with time this inconvenience
also lapsed. True, he tells us that James Lamert always continued to treat his
young relative differently from the other employees; and so does breeding tell,
or such is or was the English class system, that 'they always spoke of me as
"the young gentleman" . . . . Poll Green (one of the boys) uprose once and
rebelled against the "young gentleman" usage; but Bob Fagin (another of
the boys) settled him speedily.'

Everyone needs a role, not least a small, lost boy of awakening genius, and
Dickens's was that of doing his work well and silently, of proudly never telling
anyone of his misery, never discussing with anyone his sense of shame.
Knowing his toughness, his intense powers of application, his extraordinary
pride in later life, we may believe that he kept to that role with Spartan courage.
There is surely in the famous author's remembrance of this time a surplus of
intensity that tries to champion the boy whom everyone but he had forgotten.
'I forget in my dreams that I have a dear wife and children; even that I am a
man; and wander desolately back to that time of my life,' and 'Until old Hungerford Market was pulled down, until old Hungerford Stairs were destroyed,
and the very nature of the ground changed, I never had the courage to go
back to the place where my servitude began. I never saw it. I could not go near
it . . . . My old way home by the Borough made me cry, after my eldest child
could speak.'

As a matter of fact, in the dismal hours away from work, the 'journey home
to the Borough' came as a later alleviation. At first, when his mother and the
family moved into the Marshalsea prison south of the River Thames, Charles
was sent back to North London, to the despised Bayham Street, to lodge, along

with three other unwanted children, with an old woman called Mrs Roylance, who had once boarded children at Brighton. It is typical of the degree to which the mature author could not face the reality of those years that, when he later put this establishment into fiction as the Brighton household of Mrs Pipchin where Paul Dombey boards, he should have raised all – house, himself and other children – to the higher social level of Mrs Dickens's hoped-for establishment for the children of Anglo-Indian gentry. The journey to the Strand from this northern suburb was long and wearisome; the hungry lunch hours with his few pennies to spend on food worse.

But worst of all was his separation from his family far on the other side of the river. Sundays were a treat, when with his sister, Fanny, allowed out from the Royal Academy of Music, he spent the day at the Marshalsea Prison. His mother, a good mimic and, it would seem, a noser-out of other people's business, was able to tell him the histories of all the strange human creatures

'Until Old Hungerford Stairs were destroyed, I never had the courage to go back to the place where my servitude began.'

that inhabited that barred zoo. Also there were decent meals there, for the Customs Office (bureaucratic slowness, circumlocution sloth working this time in favour of the unfortunate) still paid John Dickens his salary, and as prison rents were low, the family lived better than they had in freedom. It is hard, I think, to forgive the self-centredness of the Dickens parents that never considered how the small Charles was living from hand to mouth in the freedom of the streets. Indeed it is easy to believe him when he wonders why the Dickens parents did not have what is now called 'a delinquent' on their hands. More importantly to us, it made him all his life ponder the springs of violence and crime in a way that has become increasingly relevant to Western man's concerns. How could he find a way to condemn the cold and dead society in which a small boy can so easily be sucked under and yet not seem to condone the callous brutality of criminals – men who were often once exactly such small, lost boys? How could he utterly refuse a sentimental forgiveness to evil men who had not shown that willpower by which he had survived those dreadful months, without losing the tender feeling which should have made all hearts melt at his childhood plight? It was an insoluble dilemma, but dwelling on it brought his thought and imagination very close to our own dilemmas, about State power that has lost all feeling and answering violence that has lost all reason.

Here we reach another paradox. In two of his novels – indeed, as soon as we set them against the facts of life we must say in two of his fantasies – we are enabled to see a child lost in a corrupt world and another child-helper who stays by her father and shares his long imprisonment. In the first, Oliver Twist is preserved from all contamination in Fagin's foul den by the grace of his gentle birth, of which he is unconscious, but which is given an outer sign by the author in the form of his uniformly standard English. Brilliant and powerful though much of this early novel is, this part of it is twaddle. If the small Charles was saved in those days from corruption, it was by willpower, an awakened imagination, and a snobbish sense of superiority, not by any innate force of gentility (for, as we know, if he had a class secret, it was the opposite of Oliver's). But in *Little Dorrit*, a novel of his maturity, he faced for the first time, as we shall see, the real moral meaning of his father's imprisonment. There is no doubt, I think, that the constancy of Little Dorrit to her father is the role that the small Charles would have wished to play to the father he so much loved – the small, brave boy standing by his father in the warm, dramatizing family circle behind bars, rather than the lonely, unnoticed boy living out his bravery in secret in the cold world outside bars. Yet it is one of the marks of the realism of *Little Dorrit* that Dickens notes how the corruption of prison had touched even that perfect heroine in blinding her moral sense to her father's frauds: 'It seems to me hard,' said Little Dorrit, 'that he should have lost so many years and suffered so much, and at last pay all the debts as well.'

The truth is that there was no easy answer in life or in fiction. If Charles had shared the imprisonment, would his strong character have been under-

'Covent Garden' by Phoebus Levin, 1864. 'Covent Garden market when it was Market morning, was wonderful company.' 'Night Walks' in *The Uncommercial Traveller*.

mined by the taint of prison morality? Or would his bitterness have been assuaged by family love without his will being sapped? Prison environment? Poor heredity? Neither will give the sort of straight moral answer that Dickens fiction demands; but, I think, *Pickwick Papers* and *Little Dorrit* both tell us, what we at any rate might guess, that the small twelve-year-old boy would rather have shared the warmth of the family fire even if the coals were prison-tainted, than have shivered outside in the honest wide world.

Yet it is necessary here, perhaps, to remind ourselves that in later life, in 1857, when he revisited the scene of the Marshalsea Prison in order to recall atmosphere for *Little Dorrit*, he was quite easily able to throw off the power of the past for the humour of the present. Despite the ruined state of the now defunct prison he located a room peculiarly nostalgic to him because it had been the room of a drunken Captain Porter whom he had immortalized in *David Copperfield*. He asked a small boy in the street: 'Who lives there?' and was answered 'Jack Pithick'. '"Who is Jack Pithick?" I asked him. And he said, "Joe Pithick's Uncle".' I quote this passage because in describing the traumatic effect of these boyhood months on Dickens, it is easy to suggest a man deeply buried in his past. Nothing could be further from the truth. His humour, his indignation, his high spirits (except in the hours of greatest depression) fed upon the present moment. The memory of his childhood, as for most novelists, was very powerful, but the stimulant to his work was the impact of the present moment, even when, as in this research visit to his father's old prison, he was delving into the cruellest past. Indeed his delight at the boy's answer may be seen as a kind of send-up of his own concern with buried sorrows.

His desperate longing for the family life eventually (the whole period, of course, was only months in calendar date; but eternity to Charles) communicated itself to his father, who procured him a lodging in Lant Street, The Borough, on the south side of the Thames, no further from the hated blacking factory than Camden Town had been, but far nearer to the loved family circle in prison. Then release came to John Dickens. 'By the death of a relative,' John Forster says in the biography; but that relative was, ironically, old Mrs Dickens, the retired housekeeper, whose thrift and respectability now left her son enough to discharge his debts (although she left more to her other, white sheep son). The family returned to Camden Town, to Mrs Roylance's (these houses seem in capacity to have been like the once popular expanding 'Revelation' suitcases of inter-war years' travel). At least Charles now shared the family food and fireside in the evening; but, to his consternation, there seemed to be no talk of his leaving the hated factory, the wretched bench that he shared with the low boys, Poll Green and Bob Fagin. Indeed, the better to get the light in the new establishment near Charing Cross to which Warren's had moved, that bench now stood in a window through which the passers-by could gaze.

Subsequent events suggest that if Charles had spoken his misery his father, at any rate, would have come to his aid, but it was a sign of love that he needed,

'Cremorne Gardens' by Phoebus Levin, 1864. 'Prostitutes in Dickens's work are never in any way associated with gaiety.' See page 95.

and signs of love must always come unbegged for. At last it came. In whatever terms, Mr Dickens sent a letter to Warren's remonstrating about his son's position. Considering all that he had done for Charles (and, no doubt, the lofty, Micawberish, Dorritian tone of John Dickens's letter), James Lamert took, not surprisingly, strong exception to the remonstrance, and, calling the boy into his office, he sent him away with angry words about his beloved father. It was then that Mrs Dickens, appalled that they might lose so good a connection when times were still so bad, anxious again to be practical, finally hurt her son too much. She secured from James Lamert a request for Charles's return. A request that John Dickens refused to consider – his pride and his love had been touched; the boy should not go back to work. The incident must have done much to confirm Dickens's determined view that a father should rule the family, a mother find her proper sphere inside the home. 'I never afterwards forgot, I never shall forget, I never can forget, that my mother was warm for my being sent back.'

In suggesting, as I shall, that these traumatic months at Warren's damaged his art and his life as well as enriching them, I do not wish to appear to judge them lightly. They were quite clearly a horrible episode in the life of a sensitive, lively child. But in all his remarks to Forster, in his abandoned autobiographical fragments, in *David Copperfield*, in the innumerable scenes of his novels where this event is reflected more tangentially, Dickens himself gives full dramatic effect to his suffering. 'In an evil hour for me', 'quick, eager, delicate and soon hurt', 'poor little drudge', 'so easily cast away at such an age', 'such a strange little apparition', 'small Cain that I was, except that I had never done any harm to anyone', 'my poor white hat, little jacket, or corduroy trousers', 'I was such a little fellow' – the phrases pour out of the autobiographical narrative so that the speaker seems like the most strange of Dickensian characters, a grown human being utterly enclosed in a vivid stylization of his childhood self, cut off from all his own everyday rational, decent 'manliness' by a lament for his own lost innocence – in short, one of the isolated, verbalizing monsters of his own novels. And so in a sense he is – a little mad about what happened to him as a child, unjust, snobbish, and uncaring for others. Yet, by jettisoning a certain fairness to reality, he undoubtedly succeeded in creating a special poetry about childhood suffering, and, by extension, about injustice generally. For all its excess of sentiment, its false notes, it vulgarity, its particular characters pitched in keys so high, so loud that they come through as blurred noises – Oliver, Nell, Floy Dombey – this indignation still makes his name a folk word for knight errantry on behalf of hard cases, a concern for the oppressed, the helpless, the abandoned and the drop-out. It is a world-wide reputation that no amount of factual detailing by scholars to show that he was often harshly just to the lost, if he thought them evil or even irresponsible, can ever alter.

For the general reader who is touched by his works, Dickens is above all funny; but, next to that, he is compassionate. And the general reader is surely by and large right – the misery of those abandoned months, the suppressed panic, the shame and loneliness, bit so deeply into him that only Dostoevsky,

Gissing and Jack London among novelists have equalled his power of absolute identification with the outcast.

He put almost every associate of these black months into his novels, but most important is his treatment of himself – from the small David Copperfield, through Arthur Clennam to Pip, he gradually sheds the romantic light in which he had viewed the episode, finally to condemn most harshly whatever there had been of inherited snobbery and gentility in his childhood self and whatever of determined material ambition those days in the abyss had left in the boy who fought his way out of it. It is evident that these months provided nearly a lifetime's impetus towards artistic creation. Without them we should not have a principal part of Dickens's novels, but with them I think it has to be said we have the final limitations of his work.

I have written of Dostoevsky as another novelist for whom the outcast and the downtrodden had a central place. Great comic novelist though Dostoevsky was, it is surely certain that Dickens is superior in comic genius; but in the last analysis Dostoevsky's world, though often more insane, more repulsive than Dickens's must be seen as more universal; in a sense, for all its madness, more mature. Dostoevsky continued to know extreme human misery on into his adult life; for Dickens it was a single traumatic experience of childhood; and although by the time he was forty-eight, in *Great Expectations*, he at last exorcised those months, it left him no time to place a full-grown man at the centre of his books, it left him no time to explore what had made Dickens the man and the great artist, for he had been too occupied in understanding how Dickens the boy could have suffered so suddenly and so hard.

Obsession with childhood is a primary defect of Dickens's world, but it is also a source of its peculiar splendour. For the second great defect of the Dickensian universe, the absence of any real sympathy with, or understanding for women, I can see no compensation. The source of this imaginative failure, which was to spoil so much of his art and make miserable so much of his life, lies six years later than the horrors of Warren's in the second great trauma of his youth – the frustrations of his passionate love for Maria Beadnell. Yet I think critics and biographers have not sufficiently realized how his mother's failure in his eyes at the time of this earlier disaster contributed towards his demanding and dissatisfied attitude towards women. When, after the death of his lawyer, Mitton, Georgina Hogarth destroyed numerous letters connected with Dickens's family, I think we may reasonably suppose that they contained sharp but very understandable complaints of constant demands upon his purse and his patience. However, if what survives of comment on his mother is the favourable part, it is certainly peculiarly slight, dismissive and reprehending; and, in general, the opinions of others, including school friends of Charles, his nurse, his brother-in-law, show a far more attractive woman than her son seemed to find her. She is called by others 'companionable', 'a good mother', 'easy going', 'good natured', 'common sensical'; she clearly had a humorous eye for life around her, and also, probably, a pleasure-loving nature, since an observer who saw her years later in 1841 at the sea-side with her famous son thought that she was too frightened of him to indulge her love of dancing save with relations. (Indeed, for Dickens, whose constant enchantment with young girls made him peculiarly hostile to mutton dressed as lamb, his mother dancing at fifty-two must have been an embarrassing spectacle.)

His father comes in for a great deal of his criticism but also for a great deal of admiring love, and his deathbed is described in terms of heroism. Far different are the few references in Dickens's letters to the lingering, senile years of his mother – three years before her death: 'My mother, who was also left to me when my father died (I never had anything left to me but relations) is in the strangest state of mind from senile decay; and the impossibility of getting her to understand what is the matter, combined with her desire to be got up in sables like a female Hamlet, illumines the dreary scene with a ghastly absurdity that is the chief relief I can find in it;' and some months later: 'I found my mother yesterday much better than I had supposed. She was not in bed, but downstairs. Helen [his widowed sister-in-law] and Letitia [his widowed sister] were poulticing her poor head, and the instant she saw me she plucked up spirit and asked me for "a pound".' To say the references are callous would be to underrate the provokingness of old age, but Mrs Dickens's senile 'thingness' seems only an extension of the alienated feelings with which her son had so long regarded her, a casting of her in an absurd, unloved role, which had begun with the portrayal of Mrs Nickleby twenty years earlier.

Mrs Nickleby, after all, thought of herself as 'companionable', 'a good mother', 'easy going', 'good natured', 'common sensical' – she felt herself the practical one of the family – all the things that more favourable witnesses had seen in Mrs Dickens. But Nicholas Nickleby, like Charles Dickens, found his mother's claims irritating and absurd. Yet, when we examine Mrs Nickleby's ambitions for her children, we may find that her main fault was to rely on 'connection', the connection with her rich, money-lending brother-in-law, whom perhaps, poor lady, she might be excused from guessing to be a Dickensian villain, a devil incarnate. Then, too, she had daydreams for her children, happy endings, but not as happy as the ending Dickens provided for the novel; for, whereas Mrs Nickleby saw her son as an usher at Westminster School, Nicholas, in fact, by getting in good with the Cheeryble brothers, ended a well-to-do gentleman, who could buy back the country estate lost by his parents' (particularly his mother's) foolish speculations. Then, too, Mrs Nickleby, at turned forty, gave her son the embarrassment of supposing herself wooed by the next-door neighbour, even for a moment causing Nicholas to think that she might have forgotten his father's memory so completely as to contemplate remarriage. It is counted against her that 'even her black dress assumed something of a deadly-lively air from the jaunty style in which it was worn. . . by a prudent disposal here and there of certain juvenile ornaments . . . her mourning garments assumed quite a new character.'

I do not write this version of a fictional character out of any sense of unfairness either to the character or to the original, Dickens's mother; indeed, if concern for the fictitious and the dead were a meaningful exercise, Mrs Nickleby provides her own defence – no sentimental picture could ever equal what Dickens did for his mother in inventing Mrs Nickleby's wonderful and absurd powers of speech. I only wish to suggest what may have been the separation between Dickens's view of life and his mother's, which caused him to see her (and subsequently so many women) only with irritated impatience. The answer, I think, is that Mrs Dickens had ambitions for him, but her ambitions were the very limited, practical ones of her class and sex. She had no inkling of his genius, nor did she feel his proud hatred of patronage. She set him at the foot of the ladder at Warren's; subsequently, as we shall see, by using her 'connections', she helped him to a higher but still very humble rung, first in the law, then in journalism. As steps to his future greatness they were important, but clearly Mrs Dickens saw them as good prospects in themselves, and thought herself a wise mother to have pulled strings, whereas to Charles they were pitiable blind alleys to bulldoze out of, and the strings distasteful attachments at the best to be remembered as obligations to be acquitted of. He recognized her kindness, her gallant gaiety and, above all, her faithfulness to his father, when he portrayed Mrs Micawber. Perhaps, if we take Mr Dorrit into account, Dickens treated his father in his fiction more cruelly than he did his mother. Certainly there are as many selfish fathers in his novels as there are selfish mothers and shrewish mothers-in-law. His parents, indeed, left him with a general dislike of the relationship. But on his mother he formed early his expectations of what a woman could fail to be.

Wellington House Academy

But now, at any rate, John Dickens earned his love. He arranged for his son to be enrolled at a nearby private school, Wellington House Academy, Hampstead Road, like much of this area soon to be broken up by the railway. Those who know the quality of English private schools might be alerted by the ostentatious patriotism of its name. It was not a good school. Much of the haphazard, desultory teaching, poor discipline punctuated by the headmaster's sadistic brutality, the seedy ushers and general run-down atmosphere, are embodied in Mr Creakle's Establishment in *David Copperfield* (one of Dickens's better names, with its overtones of a creaky, ramshackle business). Thus the school became the first of a long line of private schools to be the easy yet justified butt of English satirists; of, for example, Evelyn Waugh's Llanaba Castle in *Decline and Fall*, although I feel fairly convinced that that ardent Dickensian modelled his wonderful headmaster, Dr Fagan, and his daughters, Dingy and Flossie, upon Dickens originals from quite another novel – Mr Pecksniff and his Cherry and Merry. Years later, in a speech in 1857 at a charity banquet on behalf of The Warehousemen and Clerk's Schools, Dickens spoke very fiercely against Wellington House Academy:

> I don't like that sort of school to which I once went myself, the respected proprietor of which was by far the most ignorant man I have ever had the pleasure to know, who was one of the worst tempered men perhaps that ever lived, whose business it was to make as much out of us and put as little into us as possible . . . . In fact, and in short, I do not like that sort of school, which is a pernicious and abominable humbug altogether.

All the same, Wellington House Academy, whatever its faults in Dickens's remembrance thirty years later (after he had seen something of Eton as his eldest son's school, and had supervised his other sons' educations at expensive tutors' establishments), must have been a very heaven of interest, companionship, work and play when he came to it after the frightened months at Warren's. In his essay 'Our School', in casual references and in the recollection of his former schoolfellows it would seem to have been a typical early Victorian schoolboy's happy time, with an addition of imaginative games that one would expect from a future novelist. There were studies – their mediocre level is suggested by the triteness of Dickens's classical references – but the delights even of a meagre education to his starved, lively mind would no doubt have overcome any sense of disappointment. There were hobbies, particularly, it would seem, the keeping of pets – white mice, rabbits, birds and bees(!) wretched creatures – in school desks. There were 'accomplishments' – the violin, for which Dickens showed no aptitude; dancing with girls from the young ladies' academy nearby (where the backboard, it seems, threatened delinquents as much as a sadistic master's cane threatened the chubbier boys at Wellington House). There were fantasies about girls – an imaginary seraglio. There were school theatricals in toy theatres in which Dickens, already an old hand, led the way. There was the reading of penny 'dreadfuls', especially a penny weekly called *The Terrific Register*, whose gothic horrors and crimes probably had a less permanent effect on the 'ordinary' boy than they did upon Charles Dickens. There was the editing of a newspaper – 'Our Newspaper' – with the assistance of the boy at the next desk. There was a special, sinister playground (the site of what is now University College Hospital) called The Field of Forty Steps (reputed scene of a duel between two brothers). There was an invented language and long, shared stories in the contriving of which Dickens predictably played a leading part. There were close friendships.

There were 'accomplishments' – dancing with girls from the young ladies' academy.

But school played, no doubt, as one of his former schoolfriends, Harry Danson, suggested, a minor place in his growth: 'Depend upon it he was quite a self-made man, and his wonderful knowledge and command of the English language must have been acquired by long and patient study after leaving his last school.' To this we can add his many less important accomplishments – first-rate shorthand, very good French, adequate Italian. Indeed, for Dickens education always stands as the key to a meaningful life only if you know how to use it, that is, with other Victorian virtues of self-help, willpower, and application.

The Law

So much for school. Far different was to be the result of his experiences in the next nine years before, with the success of *Pickwick Papers*, he felt able to plan seriously for a life devoted only to writing. Warren's had been a hell that entered into the very texture of his fictional world. Wellington House, poor as it was, coming as a release from Warren's, was a glimpse of heaven that made education the central plank of his hopes for a good society. Now in a series of petty employments, on the periphery of the Law and of Parliament, his whole energies were set upon finding another outlet for his genius. This paid (poorly paid) work of his youth was no hell, only an interference, an obstacle, an irrelevance. His experiences in the legal offices and as a Parliamentary reporter do not enter into the very grain of his fictional web like Warren's, though his legal experience provided a mass of wonderful ornament, farcical and grim, to the tapestry. More important than the place of legal or Parliamentary life in his novels is the absolute contempt for the English law and the Parliamentary system with which their verbiage and dusty ceremony filled his youthful, ambitious, impatient soul. This contempt lasted all his life and lent to his social views some of their most original as well as illogical features.

Affairs in the Dickens household had not gone well. In 1825, the bureaucratic machinery of the Customs service had at last got round to noticing its employee's bankruptcy and imprisonment. John Dickens was retired at around forty years of age, with a small pension. It is true that he applied himself with energy to learning shorthand and during those school years of Charles became a shorthand reporter. But the Dickens financial position was precarious. The family was evicted from one set of lodgings. An additional mouth, the youngest son, Augustus, came upon the scene. A school friend of Charles who visited him at the Dickens lodgings in the Polygon, Somers Town, a shabby, genteel North London suburb, described Mrs Dickens as a fragile woman in delicate health.

Fragile or not, Elizabeth Dickens again appears to have been mainly instrumental, through her family, in getting her son into employment, although his new employer, Edward Blackmore, speaks of being well acquainted with both Dickens's parents. At any rate, to Ellis & Blackmore, attorneys, of Holborn Court, Gray's Inn, Charles Dickens, aged fifteen, went as a junior clerk in

May 1827. He remained there until November 1828. Then, having worked very energetically in his spare time to acquire Gurney's system of shorthand, he left what he must have felt to be a dead-end job of petty duties (very close to those of the stereotype office boy) to become a freelance reporter. He was too young (not yet seventeen) to report Parliamentary proceedings; but luckily, as chance (and his mother's good connections) would have it, a distant relative on the Barrow side, Thomas Charlton, was a freelance reporter at Doctors' Commons. Charles Dickens was able to share his box there in order to report the legal proceedings. Very absurd proceedings he found them, too.

He could hardly have seen the law from a more ludicrous angle, one more provoking, more tedious to a brilliant, ambitious young man. Ellis & Blackmore seemed, no doubt, a blind alley; but Doctors' Commons *was* a mournful backwater, even though, as time went by and he acquired a share in an office of his own, he widened his legal experience by covering cases in the magistrates' courts, when Doctors' Commons was not sitting. And this tedium went on for more than three years (a lifetime when one is suffocating with unfulfilled ambition). It is hard to say whether it was finally an advantage to Charles Dickens's art that he should have passed from the dreary and hopeless routines of an attorney's near office boy to the petty and antiquated proceedings of Doctors' Commons. Here in a court near St Paul's he was to listen for nearly four years to rambling, involved cases, mainly concerned with ecclesiastical suits pertaining to the Bishop of London's Consistory Court or the Archbishop of Canterbury's Court of Arches, with occasional excursions into marine matters in the Admiralty Court, or wills and testaments in the Prerogative Court. From those years comes the most brilliant, funny and savage picture of the machinery and furniture (inanimate and human) of the British legal system, reaching its height in the masterly *Bleak House*; but from it comes the sketchiest of outlines of the content of this absurd law or of the substance of its cases.

Dickens who, as a journalist and editor, was always scrupulous about the verification of factual details, however strong the opinions he derived from them, could not approach his fictional material in the same way. True, he took trouble and was accurate in reconstructing the events of the 1780 riots in *Barnaby Rudge*: true, his purpose was occasionally and incidentally immediate and journalistic, as with *Oliver Twist* and the Poor Law, or with Heep and Littimer in prison in *David Copperfield* as an attack on the separate system of penal confinement; but in the main his novels worked upon individuals and institutions, upon men and women and the society that bound them together, in an altogether broader way, in which detail is sucked up and dispersed, giving a sense of concrete depth to what is in fact the author's own world of fantasy.

We remember the thin gruel of Oliver's workhouse, which is derived from near fact, but somehow we remember as much if not more the white waistcoat of the hardhearted gentleman on the board of guardians – a whiteness which seems to stand for a false and cruel assertion of integrity, a whiteness that suggests stony immovability before suffering, like some white wall staring out

Doctors' Commons was a mournful backwater.

in hard sunlight. This is only one among hundreds of possible examples from the early novels when Dickens still imposed some journalistic, carefully factual description upon his fantasy; in the later novels, fact was even more dissolved into poetry.

So his life at Doctors' Commons, odd and antiquated 'Dickensian' place though it was, enters only subordinately into the world of his novels. It makes its appearance as the subject of a journalistic, humorous sketch in *Sketches by Boz*, but this is hardly fiction. It appears again in the autobiographical impressionism of *David Copperfield*, but it is no more than a location near St Paul's where David may pass his locust years in growing youthful disillusion, until Mr Wickfield's drunken ineptitude and Uriah Heep's villainy bring Aunt Betsy Trotwood's fortune crashing down and, with it, her nephew's period of wasting his time in a gentlemanly professional backwater. Of the content of all the many ecclesiastical and maritime cases that Dickens must have taken down, there appears, I think, nothing, unless it be Captain Cuttle's complete ignorance of the marine objects he lives among in Sol Gills's marine chandler's shop. As to wills and testaments, they are ubiquitous in Dickens's novels, for very good social reasons, and for the most necessary of melodramatic reasons concerned with plotting, but as to their having detailed existence *as wills* that Dickens may have encountered in his youthful work, I cannot find that any one of them (including the famous Jarndyce will) is any more than a piece of stage machinery.

Likewise with his earlier job at Ellis & Blackmore's. There are superb portraits of lawyer's clerks throughout the novels from *Pickwick Papers* to *Great Expectations*. Some of these portrayals are derisive, as of the laziness, hangovers, social pretensions and sharp dealings of the clerks at Dodson and Fogg's; some are comic, but warm and sympathetic, as of Dick Swiveller (surely a loving portrait of himself as he might have been if life had confined

Portrayals of the laziness, hangovers, social pretensions and sharp dealings of clerks.

him to the attorney's office world). That of young Smallweed in *Bleak House* is as hostile as it is contemptuous, while that of Mr Guppy in the same book is an extraordinary mixture of contempt for social pretensions (such as he must himself have had when young) and a half-checked, relenting savagery. As to attorneys (the employers) they are, with the exception of the benevolent, if cynical, Mr Perker, attorney to Mr Pickwick, a series of wonderfully portrayed scoundrels – Dodson and Fogg, Sampson Brass, Uriah Heep, Mr Vholes, Mr Tulkinghorn; relenting only at long last with Mr Grewgious in *Edwin Drood*. But, sweet and bitter alike, these young clerks and their employers are all superb and individual characters, whose physical surroundings – the rooms they work in, the eating houses they dine at, the smoking concerts they take the chair at, the courts they attend, the theatres they visit for distraction – all enclose the reader absolutely in their dusty, leathery mustiness of old books and unswept, pokey offices, of the smell of wine, of greasy, sloppy boiled meat and veg, of hot-brandy-and-water conviviality. But the work they do is just not there, save again as a plot mechanism whereby Mr Guppy may pass his professional time delving into Lady Dedlock's guilty secret.

Parliament

It is the same with experience in the House of Commons, to which, as reporter, he went from Doctors' Commons. The verbiage of Parliamentary proceedings, transferred to other settings, is facetiously imitated, I suppose, in the proceedings of the Pickwick Club and the very unfunny, irrelevant second chapter of *Nicholas Nickleby*, where we are given an account of a meeting of the United Metropolitan Improved Hot Muffin and Crumpet Baking and Punctual Delivery Company. The impression made upon him by elections gives us the Eatanswill chapter of *Pickwick Papers*, whilst the contempt of the M.P. for his electors once the election is over is satirized in Mr Gregsbury's dismissal of the deputation in *Nicholas Nickleby*. But these are very early novels, and all he had seen from the reporter's gallery of the House of Commons or at the hustings soon vanished from his world, although M.P.s and their jockeying remain a feature of his satire.

His only picture of Parliament in session is historical and seen from outside the closed doors of the Chamber. The description in *Barnaby Rudge* (1841) of the presentation to the Commons of the Protestant petition by Lord George Gordon and his mob of followers is masterly – one of the many beautifully organized and controlled crowd scenes which punctuate this mob-enthralled novel against mobs. But it is to be noted that Dickens's fictional interest in Parliament as a bulwark against the Protestant mob of 1780 came, not from any tender memory for the Parliament he had watched in action for four years, but from his alarm at the physical force element in Chartism and the violent rising of Chartists in the provinces in the four or five years before the publication of his fine historical novel. Lord George Gordon's bogus and dangerous petition must have spoken to all good, law-abiding readers of *Barnaby Rudge* as another, earlier version of the wicked Charter. Even so it is notable that the Commons themselves do little to control the mob in the novel; this is done by the bravery of an individual member, a military man, General Conway.

The historical example he chose fitted well among his own prejudices. I do not mean to imply that Dickens would have substituted iron rule for democracy. The idea sometimes put about of him as a 'crypto-Fascist' is, as I hope my picture of him will show, a false sophistication. But when it came to Parliament, his radical liberalism had a strong emphasis on the radical. In his chapter on his hero, Cromwell, in his *Child's History of England* he writes: 'As that Parliament did not please him either, and would not proceed to the business of the country, he jumped into a coach one morning, took six guards with him, and sent them to the right-about. I wish this had been a warning to Parliaments to avoid long speeches, and do more work.' This, of course, is the tone of much reporting from Parliament that we get in the newspapers today. It is the natural reaction of those who have to listen to public debates with their intermixture of so much party propaganda talk, and so much seemingly facetiously schoolboy 'House of Commons is the best club in London' wit; it is the natural reaction of those who never see the real work of Members of Parliament in committee or in constituency business. In his letters Dickens sometimes expressed grave concern for the failure of the working of the Parliamentary system; but in the fictional world this concern becomes translated into the once-for-all ironic contempt of the famous opening of the fortieth chapter of *Bleak House* (1852–3): 'England has been in a dreadful state for some weeks, Lord Coodle would go out, Sir Thomas Doodle wouldn't come in, and there being nobody in Great Britain (to speak of) except Coodle and Doodle, there had been no Government.' So much for Parliament and the party system, those bastions of the mid-Victorian constitution.

Added to his contempt for the Law, his contempt for Parliament should have made him some sort of a revolutionary, whether of left or right (as we should say now). It is indeed just what 'mature', 'responsible' men – Members of Parliament, Cabinet ministers, Q.C.s, and judges – would expect from a man whose opinion of two of the great bastions of England's society had been formed in youth from menial, irresponsible positions (or, at the best, with his reporting, purely as a spectator). It is not from office boys and clerks, or even from reporters, that mature, responsible men expect mature, responsible judgements. And in one sense they are right. For men of standing in the world of affairs, the institutions they serve are alive only in the work they execute. Of this work in any detail there is no trace in Dickens's novels.

Many reasons are given why Charles Dickens could not carry his contempt for the status quo into a revolutionary logic – the fear of anarchy of a self-made man with genteel, even snobbish frame of temper is one. But it is easy to make too much of this. Dickens earned good money, lived well, brought up his children comfortably, liked to mix with notable people. This is true. But as he came to be a world figure, he outgrew most of the snobbery which had inevitably attached to him when he was making his way. By 1860 when he wrote *Great*

'The boy with many Friends' by Thomas Webster, 1841. 'Peggoty's promised letter in a perfect nest of oranges and two bottles of cowslip wine.' *David Copperfield.*

Overleaf. 'Rat-catching at the Blue Anchor Tavern' anon, 1850–2. 'The rodent criminal world.' See page 129 on Fagin's gang in *Oliver Twist.*

Expectations he scorned gentility as fully and deeply as any hater of the social system could ask. Yet he continued always to fear deeply the overthrow of settled order. Profound disenchantment with social institutions, anxiety about any sort of social upheaval, go constantly together in his career. It is often explained by saying that he feared mobs. No doubt he did. This is sometimes said with a certain air of criticism by people who themselves would greatly fear a mob if they ever met one. And it really explains nothing. Coming from a small bourgeois family, born not twenty years after the Terror of the French Revolution, it is much more astonishing that he should espouse the popular cause at all than that he should fear its violent consequences. Yet throughout his career, and notably in *A Tale of Two Cities*, however much he warned against popular violence, he always insisted that the eighteenth-century French aristocracy had only reaped the harvest that they had sown.

The cause of his deep fear of social upheaval, which marries at times so oddly with his contempt for the social system, lies, I think, in two very differing aspects of his view of life. The first is his very real belief in evil, of which we shall see much more when we come to his great novels. But a deep-seated belief in evil, especially in evil evidenced in violence, hardly allows for social revolution. No promise of Utopia can be worth the risk of evil unleashed, that a violent revolution offers. Sympathetic though he was to the grievances of the Chartists, 'it is unnecessary for us to observe that we have not the least sympathy with physical force Chartism in the abstract,' he wrote in the *Examiner* in 1848, 'or with tried and convicted Physical Force Chartists in particular. Apart from the atrocious designs to which these men, beyond all question, willingly and easily subscribed . . . they have done too much damage to the cause of rational liberty and freedom all over the world to be regarded in any other light than as enemies of the common weal, and the worst foes of the common people.' Evil in action was for Dickens a fearsome reality – the beast unleashed.

The second was the opposite – an enjoyment of the richness and variety of life even at his most despairing moments. Dickens was not without certain puritanisms; he shared some of the prudery of his time; but he was as constant an advocate of play as he was of work. Play, enjoyment, variety, above all absurdity in variety – these are the very core of the world of Dickens. For all his radicalism, for all his deep concern to combat individual social evils, his comic sense made him – like most satirists – far more conservative than either his intellect or even his emotions often allowed him to recognize. To say all this, that his sense of evil and his sense of comedy prevented him from translating his sourness and his despair into a logical system of rejection of society, is only to say that, whatever his inclinations, thoughts and feelings, he instinctively recognized the sources of his art – the crude but powerful dramatic analysis of evil, the subtle, pervasive poetry of comic absurdity. In that scheme the Law stood, however weakly, as some negative check against ill-doing, and was an absurdity rich in comic potential. As to Parliament, it was as Law, though less important.

'The Stage Arrives' anon, c.1830. 'Yoho, down countless turnings, and through countless mazy ways, until an old Inn-yard is gained.' *Martin Chuzzlewit.*

Less important really because whereas the Law as a profession had done nothing but stand in his way in those youthful years at Ellis & Blackmore and in Doctors' Commons, his days as reporter at the House of Commons had brought him glory as a journalist and had been the immediate avenue to his success as a writer. The essential difference of how he viewed them may be seen in the way that he spoke of the two professions in after years. It is one of the curious aspects of Charles Dickens's career that long after we should consider him to be fully established as a writer, his anxieties made him speak as though he might be forced to change his occupation. Or, perhaps, if we think of the crowd of family and other borrowers that beset him, and the high expense of his household, it is not so curious. Even in his comparatively unestablished days in 1841 he immediately refused when he was invited to stand as joint candidate for Parliament with his good friend, Talfourd, at Reading. Yet as late as 1846 he could write: 'I am nominally . . . a Law Student, and have a certain number of "terms to Keep" before I can be called to the Bar, and it could be well for me to be called;' and he made serious enquiries about becoming a London stipendiary magistrate. The difference is clear, I think; he still felt the need to cancel his menial law career, but, in his mind, his career as a Parliamentary reporter needed no cancellation, it had made him a successful journalist; and journalism remained, throughout his life, some part of his great reputation.

He always thought of his reporting days with pride. In 1865 he spoke at a banquet of the Newspaper Press Fund. A passage in that speech tells us how happily he looked back on those years:

> I went into the gallery of the House of Commons as a reporter when I was a boy not eighteen, and I left it . . . nigh thirty years ago. I have pursued the calling of a reporter under circumstances of which many of my brethren at home in England here, many of my modern successors, can form no adequate conception. I have often transcribed for the printer from my shorthand notes, important public speeches in which the strictest accuracy was required, and a mistake in which would have been to a young man severely compromising, writing on the palm of my hand, by the light of a dark lantern, in a post chaise and four, galloping through a wild country, all through the dead of night, at the then surprising rate of fifteen miles an hour. I have worn my knees by writing on them on the old back row of the old gallery of the old House of Commons; and I have worn my feet by standing to write in a preposterous pen in the old House of Lords, where we used to be huddled together like so many sheep kept in waiting, say, until the woolsack wanted restuffing. I have been, in my time, belated on miry by-roads, towards the small hours, in a wheelless carriage, with exhausted horses and drunken postboys, and have got back in time for publication, to be received with never-forgotten compliments by the late Mr Black, coming in the broadest of Scotch from the broadest of hearts I ever knew.

I have quoted this extract from Dickens's speech at length, partly because it paints as well as can be done the picture of his working life from 1832 until the success of *Pickwick Papers* allowed him to give himself entirely to writing; but also because it shows, I think, by its 'old boy' tone of 'those were the days', by its pleasure in the editor Black's 'well done' that Dickens's newspaper years, however hard, were his version of happy school-days. They took place in what was really the close of the Regency world, of the pre-railway world. They tied Dickens, in his memory, with the eighteenth century, which, however he detested most of its works, was the age of his boyhood fictional heroes, of Tom Jones and Roderick Random and Humphrey Clinker.

Unlike his career in the back alleys of the Law, his reporting days were, as this extract from his speech shows, an unqualified success. Once again it had been through his mother's family, through his uncle John Henry Barrow, that the escape into a new profession had been effected. Somewhere around his twentieth year he began to work for his uncle, who was editor of the *Mirror of Parliament*, a rival to *Hansard* in reporting Parliamentary speeches. John Dickens was already working there with efficiency when his young son joined the paper. Somewhat later, early in 1832, Charles's competence won him additional reporting for an evening paper, the *True Sun*. His first reports were thus made from the old pre-Reform Act Parliament (and indeed in the old House of Commons that was burned down three years later). But he was not

'Destruction of both Houses of Parliament by Fire, on October 16, 1834.'

Holland   Melbourne   Brougham
Grey   Durham   Lansdowne   Wellesley

any more favourable to the working, the speeches and the procedure of the Reformed Parliament when it sat. He detested its architect, Lord Grey, although it was to cover the ceremony of the honouring of Grey with the freedom of Edinburgh in September 1834 that he made by sea his first journey outside England. With him on that occasion went Charles Beard, a young fellow reporter, who, best man at his wedding and a lifelong intimate friend, was the most permanent gain he made from those newspaper years. It was Beard who later said of him 'that there never *was* such a shorthand writer'. It was Beard, indeed, who a month before the Edinburgh trip had secured for Charles a post on the *Morning Chronicle* at five guineas a week. This important daily newspaper offered him steady and full employment, which meant that when the House was not in session he travelled the country – it was indeed one such trip, to the Ipswich and Sudbury by-elections, that was to serve as model for the popular Eatanswill scenes of *Pickwick Papers*. This was the first job that he had gained without the assistance of his mother's family, although even here his uncle, John Henry Barrow, with remarkable unselfishness, had earlier given a dinner party to introduce his invaluable reporting nephew to the *Morning Chronicle*'s editor, Collier. In later days Collier was to say that, in recommending his nephew, Barrow had declared that Charles had been responsible for much of the rhyming advertising copy of Warren's blacking factory. If the story is true, it is a nice ironic use to which those traumatic months of boyhood were at last put; but it also underlines the dislike

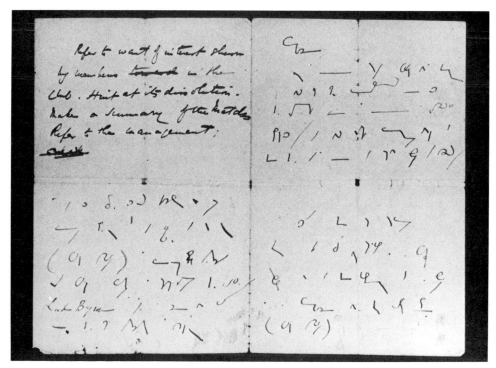

'There never *was* such a shorthand writer.' A page of Dickens's shorthand.

Opposite. 'The Reform Bill receiving The King's Assent by Royal Commission.'

that a man of exceptional attachment to truth and independence like Charles Dickens must have felt about the uneasy shifts and white lies that the poor genteel had to resort to in a world of patrons and influence.

In 1835, at the height of his reputation as a reporter, Dickens had already been publishing literary sketches for eighteen months or more, at first anonymously and then under the soon-to-be world-famous pseudonym. Before the end of 1834 he had already been pointed out to the famous historical novelist, Harrison Ainsworth, at the newspaper offices as the talented young writer, 'Boz'. In February 1836, a few months after he had led his brother journalists on the *Morning Chronicle* in a successful strike, he published his first book, *Sketches by Boz*. It was not, however, until November 1836, when *Pickwick Papers* had established his name, that he felt secure enough, with publishers' contracts, to leave journalism. He was twenty-four years and nine months old and a married man. His letter of resignation to Sir John Easthope, the owner of the *Morning Chronicle*, was a last blow against employer's patronage (to be repeated again a number of times in later years from a more independent footing, with his publishers). 'Dear Sir, if you imagine that I was the least guilty of intentional disrespect in not returning to the office the other day,' it began, and ended, 'Depend upon it, Sir, if you would stimulate those about you . . . this is not the way to do it.' The Inimitable had indeed arrived upon the scene.

But before we can assist at the glorious victory of *Pickwick Papers*, we must look at Dickens's private pleasures and sorrows during these nine years of youthful employment after he left school, for in his leisure-hour distractions and in his love life, far more than in the mainly dulling routines of his work, are to be found the social material and manners, the style and the underlying stresses, that largely compose the pictorial world of the first decade of his novels.

Chapter III
Love, Marriage, Success and Death 1827–40

uring the nine years between his leaving school in 1827 and his becoming a national figure almost overnight in 1837 the social life of Charles Dickens provided him with the material of most of his early novels, down to *Dombey and Son*, published a decade after *Pickwick Papers* had appeared.

However mythical the underlying themes of Charles Dickens's novels may be, their immediate subject is Victorian Society. It became his aim, like that of most of the other great nineteenth-century novelists, to encompass the whole of society. However some critics may cavil at his portrayal of the working classes or of the aristocracy, it may surely be said that between *Dombey and Son* (1846) and *Our Mutual Friend* (1864) he succeeded in this aim as no other English novelist had done, although, of course, the picture he presents to his readers serves the ends of his art and not of future social historians. But before 1846 the social world of Dickens's fiction is noticeably incomplete. This is true even of the England that he portrays in *Martin Chuzzlewit*, the very novel in which, after a few month's stay in the United States, he felt able to present a broad satirical portrait of the whole of American society. The England (or rather the Londoner's England) of Dickens's early novels is primarily middle-class. His few gestures towards depicting the selfish aristocracy in *Nicholas Nickleby* or the left-over Regency aristocratic society of Bath in *Pickwick Papers* are crude. There is no working class in our sense of the word, though we must except servants like Sam Weller or young Kit Nubbles, and the Marchioness in *The Old Curiosity Shop*, for it has to be remembered that domestic servants formed a very large part of the Victorian working classes. The rest of the lower social strata in these novels, almost so low as to be submerged, are those too broken to work, like the paupers in the first part of *Oliver Twist*, or those too fly to work, like Fagin's gang in the second part of the same novel.

Even in this mainly middle-class world of the early novels, save for Mr Pickwick and his three companion travellers from the Pickwick Club who, though sketchy, each gain a little flesh from their association with their great founder, the characters who stray too far into the upper reaches of middle-class gentility or affluence – the Maylies of *Oliver Twist*, the Cheerybles of *Nicholas Nickleby* – seem to fade into some rosy-hued mist that renders them almost invisible. Apart from these, this middle-class world of the good and the bad alike, the comic or the sinister, is cramped and close and isolated – it is a world of dingy counting houses and attorneys' offices, of clerks' high stools, of front parlour celebrations, of gravy-smeared boarding houses like Todger's; a world given up (where the necessities of melodramatic plot do not demand seduction or murder) to wasting your substance in fifth-rate imitation of your dandy betters as do Mr Mantalini and Dick Swiveller, or hoarding your substance in almost miserly, dusty gloom like Ralph Nickleby, or Anthony and Jonas Chuzzlewit, or Sampson and Sally Brass; an airless jungle world where young women hunt for husbands, in pairs of seeming bosom friendship but really of deadly rivalry, like Fanny Squeers and 'Tilda Price, or Miss Snevelicci and Miss Ledrook, or like Merry and Cherry Pecksniff; a world where the family hunt only for legacies, either comically, like the Kenwigs pursuing Uncle Lillyvick, or horribly, like the Chuzzlewit gang in pursuit of old Martin's cash. This is a newly emerging middle class coming out of the obscure subordination of the eighteenth century – where attorneys and ushers and doctors and curates still ranked low, where merchants and apprentices had only just separated from living together over the shop; a money-grubbing society, narrow, suspicious, worshipping mammon, sometimes with an indefinable cant of high-mindedness like Mr Pecksniff's that is not markedly religious yet certainly not secular, crude and generous in its appetite for pleasure yet disguising this greed with increasing gentility and prudery, intensely individual yet huddling together like some underground creatures not yet finally dug out of their burrows.

The left-over Regency aristocratic society of Bath.

London of the *Sketches*

Above all, the middle-class society of Dickens's early novels, though a London society, is entirely parochial, quite unconscious of the wider society of which it forms a part. When Kate Nickleby becomes companion to Mrs Wittitterly, a social climbing lady of Cadogan Place, Belgravia, we have for the first time in Dickens's novels a sense of social mobility. The Wittitterlys's social parasitism is very crudely drawn compared with the wonderful gallery of snobs and hangers-on that Dickens was to inaugurate with Major Bagstock in *Dombey and Son*, but it is there:

> 'My dear doctor,' said I to Sir Tumley Snuffim, in this very room, the very last time he came. 'My dear doctor, what is my wife's complaint? Tell me all. I can bear it. Is it nerves?' 'My dear fellow,' he said, 'be proud of that woman; make much of her; she is an ornament to the fashionable world, and to you. Her complaint is soul.'

And again:

> 'Mrs Wittitterly,' said her husband, is sought after and coveted by glittering crowds and brilliant circles. She is excited by the opera, the drama, the fine arts, the – the – the –' 'The nobility, my love,' interposed Mrs Wittitterly. 'The nobility, of course,' said Mr Wittitterly, 'and the military.'

The Wittitterlys are out after the main chance, but it is more than the greed for money that rules the lives of Bumble and Squeers and Quilp and Ralph Nickleby and Jonas Chuzzlewit or even of Montague Tigg. The Wittitterlys know and lust for the 'world', not in foolish, harmless dreams like Mrs Nickleby or Dick Swiveller, but with a life pattern that has been organized for no other purpose. The Wittitterlys are a very feeble torch that points the way out of the gloomy, airless world of the early novels to the spacious satires of all society of which the peaks are Edith Dombey's drawing room and Chesney Wold and Mrs Merdle's parrot and the silver camels on Mr Veneering's splendid dinner table.

Of course evey novelist makes social guesses. Dickens could never know the aristocracy or the working class from absolute knowledge since he had not been born into them or lived among them. But then a social novelist only needs his social worlds as the grist for his art; and to them all he will bring always his own special flavours – in Dickens's case, I think, in some part derived from the mercurial quality of his family, so that most of Dickens's characters are seen as it might be after three or four glasses of champagne. Nevertheless, to make the necessary imaginative leap to encompass a whole metropolitan society, there must be some sense of the ground beneath one, and some sense that the ground has been under one's feet long enough to be familiar to the tread. In the immediate years after the publication of *Pickwick Papers* in 1837 Dickens was in the position to be familiar with almost any branch of English society that he chose; yet it was not until 1846, after he had looked at contemporary England from the distance of the United States and

Italy, perhaps even more importantly, after he had looked at it from the past in that greatly undervalued historical novel *Barnaby Rudge*, that he was able, both technically and intellectually, to encompass the whole world he lived in. Before that, in his first five novels (I except *Barnaby Rudge*) he is working mainly upon the knowledge of the world that he gained between the year after leaving school until the year of his great success, from 1827 to 1837. The outlines of that world are to be found in the sketches, which, as he himself says in his preface, 'were written and published, one by one, when I was a very young man. They were collected and republished while I was still a very young man' – the *Sketches by Boz*.

Of their defects Dickens when he wrote this preface in 1850 was very well aware: 'They comprise my first attempts at authorship. . . . I am conscious of their often being extremely crude and ill considered, and bearing obvious marks of haste and inexperience.' Here Dickens probably refers to the very crude facetiousness of the humour, the playful, arch language of some of the passages, above all, the authorial voice of a novice, as he, indeed, sometimes calls himself: 'Scenes like these are continued until three or four in the morning; and even when they close, fresh ones open to the inquisitive novice. But as a description of all of them, however slight, would require a volume, the contents of which, however instructive, would be by no means pleasing, we make our bow, and drop the curtain.' Even the most ephemeral journalism of his more mature days never echoes such a stilted tone. He may have also been aware of the crude, truly vulgar attitude to life that marks a large number of his reflections upon human nature, a sort of vulgar, know-all attitude that used at one time to be snobbishly associated with commercial travellers. Save for the opening chapters of *Pickwick Papers* and of *Nicholas Nickleby*, he never again wrote with such unassured self-consciousness, with such obviously whipped-up desire for effect, after these early pieces, although it must be said that the sketches contain more lively characterization and certainly more first-rate journalistic description of London life than is usually allowed. But whatever may be criticized, whatever he himself looked back to with embarrassment, there are few of the elements of the early Dickens world (to say 1850) that do not make their first appearance in these sketches; and many were to remain lifelong concerns. As to the stylistic crudities, both humorous and dramatic, they were to reappear from time to time when haste prevented his great mastery from taking over. The remaining faults, as he says, are due to inexperience.

Like the later sudden and far greater success of *Pickwick Papers*, the publication of his first sketch came to him in the most delightful manner that a young author can know, towards the end of 1832, when he was twenty. His first intimation of its acceptance was when he purchased the current *Monthly Magazine* and found it there, although with an altered title, 'A Dinner at Poplar Walk'. After this he was asked to supply a series of sketches; but it should be noted that the *Monthly Magazine* did not pay its contributors. It was not long after, however, that he joined the *Morning Chronicle* and there wrote most of the pieces in the first series of *Sketches by Boz*, that was to be published collectively on his twenty-fourth birthday, only a few weeks before the first number of *Pickwick Papers* had been published in his own paper and for payment.

What sort of material is incorporated in *Sketches by Boz*? The first section, perhaps the feeblest and most ephemeral, is called 'Our Parish', and unlike the rest seems to go back for some material to his boyhood days in Chatham.

The second (and journalistically by far the best) is called 'Scenes', and embodies the fruit of all his wide, youthful knowledge of London. We may suppose that conjectures about London's poverty and crime must have already

'Public Dinners' from the *Sketches*. Dickens and Cruikshank lead the guests.

been deep in his imagination from the blacking factory days. In his journeys from Camden Town to the Marshalsea on his visits to his imprisoned father, he took in a whole segment of London which included the gentility of Bloomsbury, the depraved depths of Seven Dials, the business whirl of Charing Cross, the respectable poverty of the Borough. But in his law clerk days he enormously extended his knowledge to include all the City, the East End to the Docks and away to Greenwich, the lordly western suburbs until they became the riverside country villages of Richmond and Hampton and Chertsey, London north to Highgate and Barnet, London south to New Cross or Clapham.

A fellow clerk at Ellis & Blackmore's recalled, 'I thought I knew something of the town, but after a little talk with Dickens I found that I knew nothing. He knew it all from Bow to Brentford.'

Some of the knowledge seems already to have come from that solitary nocturnal walking that became an indispensible feature of his method of composition later in life. There are two pieces: 'The Streets – Night' and 'The Streets – Morning', which give in journalistic synopsis all that extraordinary sense of the city's life being extinguished to all but a few revellers and an army of the homeless, and of the city awaking again to the life of the markets – a city still fed by carts coming in with produce from the country – that is so essential a part of the movement of his novels. These two early panoramic sketches of London life still have a slight, rigid, tableau quality which is to be expected and found in the other set pieces like 'Greenwich Fair', 'Vauxhall Gardens by Day' and so on. But the very time change involved – the gathering darkness, and the breaking life – makes them a prelude to those great walking (or very occasionally horseback) scenes that, starting with Sikes taking Oliver Twist across London to rob the house in Chertsey, end with the pursuit along the river of Eugene Wrayburn by the murderously jealous Headstone, who in turn is dogged by the blackmailing dead-body-fisher, Riderhood, with his cap like a drowned animal. Coming from Dickens's own creatively tormented prowling through the city streets, they bring to the English novel for the first time a cinematic mobility: intensely detailed observation that swells out into dreamlike impressionism, forward in close-up focus and backward into out-of-focus, cloudlike shapes. Such passages in his work make earlier scenes of movement, even the occasionally brilliant crowd pieces of Sir Walter Scott, seem like old stills. In *Sketches by Boz* we see how a brilliant young journalist's observation of London's movement is just on the point of taking wings into imaginative art.

Continuing with the London sketches, 'Seven Dials', 'Meditations in Monmouth Street', 'Gin Shops', 'The Pawnbroker's Shop,' 'Criminal Courts' and 'A Visit to Newgate' give evidence of his early concern with the seedy and the down-at-heel, gathering up into an obsession with crime, murder and execution. Of course it must be admitted that crime and low life have been the standby of the reporting journalist from before Dickens into our own time; on the surface these articles are no more than an old recipe for giving the reader what he wants. But 'A Visit to Newgate' surely has an odd tone. It is not only that Dickens disclaims any note-taking that might weigh down his sketch, promises that no statistics shall bore the reader – 'We saw the prison; and saw the prisoners; and what we did see, and what we thought, we will tell at once in our own way.' This is no confession of sensationalism, because all his life, as we shall see, Dickens fought a battle against those who would reduce men to figures, all his life he asserted that personal experience, personal impressions, are what should guide our heads in deciding moral and social questions; our eyes tell our hearts, our hearts our heads, and this did not by any means always imply that the message would be a soft one – certainly not for most of

'Newgate: Committed for Trial' by Frank Holl, 1878. 'Would you like to have a look at Newgate? Have you time to spare?' Mr Wemmick in *Great Expectations*.

the prisoners in Newgate. The argument is familiar nowadays; it has come to have a swelling note in England as economists and sociologists are found by the general public not to have the infallibility to which they have never laid claim.

Other writers, other journalists, could wallow in Newgate and forget it; Dickens could not. The prison with its associations with executions comes up again and again in his work – in *Oliver Twist* through *Barnaby Rudge* down to *Great Expectations*. One of the best pieces in *Sketches by Boz*, 'Meditations in Monmouth Street', may, I suggest, not too fancifully, give some clue to the concern of Dickens with criminality and ultimately with execution. Monmouth Street, which is on the edge of the then criminal area of Seven Dials, must have been very familiar to Dickens from his boyhood, for it lies south of Tottenham Court Road, directly on the way from Gower Street to Charing Cross. It was in those days a street of second-hand clothes shops. In the sketches it may be associated with 'The Pawnbroker's Shop' as a place with which Dickens himself would have been familiar in his family's impecunious days. The conceit on which the sketch is based – the imagining of the previous owners of the various second-hand clothes offered for sale – is conventional enough for any light essay of the late eighteenth and early nineteenth centuries. But Dickens makes a special use of this conceit to trace, in various suits of clothes, the career from innocent boyhood to the dreadful termination of a criminal's life – not this time on the gallows, but in transported misery:

> A coarse round frock, with a worn cotton neckerchief, and other articles of clothing of the commonest description, completed the history. A prison, and the sentence – banishment or the gallows. What would the man have given then, to be once again the contented humble drudge of his boyish years; to have been restored to life, but for a week, a day, an hour, a minute, only for so long a time as would enable him to say one word of passionate regret to, and hear one sound of heartfelt forgiveness from, the cold and ghastly form that lay rotting in the pauper's grave (his mother brought low by his wickedness). The children wild in the streets, the mother a destitute widow; both deeply tainted with the deep disgrace of the husband and father's name, and impelled by sheer necessity, down the precipice that had led him to a lingering death, possibly of many years' duration, thousands of miles away. We had no clue to the end of the tale; but it was easy to guess the termination.

As well as being some very bad writing (in an article containing some rather good, lively writing), it is curiously morbid for an otherwise lively, light magazine piece (as Dickens himself seems to realize when he writes 'by way of restoring the naturally cheerful tone of our thoughts'). It does seem to pose a question about some obsession beyond the normal journalistic, even Victorian journalistic.

There are two special features of the associations in this article which may, I think, illuminate Dickens's peculiar concern with death and with crime. The first is psychological. The little piece with its bringing alive of second-hand clothing is only a small and early example of the wondrous power, that

Vauxhall Gardens. 'The temples and cosmoramas and fountains glittered and sparkled before our eyes.' Vauxhall Gardens in *Sketches by Boz*.

governs his whole fictional world, by which inanimate objects – clothing, furniture, tools – are given a life of their own. This is the key to the magic of many of his finest passages. But here we see it used to trace the opposite – the reduction of a living man to a corpse. I suggest that these two faculties are more closely connected in Dickens than has been recognized. He saw life in 'lifeless' objects, but equally he 'was much possessed by death and saw the skull beneath the skin'. An inanimate world that takes on the wild frolic dance of a nursery tale coexists for him with a world where all the human beings may at any moment be sent to the stillness of their last sleep. It remained with him always, as we may see from a curious passage in his sketch 'The Haunted House', contributed to his own magazine *All the Year Round* in 1859 when he was forty-seven:

> No period within the four and twenty hours of day and night is solemn to me as the early morning. In the summertime I often rise very early, and repair to my room to do a day's work before breakfast, and I am always on these occasions deeply impressed by the stillness and solitude around me. Besides that there is something in being surrounded by familiar faces asleep – in the knowledge that those who are dearest to us and to whom we are dearest, are profoundly unconscious of us, in an impassive state, anticipative of that mysterious condition to which we are all tending – the stopped life, the broken threads of yesterday, the deserted seat, the closed book, the unfinished but abandoned occupation, all are images of Death. The tranquillity of the hour is the tranquillity of Death. The colour and chill have the same association.

The criminal area of Seven Dials.

The other deduction I would make from his small sketch is social and biographical: it is that his fascination with the criminal world connects closely,
by way of the pawnbroker's shop, the broker's men, and the second-hand
clothes market, with the precarious world of his family. It was not just the
family life of his childhood that I have described; not just his father in the
Marshalsea, the traumatic experience of himself with common men and boys
on the warehouse bench. Save for very short intervals, Charles Dickens
continued after leaving school to live at his parent's various homes in Bloomsbury and in the socially grander area of Cavendish Square. It was a happy and
lively life from the social point of view, with his sister Fanny's friends from
the Royal Academy of Music, with his own friends from among the lawyers'
clerks and journalists of his office life, with lively, talented Barrow relations
(an aunt who painted the first portrait we have of him at eighteen, a great
uncle who sponsored him at the same age for a British Museum Reading Room
ticket). As one can see from the few surviving letters and reminiscences it was
a world of social engagements, of friends' sisters, of friends who were attached
to one's own sisters, of parties and amateur theatricals and river trips, and a
great deal of flirtation.

Dickens early made friends outside his own family, one group of whom was
to bring him the greatest emotional disturbance of his youth; but he was also
very much a family young man – indeed his family were closely interwoven
with his daily life until some years after his marriage. But the family liveliness
was only the other side of the coin to the family instability. This was not just

The new British Museum rising behind the remains of the old in 1850.

his father's improvidence; it was the economic insecurity of a whole class. His godfather became bankrupt; and his generous, talented uncle Barrow, who started the *Mirror of Parliament* so successfully, failed after a few years for a very large sum. They were not exactly bohemian; they were certainly not raffish; but they were chronically insecure. In 1834, when Dickens was already 'Boz', his father was again arrested for debt. By now Dickens was not ready to suffer passively for John Dickens's ineptitude. He put his mother with most of the family into cheaper lodgings, secured his father's release, and moved himself, with his favourite brother, Fred, into chambers in Furnival's Inn. It was the end of his living at home.

All his life he was to know both improvidence and insecurity among his family as well as many of his friends in the literary world. But it was in his youth that the thinness of the Victorian ice was first and most strongly brought home to him. And it gave him, I think, a permanently horrified, fascinated concern for the strange, squalid, criminal marine life hopelessly imprisoned beneath the ice. It made him hard towards criminals as the poor whites have been hard towards the negroes. If his dear father could have been put in prison just for debt, then surely 'real criminals' should suffer harshly for their irrecoverable evil. But it kept him, like Dostoevsky, permanently concerned with, apprehensive of, the submerged.

It also gave him a more attractive concern. If he was fierce against the criminal, he was intensely sympathetic with the pleasures of the poor, pleasures that, as a young clerk, he had shared and enjoyed. The 'Scenes' section of *Sketches by Boz* contain a number of these, for example:

> There is no master of the ceremonies in this artificial Eden – all is primitive, unreserved and unstudied. The dust is blinding, the heat insupportable, the company somewhat noisy and in the highest spirits possible. The ladies, in the height of their innocent animation, dancing in the gentlemen's hats, and the gentlemen promenading 'the gay and festive scene' in the ladies' bonnets, or with the more expensive ornaments of false noses, and low-crowned, tinder-box-looking hats: playing children's drums, and accompanied by ladies on the penny trumpet.

It is an Orwellian pleasure in working-class fun. Rather more patronizing than Orwell, as appears in the description of Rural Tea Gardens (such as the one in which the Nemesis of a warrant for arrest for costs unpaid comes upon Mrs Bardell) – 'Some of the finery of these people provokes a smile but they are all clean, and happy, and disposed to be good natured and sociable' – but then Orwell with his Eton background felt firmer ground beneath his feet than the young Dickens and could afford to insist less on his superiority.

Dickens, throughout his life, championed the right of the poor to their own enjoyments, their right to pursue them unrestrictedly in their small free time. Among his earliest social journalism, written while he was at work on *Pickwick Papers*, was the little book *Sunday Under Three Heads*. In this he attacks Sabbatarianism and urges the opening of libraries, museums, the provision of fields for outdoor games on Sundays – indeed, considering his hatred of the bad old days and above all of the Stuarts, his passionate devotion to Cromwell,

Dickens had a sneaking attachment to blood-and-thunder absurdities. Illustrations from *The Mysteries of London*.

he here paints quite a William Morris, Merry England picture of the old may-pole times now vanished. His hostility to sabbatarianism received full justi-fication much later in his life when a new Sabbatarian bill of 1855 caused serious riots in Hyde Park. He was not slow to remind his friends of the moral he had always pointed. He always championed the cheap theatres of the working people, too, however much he ridiculed the melodramas put on in them. And he steadfastly and, I think creditably, refused to support the idea that popular entertainment should be turned into an occasion for moral elevation and hidden instruction – and this perhaps particularly creditably, because the periodicals he later edited were essentially organs which contained the pill of instruction and the sugar of entertainment.

The truth is, I think, that Dickens had more than a sneaking attachment to all the blood-and-thunder absurdities of the popular theatre of his day. As late as 1850 he wrote for his newly founded magazine *Household Words* two articles entitled 'The Amusements of the People' in which he describes visits to cheap and packed theatres; his accounts of the plays shown there, especially *Gloomy Dell and Suicide Tree*, are very funny and very loving. His delight in absurdity as with many another satirist led to an affection that has almost shed its irony. The influence of this sophisticated taste for the popular accounts for much that is crudely melodramatic in his work. He has also a lifelong hankering after the theatre because it could communicate with the large illiterate popu-lation as his writings could not. As he says in these articles of 1850: 'Joe Whelks, of the New Cut, Lambeth, is not much of a reader, has no great store of books, no very commodious room to read in, no very decided inclination to read, and no power at all of presenting vividly before his mind's eye what he reads about. But put Joe in the gallery of the Victoria Theatre.' This desire for wider communication beyond print was surely powerful among the impulses

The New Cut, Lambeth, in the evening.

leading to the 'readings' of his later years. He would have delighted, I think, in television. This love of the theatre (begun as we have seen in childhood) grew to its height in the youthful period of petty employment we are considering.

It was a very low period in the history of the London theatre. Only Covent Garden, Drury Lane and the Haymarket theatres were licensed to play 'straight plays'. Other theatres, it is true, presented Shakespeare and other serious dramatists by means of converting their plays into 'burlettas' with interspersed songs and dances. Theatres, too, abounded south of the river where melodrama was given. In addition to these, there were 'private theatres', where an enthusiastic amateur could, as Dickens tells us in his sketch 'Private Theatres', play Richard III himself for £2, the Duke of Buckingham for 15s. and the Lord Mayor of London in the same play for half-a-crown. Whether Dickens actually performed as a youth in any of these theatres is unknown, but his knowledge of the workings suggest that, at any rate, he knew many who did. That it was a world of its own, as much as some teenage worlds today, we may guess by the way he tells his middle-class readers about it – that mixture of 'sociology' and shocked reprobation that is to be found in articles about 'the scene' or 'the underground' in many popular newspapers today.

The principal patrons of private theatres are dirty boys, low copying clerks in attorneys' offices, capacious-headed youths from city counting-houses . . . shop-boys who now and then mistake their masters' money for their own; and a choice miscellany of idle vagabonds . . . . The lady performers pay nothing for their characters, and, it is needless to add, are usually selected from one class of society . . . . All the minor theatres in London, especially the lowest constitute the centre of a little stage-struck neighbourhood . . . divers boys from fifteen to twenty-one years of age who throw back their coats and turn up their wristbands after the portraits of Count D'Orsay, hum tunes and whistle when the curtain is down, by way of persuading the people near them, that they are not at all serious to have it put up again.

It is hard not to think that the 'dirty boys' and 'low copying clerks' with their imitation dandy costumes must have been something akin to the seventeen-year-old Dickens and his friends. But Dickens could always be savage about a part of his life which might have held him back from the destiny of his genius – Dick Swiveller has to be reclaimed from just such innocent dissipation, as indeed Pip much later from more genteel, youthful wasting of money in the company of the Finches of the Grove. No companions, like the boy Fagin who had befriended him at Warren's, were safe from savage hindsight if their friendship had stood in the way of his real purpose in life; to this extent he was very unsentimental about his past.

But perhaps he had reason to feel superior to the wretched youths who purchased roles at the private theatres. He had developed his comic acting powers of boyhood. So glowing were the reports of his own powers that in March 1832 the manager of Covent Garden agreed to audition him for a part in the coming production of Sheridan Knowles's *The Hunchback*. The twenty-year-old boy prepared to visit the theatre with his sister, Fanny, but a heavy cold prevented him leaving his home. In his own account, 'I made a great splash in the gallery [i.e. the reporters' gallery of the House of Commons] soon afterwards; the *Chronicle* opened to me; I had a distinction in the little world of the newspaper, which made me like it; began to write; didn't want money; had never thought of the stage, but as a means of getting it; gradually left off turning my thoughts that way; and never resumed the idea.'

When one considers how much of his later life was given to acting and to concern with the theatre, this disclaimer of serious concern for a lost stage career seems at first sight somewhat disingenuous; but, in fact, I think it is broadly the truth. Dickens adored acting, even more manager-acting; into the management of and participation in large-scale amateur theatricals he put a great part of his enormous surplus energy in middle age. Amateur theatricals combined an outlet for exhibitionism (I use the word in no derogatory sense) and bonhomous camaraderie. But on the whole his gregarious need was already enough satisfied by his enormous capacity for friendship; and with the readings of his last years he found a far more satisfactory outlet for his histrionic energies. Far more satisfactory because he was working on his own creations. His was above all a creative genius combined with a talent for mimicry. The stage, unless he had also written for it, would probably have satisfied only the mimicry. And as to writing for the stage, the conventions of the day were too strong and too bad. His two earliest plays presented upon the professional stage – the operetta *The Village Coquettes* and *The Strange Gentleman*, a short play written from one of the *Sketches by Boz* – are inept, old-fashioned pieces.

As to his acting, accounts differ, and it is surely by now impossible to choose which to believe, especially as our values in acting are so totally different from those either of his youth or of his middle age. One can only say that, by even the most friendly accounts, he could gravely misdoubt his own talents in some of the roles he chose to represent in the amateur theatre, for example the young eighteenth-century fop, Lord Wilmot, in Bulwer Lytton's *Not So Bad as We Seem*, which he played before Queen Victoria in 1851. Nevertheless the impression he created was a powerful one, even upon members of the acting profession, who quite properly are seldom happy to admit amateur acting as a serious contribution to the art. He was probably at his best in melodramatic roles, as in *The Lighthouse* or *The Frozen Deep*. It seems unlikely, if he had been taken on at Covent Garden in those early years, that the stage would have kept him from becoming a novelist any more than Parliament could.

His attachment to the professional theatre, however, remained with him always. In a very wide circle of intimate friends, William Macready, the great actor-manager, was among the two or three whom Dickens respected most, partly because he admired Macready's acting so greatly, but even more, I think, because Macready gave all his energies to improving the standards of drama generally and consequently of the theatrical profession in Victorian society. It was so much what Dickens himself was bent upon doing for the profession of writing. Dickens was tireless, in a life overburdened with assisting the unfortunate, in raising funds to help actresses who had fallen on hard times or educating the children of actors who had died suddenly in a precarious profession. His speeches to the fund-raising banquets of the General Theatrical Fund were an almost yearly event from 1846 onwards. He was always conscious, I think, of how much his fiction fed upon the theatre.

Before discussing the narrow, genteel world in which the adolescent Dickens made his first romantic acquaintance with what was certainly known within its confines as 'the fairer though weaker sex', the middle-class world that makes up most of the humorous *Sketches by Boz* and, as I have said, influences all his early novels, it is worth glancing at one other sketch which may be the occasion for discussing certain conjectures that must be felt about Charles Dickens, as about almost any metropolitan eminent Victorian. The sketch is called 'Making a Night of It' and tells of two city clerks who go on a spree, and, becoming drunk, kick up a rough house, and end in the police station and the magistrate's court. It has been suggested that one of Dickens's best friends when he was a lawyer's clerk, Henry Kolle, may have had just such an adventure. Certainly we may suppose that if Dickens was an ardent cheap-theatre-going youth, and a connoisseur of London streets after dark, he was likely at seventeen to have had a few 'thick' nights.

In the course of 'Making a Night of It' we are told: 'they went into a wine vault . . . where they found a good many young ladies . . . and a plentiful sprink-ling of hackney-coachmen and cab drivers, all drinking and talking together.' But, since this was a humorous sketch, that is all we hear of the young ladies.

Prostitutes in Dickens's work are never in any way associated with gaiety, however reprehensible. More typical is the hint given in another sketch 'Shops and their Tenants'. Here we read of a poor working girl trying to earn her living by making 'some elegant little trifle for sale': 'If those thoughtless females who interfere with the miserable market of poor creatures such as these knew but one half of the misery they suffer . . . in their honourable attempts to earn a scanty subsistence, they would, perhaps resign even opportunities for the gratification of vanity . . . rather than drive them to a last dreadful resource, which it would shock the delicate feelings of these *charitable* ladies to hear named.' The passage even in full is obscure, and obscurity is not the mark of Boz in these sketches, despite all their callowness. Even hinting at the subject obviously worries the young author. Yet it sounds the only note on this theme in these early sketches. A note, however, that was to swell into an often repeated chord in Dickens's novels after the portrayal of Nancy in *Oliver Twist* in 1841.

Poor working girls trying to earn their livings by making 'some elegant trifle for sale'.

In the late forties Dickens himself drew up the rules to govern Urania Cottage, a home for fallen girls, and in the fifties he was much concerned in the management of it. From his middle years onwards he was certainly familiar with the 'wicked' side of London and of Paris life. But we can never know whether, at any period from the time of these clerks 'making a night of it' in his teens until his reports in the last decade of his life that Paris has grown more wicked, he ever in fact participated in the commercial sexual life of London or Paris which was so highly organized to cater for all sexual tastes and, because of poverty, so very easily come by. It seems to me that any reader of his works and his letters must form a strong impression at the very least that he was not a devotee of promiscuous sex; in that case, the question may seem unimportant. On the other hand, in a letter of 1840, referring to a charge that a venerable old gentleman (probably his friend Samuel Rogers) had frequented a prostitute in his youth, Dickens says, 'Good God! If such sins were to be visited upon all of us . . . what man would escape!' Complete male chastity before marriage can hardly have been common among young men of those times, who knew West End life well. Dickens and Carlyle mocked Emerson on his visit to England by telling him this. But I do not believe, as Edgar Johnson does, that they were 'pulling his leg'.

Perhaps, since we cannot ever solve the question, it may seem idle or prurient to inquire. And yet I think it is not quite so, for prostitution plays an important role in his fictional world. His prostitutes are not quite holy women, like Dostoevsky's Sonia, but their sacrifice by society does mark them out for some special scapegoat isolation; they are all oleograph Magdalens alien from the bustling vitality of the books. One and all, from Nancy onwards, they are the most unreal of his characters. Here is Martha, the Yarmouth girl turned London prostitute in *David Copperfield*, 'Making the same low, dreary wretched moaning in her shawl, she went away'; or again the prostitute who speaks to Little Dorrit near London Bridge, ' "I never should have touched you, but I thought that you were a child." And with a strange wild cry she went away.' From Nancy through Alice Marwood onwards, prostitutes in Dickens's fiction are not only not of the real world, but they are somehow not really even of his own strange world – they merely cross the stage, delicate-speaking allegories of Woman made Victim.

Certainly, as we well know, in sexual matters Victorian fiction bears no relation to Victorian real life. We should not expect the prostitutes to have any Zolaesque reality. Is it, then, that knowing the real thing and unable to say it, Dickens finds himself without his usual alchemical powers to turn the Victorian world into the Dickensian world? Or is it that he never knew prostitutes save as a journalistic observer or a strict manager of their reform at Urania Cottage? A rather sad little passage in a letter to Wilkie Collins from wicked Paris in 1856, when he was forty-four, suggests to me that his relation with the demi-monde was governed by timidity as well as by the fastidiousness one would anyway expect from him:

On Saturday night I paid three francs at the door of that place where we saw the

His prostitutes are oleograph Magdalens.

wrestling, and went in, at 11 o'clock, to a Ball. Much the same as our own National Argyll Rooms. Some pretty faces – but all of two classes – wicked and coldly calculating, or haggard and wretched in their worn beauty. Among the latter was a woman of thirty or so, in an Indian shawl, who never stirred from a seat in a corner all the time I was there. Handsome, regardless, brooding, and yet with some nobler qualities in her forehead. I mean to walk about tonight and look for her. I didn't speak to her there, but I have a fancy that I should like to know more about her. Never shall, I suppose.

As she stands this woman would seem to have gone about her commerce as only a Dickens prostitute could, but surely if he had known more . . . but he certainly never *did* know more in his novels. Perhaps he hoped for something more when he wrote to a French friend in 1855 on a proposed visit to Paris with Wilkie Collins, 'I want it to be pleasant and gay, and to throw myself *en garçon* into the festive diableries de Paris'.

But I doubt it. Perhaps, however, there is a third solution to the problem; perhaps, knowing these unfortunates as well as he did most other classes in Victorian society, he read into the nullities, which were all Victorian propriety allowed him to create in his novels, what he had omitted, and he expected his male readers would do the same. Certainly his worldly friend, the novelist Wilkie Collins, who must have known the reality of such women, read something that we cannot see into the cypher character of Nancy: 'The character of Nancy is the finest thing he ever did. He never afterwards saw all sides of a woman's character – saw all round her.' Or perhaps Collins felt that within the Victorian limits of discussion, Nancy was more real because she had a fierce attachment to her ponce, Sikes.

The question is insoluble, but it remains of real interest. Thackeray, in suggesting the lower depths to which Becky Sharp (1848) is driven when fortune turns against her, does not say much, but he tells us enough and does not, as he so often does with respectable women, equivocate. Meredith in his portrayal of Mrs Mount, the reckless, expensive cocotte of *The Ordeal of Richard Feverel* (1859) tells us really all we need to know; Dickens, wishing to speak of a much lower sort of prostitute, fails completely. Is it simply that a certain degree of coarseness cannot even be suggested in association with a female character in Victorian fiction? Or is there some deeper, unrealized bad faith here that, consciously supposed to champion the fallen girl, really betrays her more completely by removing the least traces of humanity by which she might hope to win the reader's sympathy? When we consider how little the censorship of Victorian prudery prevented him from suggesting the eroticism, the perversities even, of his 'respectable' characters, there remains some curiosity about his total failure to give life to the harlots whom, obedient to his New Testament creed, he calls to repentance and to our shamed forgiveness. But perhaps it is only an extreme example of the general denial of real humanity to young women (despite many very brilliantly drawn female characters) that mars his fictional world. The prostitutes of his novels are merely Magdalen models, as his heroines are largely Victorian illustrations for the story of Mary and Martha.

The rest of *Sketches by Boz* – the sections called 'Tales' and 'Characters' – bring us immediately up against this defect, although it may be less noticeable in this immature, largely feeble work than in his later novels of genius. The reasons for it lie very close at hand. When we compare the few letters of his late teens, the accounts of home theatricals, the general picture of a lively circle of young people crowding as much good time into their leisure hours as they can, with the humorous picture of this world given in *Sketches by Boz*, the contrast is quite considerable. 'A chosen few to join in a friendly quadrille', 'We can mount, dismount and ride eight or ten miles without seeing a Soul the Peasantry excepted', 'We intend asking Charles Ross and one or two fellows on Saturday Evening next, and to knock up a chaunt or two', 'Get one or two young men together for the purpose of knocking up a song or two', 'Is it of any use asking you and "a Brother or two" to look in and take a glass of Punch and a Cigar tomorrow?' – these are the phrases of the few letters.

The world of the *Sketches*, although consistently facetious, is quite different in tone. To begin with, unlike the pleasures of the poor at Astley's or Greenwich Fair, everything in the middle-class celebrations goes wrong. This is partly the necessity of farce. But nevertheless this part of the *Sketches* is a sad book for a very young man – of sour high spirits, in which the high spirits seem forced, but the bilious taste of the morning after seems persistent. There's Miss Martin, the milliner, who has ambitions to sing – '"Off, off, off," cried the rest of the audience . . . . It wouldn't do – Miss Amelia Martin left the orchestra, with much less ceremony than she had entered it; and as she couldn't sing out, never came out.' There's Mr Augustus Cooper, a young man who takes dancing lessons and finds himself threatened with breach of promise – 'And Mr Augustus Cooper went back and lived with his mother, and there he lives to this day; and as he has lost his ambition for society, and never goes into the world, he will never see this account of himself, and will never be any the wiser.' There are the good-natured, vulgar, *nouveaux riches* Tuggses who, on holiday in Ramsgate, are led into disastrous amours and financial adventures with some impostors, Captain and Mrs Waters and Lieutenant Slaughter. There is Horatio Sparkins, whose deception of the Madderton girls is discovered when they find him behind the counter at the draper's shop. There is Mr Percy Noakes who 'used to talk politics to papas, flatter the mamas, do the the amicable to their daughters'. He arranges a quite disastrous boat trip in which every species of feminine jealousy and spite, of masculine vanity and deceit is brought to a sad close by universal, highly comic seasickness. Then there is Mrs Joseph Porter at Rose Villa, Clapham Rise, whose snobbery, backbiting and envy are given successful outlet by the Gattleton family's calamitous amateur production of *Othello*. There is Mr Watkins Tottle, a shy bachelor, who over many long passages is persuaded into declaring his love for Miss Lillerton, only to receive a flea in his ear. The story ends with a facetious account of his suicide.

But this is enough to give an idea of this world where young men and women (to say nothing of jolly old bachelors and old maids with a bit of money) must watch like hawks to see that persons of lower social origins, or impostors, or fortune hunters of both sexes do not catch them unawares. (And 'unawares' means whenever gaiety or festivity has lulled them out of the necessary vigilance.) Where everyone is on the make. Where children are used to please the money out of the pockets of rich bachelor uncles. Where every mother with daughters to marry off is ready to pounce on the humiliation of every other mother with daughters to marry off. Where expeditions or parties or festivities are the cover for designs on hearts or pockets. Where to marry and have no end of children and no end of bills to pay is the only alternative to being left on the shelf, ridiculous and sour.

How is this world to be accommodated to the world of the Dickens children and their friends, lively, intelligent, fond of each other and (at this stage, decades before his brothers Fred and Augustus proved to be 'hopeless') a talented, promising family? In part, I think, we must see *Sketches by Boz* as the rejection of a world, however lively, that he found too petty, by a man possessed of imagination that would have broken to pieces a far larger world. Partly, I think, that there was a mercenariness, particularly within families and between the sexes in early- and mid-nineteenth-century England that percolated from the as yet uncivilized commercial middle classes through every section of society save to the very poor, who had nothing to expect. It can be seen in different pictures and through various eyes from Jane Austen's *Pride and Prejudice* (1813), through Thackeray's *Vanity Fair* (1848), to George Eliot's *Middlemarch* (1872) and Trollope's *The Way We Live Now* (1875). The only distressing part of *Sketches by Boz* is that the young Dickens sees all this with the easy cynicism of a more shrewd member of the very world he is attacking. Mothers-in-law, matrimony, rich uncles, spinsters, calf love – all the sort of humour of Victorian *Punch* at its worse. These vulgar images were to take a long time dying away altogether in his work (though another version of this facile worldly shrewdness is far more common in Thackeray's periodical journalism like *The Book of Snobs*), but what is most remarkable is that in *Pickwick Papers* Dickens was able totally to transcend this spirit; and to do so not really by escaping into a wider world, but by probing (however unconsciously) far deeper into himself. Yet many of his most grating cocky sketches – 'Sketches of Young Gentlemen', 'Sketches of Young Couples' – did not appear until after the publication of the full edition of *Sketches by Boz*, when *Pickwick Papers* was some years behind him.

Maria Beadnell

Critics, on the whole, have preferred to pass over the *Sketches* as a young man's book and go straight on to the glory of *Pickwick* by a man only a year older. To do so, I think, is to lessen the extraordinary force of *Pickwick*. It is also to leave unexplored the immediately powerful effect of one episode of his adolescence – an episode that has for long been recognized to have affected all his fiction and the whole of his life at a deeper level. When Dickens, in 1845 or 1846, wrote down the fragment of autobiography in which he first recapitulated to himself the shame of his father's imprisonment and of his own employment at Warren's, he left off because he saw looming before him an event far more devastating, too painful to recall. It was his passionate devotion to Maria Beadnell, a girl a year older than himself, whom he probably first met in 1829 when he was still only seventeen. How exactly he met the Beadnells is not quite clear, although at least two of his close male friends formed part of the circle that clustered round Maria and her sister. One of these, Henry Kolle, acted as go-between for Dickens when his feelings for Maria became a matter for the disapproval of the Beadnell parents. Kolle subsequently married Maria's sister, Anne. Another, Henry Austin, who painted portraits of the Beadnell girls, subsequently married Dickens's younger sister, Letitia.

The Beadnells' was just the house for eligible young men, and also, as Mr and Mrs Beadnell saw it, for some who were not eligible. There were musical evenings at their Lombard Street home, next door to the bank where Maria's uncle was manager, and Maria's father was later to succeed him. After the insecurity of the Dickens and the Barrow households, the Beadnells' had the charm of solidity and of the greater elegance that opulence can bring.

There is little doubt, however, that Charles Dickens cared for 2 Lombard Street only because Maria was there and that he had fallen very deeply in love with her. A few years later he would have been a welcome suitor to the Beadnell parents, but now, alas, as his affections grew warmer for Maria, he sensed that Lombard Street became colder. He remembered always every detail of his treatment of those passionate days; nearly a quarter of a century later when Maria appeared on his scene again, a stout married woman with a child, he wrote to her: 'I escorted you with native gallantry to the Dress Maker's door, and your mother, seized with an apprehension – groundless upon my honour – that I might come in, said emphatically: "And now Mr Dicken," which she always used to call me, "we'll wish *you* good morning." ' The recollection of the typical upper-middle-class brush off, including the inevitable mispronunciation of the name, is complete.

Things were not made easier by a girl friend of Maria's, Marianne Leigh, whose ambiguous, semi-flirtatious encouragement of Charles's passion for her friend alternately made the youth hopeful and desperate. Miss Leigh's part in the unhappy love affair had a general influence on his attitude to women. It increased his belief, so often reflected in the early novels, that young women (indeed all women) were in a general alliance against men – a conspiracy which any one of them always betrayed when she thought she had made the catch she was after. No doubt it had some solid foundation in the society of his time, but the events of 1831 and 1832 must have given the alliance sinister and conspiratorial proportions in his mind.

There survives a poem (a somewhat embarrassing one) called 'The Bill of Fare', which the young Dickens wrote to amuse the guests at a banquet given by the Beadnells. The praise of his host and hostess, and, of course, of their daughters, is almost fulsome; but he feels free to attack somewhat savagely Marianne Leigh and her parents – did he perhaps count on the essentially hostile nature of most social friendships as he portrays them in the *Sketches* to mean that the Beadnells would be pleased with malice against their friends the Leighs? Certainly both Mr and Mrs Leigh are attacked in some tales that appear in the *Sketches*.

Whatever the feelings of the Beadnells about the young man's poetry, they seem to have felt it wiser to separate him from their daughter; it is conjectured that they had heard unfortunate stories of Dickens's father's financial instability. At some point in 1832 Maria was sent to Paris for some months to 'finish' (this alone suggests the social grandeur of the Beadnells). He remembered it bitterly twenty-three years later, for when Maria reappeared in his life he was just about to set off for Paris himself: 'When I was writing the word "Paris" just now, I remembered that my existence was once entirely uprooted and my whole Being blighted by the Angel of my soul being sent there to finish her education!' On her return, the vigilance of her parents seemed much greater and her own feelings seem to have cooled – the little trip abroad, so old a device of parents in such situations had, in fact, worked. It was then that Dickens entered into a clandestine correspondence with her, first through his friend Kolle, whose wooing of her sister was acceptable to the Beadnells, then through her maid. In March 1833 with a letter that rather touchingly tries to preserve his dignity while declaring his continuing love and his hurt feelings, he returned her letters and some small present she had given him; this was after she had shown particular unkindness to him at his twenty-first birthday party celebrated at his parents' home. Sometime that spring Marianne Leigh seems to have persuaded him into a 'heart to heart' about his feelings, which she then retailed to her friend Maria, for in May he writes twice to Maria to vindicate himself from Marianne's slanders, and to Marianne herself he writes a bitter letter, 'inclosing your Album (which I regret to say want of a moment's time has quite prevented me writing in)'. After this there was little left but to return home from the House of Commons at night a very long way round, past the Lombard Street window of the room where Maria was sleeping.

The letters are the pitiful letters of a young lover, attempting to unravel knots of circumstantial misunderstanding in which his favourite sister, Fanny, was also involved, as though these could somehow solve the problem of a love that was no longer reciprocated. What happened? Did he press his suit upon her too hard? Very possibly. He was to do so again in his life. Although in later years when he was famous and she was a respectable stout matron, Maria implied romantically that she had always loved him and if only he had pressed . . . it is surely more likely that her youthful attraction to an unusual, lively, talented youth from outside her own usual circle was dissipated as her parents sensibly expected by a change of scene, a bit of mischief-making by her girl friend, and perhaps a little influence of the worldly advice of her parents. If Dickens's rather facetious sketch 'A Birthday Party' written in the fifties refers to his own twenty-first birthday party then: 'What passed, I cannot as a man of honour reveal. She was all angelical gentleness [Angelica, or angelic are the words always applied to Maria in his few fictitious sketches about the episode] but a word was mentioned – a short and dreadful word of three letters, beginning with a B. – which, as I remarked at the moment, "scorched my brain".' That he was after all still a mere boy sounds uncommonly like the retailing by a girl of her parents' warning.

What no one could guess was that the love affair would have bitten so deeply into Dickens's soul. We have the statements that he made to Forster about the impossibility of writing his autobiography to include the event, and the direct confession he made years later in letters to Maria when she reappeared in his life. The phrases here are strong:

I have always believed since, and always shall to the last, that there never was such a faithful and devoted poor fellow as I was. Whatever of fancy, romance, energy, passion, aspiration and determination belong to me, I have never separated and never shall separate from the hard-hearted little woman – you – whom it is nothing to say I would have died for, with the greatest alacrity! I can never think, and I never seem to observe, that other young people are in such desperate earnest or set so much, so long, upon one absorbing hope. It is a matter of perfect certainty to me that I began to fight my way out of poverty and obscurity, with one perpetual idea of you. This is so fixed in my knowledge that . . . I have never heard anybody addressed by your name, or spoken of by your name, without a start. The sound of it has always filled me with a kind of pity and respect for the deep truth that I had, in my silly hobbledehoy head, to bestow upon one creature who represented the world to me. I have never been so good a man since, as I was when you made me wretchedly happy. I shall never be half so good a fellow any more . . . . I have a strong belief and there is no harm in adding hope to that – that perhaps you have once or twice laid down that book [*David Copperfield*] and thought: 'How dearly that boy must have loved me, and how vividly this man remembered it'.

And again,

My entire devotion to you, and the wasted tenderness of those hard years which I have ever since half loved, half dreaded to recall, made so deep an impression on me that I refer to it a habit of suppression which now belongs to me, which I know is no part of my original nature, but which makes me chary of showing my affections, even to my children, except when they are very young . . . .

All this is very pathetic and not a little sickening from a man of forty-three; from a very great and fulfilled artist. But he was not fulfilled in his marriage; in three years' time it was to break up. And the statements, though self-pitying, are true – truer than perhaps he had faced then, possibly ever faced. He had tried to make sense of it all in *David Copperfield*, and he had made a fine novel that yet is somewhere false. Maria Beadnell had paid her price to him and to posterity by providing the model for the true, revealing character of Dora, as later, now Maria Winter, she was to provide the model for one of his great comic creations, Flora Finching.

Admirers of the Dickens world should be grateful to her. But Dickens could hardly be so; not even as much as his sense of his own faults suggested in his fictional pictures of her, for the wounds (however self-inflicted) of the break-down of his romantic dream of love for her left him a man who divided women all his life into diminished categories, while preserving a self-indulgent ideal of what he wished from them. More importantly, it had a curious effect on his fiction; from this categorizing of women we have some of the finest humours of women's various vanities and sillinesses to be found in any novels, but in all the rest, whether woman scorned and dangerous, woman the wise counsellor and thrifty housekeeper, or – most extraordinary and yet most distorting – half girl, half angel, who by her purity and love keeps clear Man's Path to Heaven, we have nothing that gives woman the true dignity of a whole body and a whole mind. It seems extravagant – and will be thought so by many – to attribute to a commonplace little middle-class teenage love episode the gulf that divides a writer of Shakespearean potentialities (indeed in his comic language and portraiture, Shakespearean in fulfilment) from Dickens's great but unequal achievements. Yet, given the degree to which Charles Dickens, as evidenced in his letters and his talk, hugged his past self to him, I do not think it more than a meaningful simplification.

However, as he rightly says, in his letter to Maria so many years later, from that bitter youthful time dates the full determination of his ambition. For a man like Dickens, such hope of achievement in life meant domestic ease – a wife to maintain a decent, orderly household, a hostess to entertain his growing circle of friends, someone certainly to satisfy his love (and there is no need, I think, to scan that word too closely), someone to bear him children (though surely in his schemes, not to be the mother of eleven). This girl appeared on the scene three years after his final break with Maria.

The David Copperfield Polka – 'My child wife Dora'.

The Hogarth Sisters

In 1835 the proprietors of the *Morning Chronicle* launched an evening paper. They appointed to be its editor George Hogarth, an Edinburgh man, who until middle life had been a lawyer, a Writer to the Signet. In middle age, seeing himself a failure in law, he had become a journalist. By his editing of a Halifax newspaper he had helped to win that notoriously Whig Yorkshire constituency for the Tories. Hogarth took immediate notice of his young colleague, Dickens, by commissioning from him contributions for the journal. The sketches supplied by Dickens were his London pieces which appeared later among the *Sketches by Boz*. Indeed they were published in the *Evening Chronicle* under that pseudonym, and Dickens's weekly salary went up from five to seven guineas.

It was not surprising that Dickens should have inclined towards this cultivated, older man. But there were more reasons than patronage for his pleasure in visiting Hogarth's house in Fulham, then a London suburb of gardens and orchards. George Hogarth was of intellectual interests, an excellent musicologist, one of the founders of the Edinburgh Festival. His wife's father had also been an eminent musical scholar and a friend of Burns. But there was a further aspect of Hogarth's past that must have outshone all this. He was related to Scott's publishers, the Ballantynes, but, despite all the litigation that arose between the great novelist and that family after the bankruptcy which crippled the end of Scott's life, Hogarth had remained Scott's legal adviser and friend. Most writers have some predecessors to whom they look back with special reverence. Dickens revered Scott, not only for his novels but for the dignity, the dedication and the industry with which he had followed his profession of writer. It is true that he must have had reservations about Scott's tendency to decry his professionalism – something that Dickens hated in Thackeray; on the other hand he would have felt more sympathy than he would perhaps have admitted for Scott's desire to be a landed gentleman. In any case he owed much to Scott, for it was the literary influence of Scott that lay behind *Barnaby Rudge*, the novel that first emancipated Dickens from the loose-knit, wandering narratives he had inherited from his earlier gods, Fielding and Smollett. In 1835, when Dickens met Hogarth, Scott had only been dead three years and was not only the most renowned novelist in Britain, but, with the late Lord Byron, the most renowned British writer on the Continent. For Dickens the Hogarth household was a meeting place of culture and good breeding – something very different from the rather philistine opulence of the Beadnells. It was also a somewhat impecunious household, but Dickens surely would not have been surprised at this touch of the atmosphere of his own home.

Here he met, wooed and married the eldest Hogarth daughter, Catherine, with momentous and ultimately unhappy results.

Catherine was twenty when he met her. She had heavy-lidded eyes and a certain secretive beauty of languor that was perhaps bound to disappoint – as do so many women whose enigmatic, Mona Lisa smiles disguise the comparative vapidity that lies behind them. Dickens's attentions, no doubt, drew her out further than he or she expected. She could be funny in an absurd, punning, unexpected way. Although his letters to her, almost from the start, lack passion, there was, I suspect, a bond of humorous vision of life between them (the stronger at first because so unexpected from her, but a fragment of a letter to her cousin written before her marriage suggests a lively, gossipy, almost maliciously humorous girl – 'heaven knows she was quite convinced that she was to be my bridesmaid until I quickly undeceived her the other day. The old Mother is always dying but never dies . . . .'); yet it wore away gradually as their temperaments grew more set and more divergent.

Many factors, indeed, told against the success of their marriage. Her family

'My marriage with . . . the daughter of a gentleman who . . . was the most intimate friend . . . of Sir Walter Scott.' Abbotsford, home of Sir Walter Scott.

home, for all its cultivation, was disorganized and untidy, features which were certainly not going to be tolerated in Dickens's future plans for success. He had disciplined himself away from the hand-to-mouth improvidence of his own family; he would help his bride to discipline herself away from the bohemian muddle of her home. And so he did – or rather he disciplined, almost cowed her, but at the eventual cost of the emerging personality that had attracted him, at the cost of her reverting into a comfortable, easy indolence hardly different from the negligence of her parents' home.

When he became engaged to Catherine he was a young journalist, who had made a name for himself by the periodical publication of some sketches. His acquaintance with the literary and artistic world was to come. By the time they were married, rather quietly at Chelsea in April 1836 (with a special licence since Catherine was under age) much had changed. He had met, through the popular novelist, Harrison Ainsworth, the famous cartoonist, Cruikshank. What was more, Ainsworth's publisher, Macrone, had suggested that the young Dickens should collaborate with Cruikshank to produce an illustrated book of his journalistic sketches, and commissioned further work from him. This book, published as *Sketches by Boz*, had already run into two editions. And now Mr Hall, of the publishers Chapman & Hall, had descended upon him in his chambers in Furnival's Inn and as a result he was engaged to produce a monthly serial to accompany a series of sporting drawings by the artist, Robert Seymour (suggested title *The Nimrod Papers*). In fact *Pickwick Papers* had been born.

These were all happy auspices for the wedding. They were certainly no less than Dickens had planned or expected. He was, externally at any rate, very sure of himself. For instance he wrote to Macrone complaining that Cruickshank – the famous man with whom he should have been flattered to work –

'requires the spur'. When Catherine, during their happy, loving engagement, showed some disposition to resent the hours he spent away from her, working, his response was usually kind but firm:

> If you knew how eagerly I long for your society this evening . . . you would believe me sincere in saying that necessity alone induces me to forego the pleasure of your companionship for one evening in the week even. You will never do me the justice of believing it, however, and all I can do until my book [*Sketches by Boz*, first series] is finished, will be to reflect that I shall have (God willing) many opporunities of shewing you for years to come how unjust you used to be, and of convincing you then of what I would fain convince you now – that my pursuits and labours such as they are not more selfish than my pleasures, and that your future advancement and happiness is the main-spring of them all.

Such notes continued right up to their marriage – firm, definite admonitions to his 'dearest Mouse' or 'dearest Pig' – 'Why then, my dear, you must be out of temper, and there is no help for it.' *She* had from the start, it is clear, a tendency to be 'Cwoss' (as the baby language of his engagement letters calls it) and out of spirits; *he* was not going again to be the prey of a woman's whims.

The lesson would probably have not been impossible for Catherine to absorb, and to absorb without losing her identity, if events had moved less speedily. A successful book published, a new one on the way, fame as a reporter, a gradually expanding circle of distinguished friends   all this Catherine might have taken happily and survived well. But what came with *Pickwick* was an avalanche of success – an avalanche that, despite Dickens's real concern for some domestic privacy, took him away from her into more and more work, into even wider social spheres where she often found it difficult to follow him. I do not suppose that she ever entirely disliked the position and affluence that being Mrs Charles Dickens brought her, although twenty years later, so Dickens said, she urged her own departure from a household in which she felt ill at ease. But though many liked her, few seem to have done so without a certain patronage.

Success and prosperity came too quickly for her to learn to earn it; she fell back upon passively accepting it. If Dickens resented this – and he did – he probably also guessed that his firm, authoritarian methods with her, while serving his immediate purpose of preventing her interference with his rapid climb to fame, had also killed the little that was different in her, that might have contributed instead of taking. And, although at the time of the marriage he wrote with evident pride to his uncle Thomas Barrow, 'My marriage with Miss Hogarth – the daughter of a gentleman who has recently distinguished himself by a celebrated work on Music, who was the most intimate friend and companion of Sir Walter Scott, and one of the most eminent among the Literati of Edinburgh,' in six months' time this was all very small beer to the Inimitable Boz, the nationwide notable author of *Pickwick Papers*. Yet, as the years went by and relations between Dickens and all but one of his in-laws grew worse, it must have been a solace, if a hardly helpful one, to Mrs Hogarth, the mother-in-law he disliked, that the Hogarths had contributed breeding and culture to

Kate and Mary Hogarth.

a tyrannical parvenu who could not appreciate them – but not to Catherine, for whatever else went wrong with his teaching of her, she never ceased to revere him with worried perplexity. As to his fiction, she almost completed the circle of his ill education in the nature of women, for in the end she confirmed much of his fear that the sex which he placed upon a pinnacle was all too often unworthy of his worship.

Luckily – or perhaps very unluckily – Catherine had younger sisters, who in turn would sustain his hugged ideal of all that Woman could be for Man if she tried. After a short honeymoon in a village near Chatham, the scene of Dickens's happy childhood days, the couple returned to live at his bachelor chambers in Furnival's Inn. Here they were joined by Catherine's seventeen-year-old sister. The arrangement of an unmarried girl joining her married sister's household was a fairly usual practice in nineteenth-century England. Nevertheless the bachelor's rooms must have been crowded, for Dickens's young brother, Fred, remained on.

It must have been a deliriously happy period. Dickens and his bride were newly wed lovers. *Pickwick Papers*, after a certain initial lagging, soared to dizzier sales each month. Dickens had a play and operetta put on the stage, and, if they were not overwhelmingly successful, they went well enough to make the theatre seem a probable additional means of livelihood. Publishers were thick on the ground with contracts, and although this proliferation of commitments was to give Dickens serious problems in the next few years, at the time he thought that he had untangled any constricting knots. By November 1836 he had agreed with the publisher Bentley to edit a new magazine, *Bentley's Miscellany*, and when the first number appeared in the new year it was an instant success. Already he had felt able to resign from the *Morning Chronicle*, with the sharp letter to the owner we have seen. His circle of friends was expanding. In January 1837 he was elected to the Garrick Club. *Pickwick*

Opposite. Charles Dickens in 1839 by Maclise.

was on everyone's lips; but what counted more, I imagine, was that by February 1837 the first number of *Oliver Twist* appeared with a good deal of acclaim (mixed with just a little sharp criticism). It banished that most frightening of nightmares for a young novelist, whose first book has been a success; the public was not making of him a one-day wonder.

It was a glorious time. Gone were the boredoms and claustrophobias of Parliament, the discomforts and pains of high-speed coach travel, however he might later look back on them. Present were days of happy domestic absurdities and prides, and of ever-expanding new horizons. True there was too much work – in a wickedly overworked life Dickens never worked so hard again as in those first years of *Pickwick* and *Oliver* – he was producing two monthly serial novels at the same time, as well as editing a monthly magazine and carrying through some commissioned chores like an edition of the auto-biography of Grimaldi the clown. He worked at night as well as by day – something he was never to repeat after those years. But everything was done in high spirits and high hopes.

The presence of the two younger people in the cramped rooms surely helped the young couple to make a happy holiday of this year. Fred Dickens was a lively youth of sixteen, friendly, funny, a good mimic, kind and attentive – his irresponsibility and weakness had not yet shown themselves. Mary was a pretty, lively, intelligent girl who adored her famous young brother-in-law. In January 1837 Catherine gave birth to their first child – a son, Charley. For a day or two the mothers-in-law took over, but Dickens took refuge from this maternal invasion by a youthful, high-spirited expedition with his young sister-in-law to buy a table for his wife's room. When Charles and Catherine returned that year to their honeymoon village for a short holiday they took Mary with them. And when, with a more assured income, they leased a house in Doughty Street, Bloomsbury, it was taken for granted that both Mary and Fred should live there. The first weeks of the oddly assorted group of four were bliss – happy, entertaining family evenings, steady successful work. Charles's delight in his young sister-in-law's admiring and quickly comprehending companionship was keen; it would no doubt have found a proportioned place in that regular but controlled enmeshment of close friendships that was always the pattern of his life, a pattern the more satisfactory because all friendships were subordinate to his work. But his feelings for Mary Hogarth, like his feelings for Maria Beadnell, were to get out of hand, once again to dominate and distort his attitude to women, especially in his fiction, because, as with his relationship with Maria, he was not given time to resolve his relationship with Mary into his overall scheme of life. For Mary died very suddenly in May 1837, after returning with Dickens and his wife from a happy evening at the theatre. She was only seventeen. And she died in Dickens's arms.

The family grief was great. Catherine, slightly, one guesses from the tone of his comment, to Dickens's distaste, recovered the most easily. Mrs Hogarth, the girls' mother, was for many months prostrated. It was not in Dickens's nature to be physically prostrated, but his grief was violent. For the only

'Many Happy Returns of the Day' by William Frith, 1856. 'Life I supposed to consist entirely of birthdays.' 'Birthday Celebrations' in *The Uncommercial Traveller*.

time until the last decade of his life he failed to produce the monthly issues of his serials. The June numbers of *Pickwick Papers* and of *Oliver Twist* – a peculiarly heavy dual burden – did not appear. A small note of explanation to readers begins that close connection between his person and his reading public that came to matter so much to Dickens. He wrote ten days after Mary's death to his friend Beard: 'The first burst of my grief has passed, and I can think and speak of her, calmly and dispassionately. I solemnly believe that so perfect a creature never breathed. I knew her inmost heart, and her real worth and value. She had not a fault.' Such a remark conventionally means that intense grief is past and over; but for Dickens this was not so. As late as 1855 in *The Holly Tree* he tells what is confirmed by many of his letters:

I had lost a very near and dear friend by death. Every night since, at home or away from home, I had dreamed of that friend; sometimes as living; sometimes as returning from the world of shadows to comfort me; always a being beautiful, placid and happy, never in association with any approach to fear or distress. It was at a lonely Inn in a wide moorland place, that I halted to pass the night. When I had looked from my bedroom window over the waste of snow on which the moon was shining, I sat down by my fire to write a letter. I had always, until that hour, kept it within my own breast that I dreamed every night of the dear lost one. But in the letter that I wrote I recorded the circumstance, and added that I felt much interested in proving whether the subject of my dream would still be faithful to me, travel-tired, and in that remote place. No. I lost the beloved figure of my vision in parting with the secret. My sleep has never touched upon it since, in sixteen years, but once. I was in Italy, and awoke (or seemed to awake), the well-remembered voice distinctly in my ears, conversing with it. I entreated it, as it rose above my bed and soared up to the vaulted roof of the old room, to answer me a question I had asked touching the Future Life. My hands were still outstretched towards it as it vanished, when I heard a bell ringing by the garden wall, and a voice in the deep stillness of the night calling on all good Christians to pray for the souls of the dead; it being All Souls' Eve.

The dreams were of Mary Hogarth. The person to whom he communicated the circumstances, after which the dreaming ceased, was Mary's sister, his wife Catherine. This was in 1838 when he was travelling in Yorkshire to collect information for Dotheboys Hall in *Nicholas Nickleby*. He wrote a full account of his later Italian experience from Genoa to his friend, John Forster, in 1844. The story is full of incidental peculiarities that give it verisimilitude, and his explanation of them satisfies. It is also to be emphasized that Dickens was markedly sceptical of spiritualistic phenomena, and wrote many articles attacking well known mediums. There is one peculiar feature to notice, however: 'I said, sobbing, "Oh give me some token that you have really visited me!" "Form a wish," it said. I thought, reasoning with myself: "If I form a selfish wish it will vanish." So I hastily discarded such hopes and anxieties of my own as came into my mind, and said, "Mrs Hogarth is surrounded with great distresses," – observe, I never thought of saying "your mother" as to a mortal creature – "Will you extricate her?"'

Hampstead Heath by John Linnell, 1831. 'Somebody to walk with me in the snow to Hampstead Heath and have a chop at Jack Straw's Castle.' Diary, 1838.

Apart from the lasting influence Mary Hogarth's sudden and early death had in making more peculiar and inhuman Dickens's ideal of woman both in life and in fiction, the other incidental, but certainly unintentional result it had, I think, was to begin his disenchantment with Catherine's family. In particular, perhaps, with her mother, who alone shared his violent grief. It is true that they exchanged mementoes of the dead girl for some years to come; it is true that Dickens thought that he wished to share his grief with his mother-in-law: 'It will be a great relief to my heart when I find you sufficiently calm upon this sad subject to claim the promise I made you when she lay dead in this house, never to shrink from speaking of her as if her memory were to be avoided, but rather to take a melancholy pleasure in recalling the times when we were all so happy.' He may have wanted this dialogue; it is more doubtful if Mrs Hogarth found him the most welcome or the most appropriate member of the family to enter her most private feelings. Certainly, nearly a year later he notes in a rare diary entry: 'I wrote to Mrs Hogarth yesterday . . . imploring her . . . not to give way to unavailing grief. Her answer came tonight, and she seems hurt at my doing so – protesting that in all useful respects she is the same as ever. I meant it for the best and still hope I did right.' As too often when Dickens thought people had judged him unfairly, he sounds more like Mr Pooter than the man of extraordinary insight that he was.

The relations with the Hogarths were not improved by the fact that Mary's grave in Kensal Green Cemetery was bought and owned by him. There is no doubt that he hoped to be buried with the dead girl. However, in 1841 Mary's brother, George, also died, only a very young man. We can judge from Dickens's letter to his friend, Forster, how much like the muddle of his own family the Hogarth's inefficiency at this juncture seemed to him, though he at once arranged for his brother-in-law's burial in Mary's tomb:

As no steps had been taken towards the funeral I thought it best at once to bestir myself . . . . It is a great trial to me to give up Mary's grave, greater than I can possibly express. I thought of moving her to the catacombs and saying nothing about it . . . . The desire to be buried next her is as strong upon me now, as it was five years ago; and I *know* (I don't think there ever was a love like that I bear her) that it will never diminish. I fear I can do nothing. Do you think I can? They would move her on Wednesday, if I resolved to have it done. I cannot bear the thought of being excluded from her dust; and yet I feel that her brothers and sisters, and her mother have a better right than I do to be placed beside her. It is but an idea. I neither think nor hope (God forbid) that our spirits would ever mingle there. I ought to get the better of it, but it is very hard.

It was hard, indeed, for Dickens ever to restrain his own masterful egotism. And the Hogarths, like his own family, also paid a price for lazy cadging. When, over twenty-one years after Mary's death, Dickens was searching for excuses for separating from his wife, he believed that his young sister-in-law had already seen the incompatibility of his temperament with Catherine's. For the rest, and most importantly, the deep impact of Mary's death made

what was already weak in the novel *Oliver Twist* grotesquely feeble, and
helped a later novel, *The Old Curiosity Shop*, to become one of the most peculiar
novels ever written.

Pickwick

It is time now to examine the novels that had brought 'fame and prosperity'
to Dickens at such an early age. *Pickwick Papers* is one of those books so
world-famous, in a few parts so bad, and in all parts so unlike what adult
readers of our century expect to read, that an honest critic today must surely
approach its reputation with scepticism. It is a book, save by a few enthusiasts,
remembered usually with delight, occasionally with irritation, from childhood.

Pickwick Papers: frontispiece of Sam and
Mr Pickwick by Phiz.

Any sensitive, fair-minded person, I think, who re-reads it with care, will at the end have seen that it is an exceptional, a truly wonderful book.

It raises, right from the start of Dickens's work, the question of how far his novels can be seen as a broad design and how much is improvisation. Since the publication of Sir Walter Scott's *Kenilworth* in 1821 it had been the habit – a habit that suited the circulating library – to publish novels in three volumes. Some more journalistic books, books like the popular Pierce Egan's *Tom and Jerry*, sketches of sporting and man-about-town life, had been published in monthly parts as a serial. When in 1836 Mr Hall suddenly proposed that he should write for a series of sporting drawings, Dickens already had in mind a three-volume novel, which would start him on the career of novelist in the honoured tradition of Scott. Now, in order to accept this new, financially very attractive offer, he had to agree to a method of publication which, 'My friends told me . . . was a low, cheap form of publication, by which I should ruin all my hopes.' Writing *Pickwick Papers*, then, was in a way (despite the fact that it meant giving up the idea of a third series of *Sketches by Boz*) a commitment to 'journalism' rather than to his ambition to establish himself as a conventional novelist.

For reasons I have already suggested Dickens found this serial method of publishing very congenial and continued to use it all his life – varying only because of occasional special demands with the even more extraordinary method of weekly publication. Such a method – with its demands for copy, the pressure of reader response, the inevitable temptation to alter one's scheme because of comment or criticism – encourages improvisation.

From the start Dickens probably had some strong sense of artistic unity within novels, but this sense, and more certainly the technical skill to maintain it by elaborate notes and schemes made in advance to establish the track of narrative while at the same time meeting serial demands, only developed with his experience. The earlier novels have much more of improvisation. As a point of fact *Pickwick Papers* was the most completely improvised of them all. With his other early novels he had enjoyed some interval between signing the publishers' contract and issuing the first serial number, which allowed him to incubate his design – for *Oliver Twist* six months, for *Nicholas Nickleby* four months, for *Barnaby Rudge*, his first fully planned and organized novel, five years. After 1846, with *Dombey and Son*, he always had a few numbers written before publication began. But with *Pickwick Papers* the publishers' offer came on 10 February 1836, he accepted on 16 February, began writing on 18 February, and the first number was published on 31 March.

It is not surprising then that the early part of *Pickwick Papers* is journalistic and episodically jerky, since the only unity that it has is the travelling of the Pickwickians by coach – which is perhaps not inappropriate. Indeed Dickens seems to have had some idea that each number should be self-contained. Nevertheless, after the first disastrously facetious chapter the style and presentation of the narrative is self-assured far beyond anything in *Sketches by Boz*; he clearly feels that he has time ahead to develop what he is saying, that it is no mere occasional piece for a magazine.

The London–Canterbury–Margate–Dover coach.

Robert Seymour was a sporting artist and he wanted sporting text. But Dickens tells us in the preface he later wrote for *Pickwick*: 'I objected, on consideration, that although born and partly bred in the country I was no great sportsman except in regard of all kinds of locomotion . . . that I would like to take my own way, with a freer range of English scenes and people . . . . My views being deferred to, I thought of Mr Pickwick and wrote the first number.' This is more simple than absolutely true. He undoubtedly recognized that this could be his big chance; he undoubtedly did overrule his illustrator's wishes in a way extraordinary for a young, comparatively untried writer.

Seymour's suicide in the very early stages of the novel, although it was the result of a congenital depression, was perhaps also brought on somewhat by Dickens's masterfulness. This has led critics to see only the way that Dickens controlled the scheme of his illustrator and not to note the degree to which the scheme controlled Dickens. For it was not only the serial method that he gave way to in writing *Pickwick*, not only more use of sporting events – the cricket match, the skating, the shooting expedition in Suffolk – than he would surely have chosen for himself, but the setting of the countryside, which he knew only from childhood memory, from reporters' rapid journeys, and from a few Cockney expeditions.

Considering how small his knowledge was of England outside London, it is remarkable how, by variation of scene and, above all, by his extraordinary power of conveying the sense of travelling, he does succeed in making the reader feel that he has covered a large area of English life and locality. Yet a good part of it is journalistic writing up of his journalist's experiences – the Eatanswill election, the Ipswich magistrate, provincial newspapers, above all the many scenes in coaching inns; and the rest – especially the Rochester, Dingley Dell and Muggleton scenes – is surely embroidery in imagination of scenes known in childhood. His eye for the country and country life is not as exact as it is for London scenes; his feeling for it, throughout his life and works, is that of a Cockney on holiday. The result, though never gripping, sometimes even perfunctorily pastoral, is always genuinely full of the joy of living, of carefree, happy tranquillity. The country is a conventional but adequate symbol in his work for the innocent happiness of life. Never again, however, was he to use it so fully and so successfully as in *Pickwick* as a ground-work for his account of life.

It is not the theme to which he seems originally to have inclined. The first chapter of *Pickwick* – one of the worst, most facetious chapters he ever wrote – is an account of a meeting of the Pickwick Club, and as whenever Dickens has to use debate, which he despised and hated so much from his Parliament days then only just behind him, his normally exact ear seems to fail him. But the theme of the quarrel between Mr Pickwick and Mr Blotton in his bad first chapter appears to be one of Dickens's perennial concerns – the contrast of the Right, that is, fancy and imagination, versus the Wrong, facts and figures. As he was to use this anti-intellectual theme so often again in his work, from his next novel *Oliver Twist* onwards, we may be quite happy that he renounced it here. In the next chapter, with its easy assurance of writing, the Pickwickians

'The Successful Candidate' by Phiz.

leave London for the country, which, despite many of the petty evils of provincialism, is to be an endless unfolding of festive scenes and innocent happiness.

Mr Pickwick, a retired business man of means, is accompanied by the middle-aged Lothario Mr Tupman and the younger Mr Snodgrass, of poetic interests, both presumably gentlemen of means, otherwise whence comes their leisure? The fourth member of the party, Mr Winkle, a sportsman (or rather, like Dickens trying to write about sport, an imposter pretending to sporting prowess) is the young son of a Birmingham businessman, who has been given money to explore the world before he joins his father's business. It is hardly a group of which Dickens could have had much knowledge. Leisure he could ill afford; perpetual leisure he would have found most irksome; gentlemen would have doubted whether he knew their species. As to the sort of random adventures that the Pickwickians in their travelling sought, Dickens's family life had already provided him with all the randomness that he hoped ever to meet; discipline and order were his demands from life. Above all, the Pickwickians on tour cut out all the social concerns for the poor and submerged that Dickens's childhood had given him, all the obsessions with crime and evil. To this extent it promised a diminution of the London world of some of the *Sketches by Boz*.

It is usually said that these more sombre or macabre notes are provided by the rather garish, ill-written melodramatic stories that are interpolated mainly into the first half of *Pickwick*. I cannot agree with this at all; the sombre side of life, the shadows which are gradually to grow around Mr Pickwick until he is wrongfully imprisoned for debt in the dreadful darkness of the Fleet prison, those shadows which make the high spirits of the first three quarters of the novel and its emergence into a sunny ending so significant and so acceptable, are present in various ways from early on.

Mr Jingle, music hall comedian though he is, represents much of the dark truth of London (with his greasy, splitting clothes and the wretched little brown paper parcel with which he must face the world) to accompany this Cockney idyll into the country. He is a scoundrel, as we think, for his playing upon the wretched old spinster Rachel Wardle's romantic feelings, but Dickens obviously thought that part of it a jolly good music-hall joke about spinsters. Luckily, however, women play only a small part in *Pickwick* (where they do, the tone is on the whole the young, soured Dickens at his worst). It is with Mr Pickwick, the retired business man, that we have to identify ourselves, and, I think, our sympathy can only gradually be won. To begin with, although he is infinitely gullible about what lies in the great world outside his counting house, he is not all innocence; occasionally he comes forward with a piece of worldly wisdom, and when he does so, it does not belong to the brave, dignified man we come to love, but to a very inferior, prosaically cynical plain man. Such is, for example, his famous advice about its always being best to do what the largest mob does; it is he again who thinks to bribe Sam Weller into revealing the whereabouts of the eloped Jingle and Rachel Wardle – 'I made use of the argument which my experience of men has taught me is the most likely to succeed in any case.' But, little by little, we are won to his side – by his continual high spirits (but Mr Wardle has those and he can be very exhausting), by his consideration (for example to old Mrs Wardle), by his continuous courtesy and gallantry, by his readiness to look an ass in order to assist any social occasion, by his determination to pursue what he feels to be justice, by his romantic spirit above all, and by his total refusal to be subdued by authority. He has, in fact, turned a large part of his rentier, elderly, portly, gentlemanly self into a high-spirited, schoolboy knight errant. Already by the Suffolk scenes of the novel our attitude to Mr Pickwick has changed. When the country mob call out to him as he awakes to find himself in a wheelbarrow in the village pound, 'You ain't got no friends, hurrah,' we want, I think, almost as in panto-mime, to hiss them for their unkindness. Mr Pickwick *has* friends; we, his readers, are they. Shortly after, when he exposes Mr Jingle before Mr Nupkins, the magistrate at Ipswich, we do not care that Mr Nupkins has been saved from being defrauded; in fact we are probably rather sorry; but when Jingle patronizes Mr Pickwick as he leaves: 'Good fellow, Pickwick – fine heart – stout old boy – but must *not* be passionate – very bad thing,' we no longer half sympathize with Jingle as the representative of poverty and reality, we know that if reality says that Mr Pickwick should not be passionate, then reality is wrong. For we have learnt the cry, 'Pickwick and principle!'

It is Sam Weller, of course, who teaches us that Pickwick is principle – and Sam Weller, indeed, who voices for us our gradual realization of the growth of Mr Pickwick's moral stature, until at last he can tell Job Trotter, 'I never heard, mind you, nor read of in story books, nor see in picters, any angel in tights and gaiters, nor even in spectacles, as I remember . . . but, mark my words, Job Trotter, he's a reg'lar thoroughbred angel for all that.' But then the relation of Sam Weller and Mr Pickwick is the central theme of the book, to which the underlying theme of country (holiday happiness) and London (the horror of reality) is subordinated.

The two are beautifully married in a too-little-noticed episode in the novel – one that occurs long before the simultaneous publication of *Oliver Twist*, by which Pickwick's darkening shadows are often accounted for. When Mr Pickwick and Sam leave Eatanswill for Bury St Edmunds in pursuit of the scoundrel, Jingle, they pass through a lyrical scene of country life:

> As the coach rolls swiftly past the fields and orchards which skirt the road, groups of women and children, piling the fruits in sieves, or gathering the scattered ears of corn, pause for an instant from their labour, and shading the sun-burnt face with a still browner hand, gaze upon the passengers with envious eyes, while some stout urchin, too small to work, but too mischievous to be left at home, scrambles over the side of the basket in which he has been deposited for safety, and kicks and screams with delight.

It is exactly in this pastoral scene that Sam, delighting in the happy day, nevertheless tells Mr Pickwick of his glum childhood: 'Afore I took up with the vagginer, I had unfurnished lodgings for a fortnight . . . the dry arches of Waterloo Bridge . . . it's generally the worn out, starving, houseless creeturs as rolls themselves in the dark corners o' them lonesome places.' I do not

'I had unfurnished lodgings for a fortnight . . . the dry arches of Waterloo Bridge.'

believe that, for all Dickens's improvisation, this juxtaposition is a fluke. Here in the central relationship of Mr Pickwick and Sam is brought alive the conflict between idyllic country (Dickens's Cockney country ignores rural poverty, although Dickens knew its poet Crabbe's works well) and cruel town. Sam, the mentor of Mr Pickwick, his guide to the world, uses the same black humour as Mr Jingle does, although with a different and generous intent. But Mr Pickwick is also the saviour and, in a sense, the mentor of Sam, for he brings him into the happy holiday air of the country, where he immediately thrives – at Christmas at Dingley Dell, for example, 'Sam had managed to become mighty popular already, and was as much at home as if he had been born on the land.' No wonder that a partnership so profitable to both parties cannot be ended by the Fleet prison, that Sam must get himself arrested to be there with his surrogate father, who needs his care, and that he does this with his own real father, Tony Weller, as his accomplice, for Tony is a man equally full of benevolent wisdom and equally in need of Sam's worldly guidance as is Mr Pickwick.

Professor Stephen Marcus is surely right to suggest that this meaning lies deep in Dickens's own self. Most first novels are patently autobiographical. *Pickwick* only *seems* to defy this rule. Indeed it seems to me that Professor Marcus's fruitful analysis of the novel can be pushed even farther than he extends it. In *Pickwick* surely Dickens relives the cruel months of his father's

The interior of the Fleet prison – the rackets court.

first imprisonment and solves them as he would like them to have been solved. In this fictional version the young boy Dickens (Sam) stays with his father in the Marshalsea and yet guides and befriends him with the worldly knowledge he had so cruelly gained as he tramped the streets during his luncheon hours at Warren's. Surely such a happy dream deserves the happy effect it has upon its readers.

With the eleventh number of *Pickwick*, Dickens began the publication of his second novel, *Oliver Twist*. Before *Oliver Twist* was complete the serialization of his third novel, *Nicholas Nickleby*, had started. But it was not only an incredible load of work that pressed upon Charles Dickens in those amazing first years as a writer. He was also playing hard: an immensely gregarious man, with an extraordinary gift for maintaining not just a display of social acquaintanceship but of keeping alive, like some brilliant juggler with variously coloured hoops, the most diverse intimacies at the same time and over many, many years, he extended his range of human knowledge enormously at this time. By 1841 when he began the publication of *Barnaby Rudge*, the novel that had been making so long, his place within the social world of arts was more than secure, rather, it was outstanding. He had arrived in time to participate in what remained of the Regency world in which the Romantics had flourished – his friendships with Walter Savage Landor and Leigh Hunt linked him to Shelley and to Byron (whose influence and popularity he had already mocked with distaste in a sketch of a poetical young man in *Sketches by Boz)*; he was connected not only by these but by attending the last years of the famous breakfasts of Samuel Rogers, the Regency wit and poet, and by the favour of the formidable Lady Holland, who from her great Whig mansion had ruled the fashionable cultural world for many decades. More insecure, more what in our times has been called 'café society', but no less fashionable, were Lady Blessington and Count D'Orsay at Gore House. He knew well the Scottish critic, Lord Jeffrey, the famous lawyer, Talfourd, and the literary host and politician, Monckton Milnes. He knew most of the principal painters, and was already a close friend of Macready, the actor. Of the figures of the future he knew Thackeray and Browning, although not as yet Tennyson, whose work was to influence him more. He knew the young millionairess and philanthropist, Angela Burdett-Coutts, who was to give him practical outlet for his social reforming and charitable interests.

All in all, he knew 'everybody that counted', although it has always to be remembered that the artistic world was far closer to journalism, far further from the universities, from learning or serious philosophical thought, than even a hundred years later, and certainly than now, when 'men of letters' who are not connected in some way with academic life are a vanishing species. This makes it necessary to point out that many of the nineteenth-century figures who now seem to us at the centre of serious thought – John Stuart Mill,

A world of long walks with huge meals at the end of them, above all at the Star and Garter.

Matthew Arnold, John Henry Newman – were never among his many circles of friends. But as far as contemporary England saw its cultural 'Establishment', Dickens already encompassed it by 1841, five years after the success of *Pickwick*.

The new social ties did not cut him off from an active, lively social relationship with old friends or his family; his parents, indeed, produced a new financial crisis in the summer of 1839. 'I am sick at heart with both her and father too,' he wrote of his mother. He acted immediately, packing them off to a cottage near Exeter that he bought and furnished for them. It is perhaps typical of the way in which he felt a need to sweeten his own masterfulness even to himself that at the moment when he was sending his parents unwillingly to country exile in Devonshire, a place with which they had no connection of memory, he was making that county the scene of the happy ending of *Nicholas Nickleby* where 'nothing with which there was any association of bygone times was ever removed or changed'.

All his social life, pleasant though it must have been – a world of dinner parties, theatre-going, impromptu long rides or long walks with huge meals at the end of them, above all at the Star and Garter, Richmond – was something of a strain even on so energetic a young man. And to them was added an appalling net of publishers' contracts, by which at various times he found himself pledged to write books for three different firms. It was one of the new friends out of his great new world who helped him out of this publishers' tangle; and to John Forster, his future biographer, he remained more deeply attached, at any rate until his middle age, than to any other friend. In Forster he found a man whose wit, interests, social views, and, above all, ethics spoke to his own. Soon Forster was reading all his proofs, advising him in detail about his work as he wrote it, perusing all his contracts, hearing all his inmost fears and worries. Only when, as the years advanced, Dickens's restlessness grew almost frenetic, and Forster became more conventionally marked with the pomposity of middle age, did their great intimacy weaken; and it never broke. Forster's rather overwhelming solidity, indeed, was a necessary buttress in these extraordinary years between *Pickwick* and *Barnaby Rudge*.

Oliver Twist

The effect of such pressures in life, perhaps with the blow of Mary Hogarth's death added, does tell in *Oliver Twist* and *Nickleby*. In a sense, by preventing him from advancing his art as a novelist, it makes the first the remarkable work it is, but it spoils the second.

Oliver Twist is surely one of the great popular works of art of all time – rightly seized upon by film, stage and television producers, rightly made the prey of pop composers. It is two novels which Dickens, without the technical powers needed, attempts but fails to join together by a preposterous plot of coincidence and improvised mystery. The first part lies nearer to his journalism; but in its assured, controlled and concise language (even when it is most sentimental) it is journalism of genius. The story of Oliver, the illegitimate

'Come unto these Yellow Sands' by Richard Dadd, 1842. 'All I can say is, with my friend Shakespeare, that it's like the shadow of a dream.' Cousin Feenix in *Dombey and Son*.

Overleaf. 'The Thames at Twickenham' by Gerald Barrett II, c. 1850. 'And he thought that it might be better to flow away monotonously like the river.' Arthur Clenham at Twickenham ferry in *Little Dorrit*.

orphan, first at the baby-farmer's, then at the workhouse, and finally in the wider world apprenticed to the undertaker, is a story of the routine cruelty exercised upon the nameless, almost faceless submerged of Victorian society by a system, which would be harsh if efficient, and, given the built-in inefficiency of human beings, is deadly. That it was an attack upon the ideas of serious, intelligent, educated and well-intentioned men presented with an intractable social problem, is not relevant to modern readers, nor even that Dickens in his often wrong-headed attack upon them largely saw the truth instead of the statistics which obsessed the legislators. What matters is that it is one of the most successful social satires, which, in great degree, deals not in personalities but in human anonymity, in the 'crowd', in 'society'. To my own taste, the achievement is made at the cost of Dickens's greatest gifts of dialogue and characterization; it is also done by a profuse use of that heavy irony which marks all his novels down to *Dombey and Son*.

It is unlikely however that I should entirely favour this first part, for I am entirely seduced by the second – the strange evil world which encloses the ridiculous melodrama of little Oliver fallen among thieves. This part has many more glaring faults than the first: an army of good, genteel characters, all finally by far-fetched explanations to prove related to the little boy they have befriended, an army which is totally vapid when it is not mawkish or playfully whimsical; a long, irrelevant illness given to the heroine, Rose Maylie, simply as a result of the impact of Mary Hogarth's death upon the author; and even among the glamorous, gamey, stinking set of petty thieves and brutal robbers a key character, the prostitute Nancy, who, to my thinking, has only the shadowiest existence. Fagin, Sikes, Charley Bates, Noah Claypole and above all, the Artful Dodger (Sam Weller gone downhill from his unfurnished lodgings underneath the arches to pit all his Cockney liveliness against Mr Pickwick's decency instead of on its behalf) – these are superb individual characters; but they are also a superb gang, perhaps the first and the best of all the thousands of fictional gangs to follow them, because the gaiety, the high spirits of desperation never conceal for a moment the total brutality and treachery of these men and boys, for whom the Golden Rule is the reverse of the Sermon on the Mount, 'Look after Number One'. But a collection of characters, even a gang, cannot account for the extraordinary effect of the second part of this novel. This comes from the masterly incorporation of the human characters into their physical setting – a gang constantly on the move, slithering, squeaking and scuttling from one unoccupied, rat-ridden old London house to another, like the vermin themselves.

The rodent criminal world, indeed, is unnoticed by the indifferent crowd until the cry of murder goes up. Then a bloodthirsty rat-hunt is immediately on, with all the world ready to lynch Sikes or Fagin; the indifferent, respectable, everyday workpeople of society have turned avenging mob. The picture is stylized, an injection of real delight into mythic story, but it has an extraordinary surrealist, nightmare conviction.

These two parts *are* joined; not by the plot, but by the figure of little Oliver,

'Autolycus' by Augustus Egg, 1845. 'Shakespeare . . . though he died a commoner . . . nevertheless did the State some service.' Speech, 1856.

A gang constantly slithering from one unoccupied, rat-ridden old London house to another.

the orphan boy fallen among thieves, who speaks and behaves with absolute gentility. Oliver is a vacuum. But so he has to be. All through his life Dickens hammered home the point that crime was the result of the terrible Poverty and Ignorance in Victorian society. He worked hard on society's compassion in order to diminish the poverty and the ignorance; but with minor exceptions he did not wish to rouse its compassion for the criminals whom he declared to be the result of these evils. He was concerned for justice, and believed, as he says in the preface to this very novel, 'I fear there are in the world some insensible and callous natures, that do become utterly and incurably bad,' And, as we see from his gloomy account of young delinquents in the 'Newgate' piece of *Sketches by Boz*, he saw total corruption taking over at a very early age in the criminal mind.

There is a gulf between the corrupting causes of crime and the absolutely evil nature of most criminals, a gulf that cannot easily be crossed. For this reason it is as well that Oliver, who is intended to act as the bridge, should have no reality, should be merely an image of humanity worked upon by external forces. He rouses in the first part our hatred of a system which is cruel, which exploits poverty and ignorance; he rouses in the second part our fear of those people who fight that system by means of the evil, violence, and brutality within themselves – the criminal gang.

But the good, genteel people in the second part – Oliver's friends – belong, whether Dickens likes it or not, to the anonymous society that exploits the poor and ignorant in the first part – that is perhaps why they are so null and void, these sweet Rose Maylies and jolly old Mr Brownlows, that they are almost anonymous too. Mr Brownlow, the kind old gentleman who befriends

Oliver Twist: 'Monks and the Jew'; 'Fagin in prison' by Cruikshank.

Oliver, is only another mask for the gentleman in the white waistcoat on the board of guardians, who in the first part fails to realize that Oliver is human. Inevitably, then, although Dickens by the force of his powers of rhetoric and narrative can rouse us to join the rat hunt against Fagin and Sikes after the murder is known, for the most part we find ourselves, however we shrink from their brutality, treachery and filth, living the second half of the novel *with* the gang, for they alone are alive, they alone share the author's power of laughter, however devilishly. And we cannot but suspect that, somewhere in himself, though Dickens feared them and implacably condemned them, he participates with the villains of the second part (Fagin, Dodger & Co.) in their fight against the villains of the first part (the gentlemen who run society for their own well-being).

The book is in two parts, in fact, because the problem of crime as a social waste cannot be reconciled with crime as a deadly poison. And this surely, apart from the wonderful characterization and atmosphere, is why *Oliver Twist* is a great 'pop' novel, for the public at large (we, that is) by instinct want to feel compassion for the exploited, but does not want to face the difficult problem of exploring the results in detail. It wants to pity Oliver, but he must not be real, for then he might be corrupted and brutalized into Fagin, whom it must loathe. The public wants, also, to join in the hue and cry against the gang when the moment comes to hunt them out; yet in its imagination it wants to share in the gang's violence and glamour (however squalid, perhaps nowadays the more squalid the better) and feverish, doomed fun.

Nicholas Nickleby

In writing *Oliver Twist* Dickens had exploited a fashionable *genre* of novel, the 'Newgate' novel in which both his popular contemporaries, Ainsworth and Lytton, had shown their mastery, although, as he strongly protested in the third edition's preface, he had sought to avoid the sentimental romanticizing of criminals into which most of the 'Newgate' school fell. In writing *Nicholas Nickleby* he returned to the old wandering adventures of a young hero that he had inherited from the last century, from Fielding and Smollett; but he tried to give them a unity of plot. Although in Nicholas Nickleby he created a young hero with more of his own humour, his own sense of the ridiculous and his own natural flirtatiousness than any of his later heroes, the novel as a whole fails.

It has magnificent features. Mrs Nickleby is a great comic creation and the central image of her ceaseless chain of speech is genteel, wounded egotism. On any subject under the sun, she, and by implication her class, have been slighted or deprived; all is past glory. Hear her on the Corn Laws, coming to them from a swollen face she had once received from draughts in a hackney carriage: 'If they hadn't charged us a shilling an hour extra for having it open, which seems to be the law, or was then, and a most shameful law it appears to be – I don't understand the subject but I should say that the Corn Laws could be nothing to *that* act of Parliament.' But one brilliant character cannot

Nicholas Nickleby: 'The internal economy of Dotheboys Hall'; 'Nicholas astonishes Mr Squeers and family' by Phiz.

save a novel and Mrs Nickleby is almost sucked down by the melodrama and the shapelessness of the whole (in this respect, her wonderful monologues are almost a parody of the novel).

Much praise has been given to Squeers and Dotheboys Hall, but this is surely no more than good imaginative reporting. Unlike the first part of *Oliver Twist*, the total anonymity of the boys set against the strong characterization of their tormentors, the Squeers family, fails to stir the reader. Indeed I suspect that most readers of the novel will remember Dotheboys Hall from the two wonderful illustrations by Phiz rather than from Dickens's text. Perhaps this is the place to say that, with inevitable failures, the illustrations of Phiz (Hablot Browne) who, after joining Boz in *Pickwick*, remained his principal illustrator until late in his career, seem to me frequently to add a dimension (and an imaginatively valid one) to Dickens's fictional world. I do not exempt the superior draughtsman George Cruikshank, illustrator of *Oliver Twist*, from the preference I give to Phiz over all other Dickens illustrators – but Phiz's failures do tend to reinforce Dickens's weaknesses, for they are markedly in the 'realistic' and sentimental characterization of the books. In such scenes as Dotheboys Hall he lends particularity to the crowd (the boys) where Dickens's text blurs. For better or for worse, our conception of the Dickensian world is tied up with Phiz. Who can separate Phiz's vision of

Pecksniff or Mrs Gamp, of Mrs Skewton, Major Bagstock, of Mr Micawber, or of Steerforth defying Mr Mell; or indeed, in more dramatic mood, of Mr Carker in flight, or of Tom All Alone's from Dickens's text? Indeed, when we consider Dickens's close supervision of the illustrations, who would wish us to?

One part of *Nicholas Nickleby*, however, is superb – the Crummles episodes. Nowhere does Dickens pay such splendid tribute to the theatre as in this description of the little world of the fourth-rate touring company. He gets full effect from their absurdities, their vanities and their egotism. No one is immune from criticism except perhaps that marvellous figure of all work, Mrs Grudden. Vanity is their mainspring, as it must be for all theatre people who are offering what is so poor; but they also know that what they offer has its spring in fancy and imagination, which make it worth more than all the values of the wretched local bourgeoisie to whom they have to beg for patronage. No one, not themselves, can say how much of what they do and say is sheer fraud, for who can say how much better they could realize their dreams of being true artistes if circumstances were not so hard, if they had larger and more discriminating audiences, if they didn't have to make purses all the time out of sows' ears? Probably they have a natural taste for the bad and the improvised, for upstaging and for cheap effects? But who can say how much their grand image of themselves once had validity? Mr Crummles, with his exploited daughter, the Infant Phenomenon, above all, is one of the few unsentimentalized, greatly likable old frauds in fiction. While Nicholas is with them as Mr Johnson the book takes on an extra dimension of vitality and of affection laced with cunning (a rare quality in Dickens's work). If *Nicholas Nickleby* could have been Dickens's 'theatre novel' as *Bleak House* is his novel of the Law it could have been a comic masterpiece. Some recent admirers of the book have attempted to suggest that this is so – that the melodrama of the main plots connected with Ralph Nickleby, the miser Gride's pursuit of Madeline Bray, Nicholas's love, and of the rake Sir Mulberry Hawk's pursuit of Kate, Nicholas's sister, are purposely theatrical and set purposely against the Crummles. But this, I think, is an ingenious excuse for Dicken's poor melodrama. Much might have been done to set the play-acting characters like Mrs Nickleby, Mrs Wittitterly and the Mantalinis against the real players of the Crummles world – and it is noticeable that the funniest conversation about Shakespeare in all Dickens's work – and Shakespeare is the source of much of his funniest comedy – is held between Mrs Nickleby and Mrs Wittitterly:

> 'I'm always ill after Shakespeare,' said Mrs Wittitterly. 'I scarcely exist the next day; I find the reaction so very great after a tragedy, my lord, and Shakespeare is such a delicious creature.'
>
> 'Ye-es!' replied Lord Frederick. 'He was a clayver man.'
>
> 'Do you know, my lord,' said Mrs Wittitterly, after a long silence, 'I find I take so much more interest in his plays, after having been to that dear little dull house he was born in! Were you ever there, my lord?'
>
> 'No, nayver,' replied my lord.
>
> 'Then really you ought to go, my lord,' returned Mrs Wittitterly, in very languid

and drawling accents. 'I don't know how it is, but after you've seen the place and written your name in the little book, somehow or other you seem to be inspired; it kindles up quite a fire within one.'

'Ye-es!' replied Lord Frederick. 'I shall certainly go there.'

'Julia, my life,' interposed Mr Wittitterly, 'you are deceiving his lordship – unintentionally my lord, she is deceiving you. It is your poetical temperament, my dear – your ethereal soul – your fervid imagination, which throws you into a glow of genius and excitement. There is nothing in the place, my dear – nothing, nothing.'

'I think there must be something in the place,' said Mrs Nickleby, who had been listening in silence, 'for, soon after I was married, I went to Stratford with my poor dear Mr Nickleby, in a post chaise from Birmingham – was it a post-chaise though?' said Mrs Nickleby, considering, 'yes, it must have been a post-chaise, because I recollect remarking at the time that the driver had a green shade over his left eye; – in a post-chaise from Birmingham, and after we had seen Shakespeare's tomb and birth-place, we went back to the inn there, where we slept that night, and I recollect that all night long I dreamt of nothing but a black gentlemen, at full length, in plaster-of-Paris, with a lay-down collar tied with two tassels, leaning against a post and thinking; and when I woke in the morning and described him to Mr Nickleby, he said it was Shakespeare just as he had been when he was alive, which was very curious indeed. Stratford – Stratford,' continued Mrs Nickleby, considering. 'Yes, I am positive about that, because I recollect I was in the family way with my son Nicholas at the time, and I had been very much frightened by an Italian image boy that very morning. In fact, it was quite a mercy, ma'am,' added Mrs Nickleby, in a whisper to Mrs Wittitterly, 'that my son didn't turn out to be a Shakespeare, and what a dreadful thing that would have been!'

Jean Davenport, original of Mr Crummles's daughter, the Infant Phenomenon.

But the villains, Ralph Nickleby, Gride, Bray, Hawk, are not play-acting at all, they are (save for Bray) not self-deceiving, they are merely stagily presented, so that their contrast with the true world of play-acting has no such force as modern apologists for the novel proclaim. Given the pressure of work and the pressure of new experience upon the young Dickens, *Nicholas Nickleby*, crammed with good stuff, crowded and jostled into a meaningless muddle by undigested material, is exactly the sort of magnificent failure that could be predicted. But the novel of the theatre that is lost in the washing is sad to think of. There is a certain irony in the dedication to his great actor friend, Macready.

Mr Macready as Hamlet and as Macbeth.

The Old Curiosity Shop

A quite different sort of mixture is *The Old Curiosity Shop*. Before *Nicholas Nickleby*'s serialization was complete the overworked Charles Dickens thought that he had seen how to meet the rising cost of his way of living, of his growing family (his third child, Katey, was born the month after *Nickleby* ended), and the ever-swelling number of his dependants (the battle, as a matter of fact, went on in one form or another, desperately, for all his life). He put before his publishers, Chapman & Hall, a scheme for a sort of *Arabian Nights Entertainment* of Dickens fiction. It was, it must be confessed, a lazy scheme of an over-

The Old Curiosity Shop: 'Waiting at the grave' by Cruikshank.

pressed young man in which he hoped to use the popularity of Mr Pickwick and Sam Weller all over again; in which a quaint old narrator, Master Humphrey, should link a series of stories; in which a contemporary taste for whimsical legend (typified in *The Ingoldsby Legends* of 1837) should be exploited by making the mythical giants of London, Gog and Magog, tell many of the tales; in which travel sketches like those made so popular by the American writer, Washington Irving, would give reason for Dickens the editor to travel in Ireland and America. *Master Humphrey's Clock*, as the periodical was called, had four major advantages in Dickens's mind: it would secure his continuous relation with his public; by sharing in the profits he would become more independent; it was to include contributions by other writers; it would allow him time, he believed, to produce the full-scale major novel (finally to emerge as *Barnaby Rudge)* he had borne inside himself for so long. There were, as it transpired, two overwhelming defects – it was to appear weekly, and by its third weekly appearance in the spring of 1840 it was quite apparent from the serious decline in sales that it was not what his public wanted from him.

Immediately, as many times later in his career, Dickens leapt to meet the challenge. He had earlier thought, while staying at Bath, of 'a child's story' to fill one of the numbers; now, his imagination possessed by the story of Little Nell, he decided to expand the story to novel length and save his magazine enterprise. After appearing intermittently in the magazine for some weeks, the new story took over. The success of *The Old Curiosity Shop* among all classes of readers, both in Great Britain and the United States, fully justified his hopes.

The story of Little Nell, 'a small and delicate child of much sweetness of disposition', and her journeyings through the West Midlands with her senile, cunning, gambling-crazy grandfather, is one of the most difficult fictions for a modern reader to appreciate. The other part of the novel – the story of the wicked dwarf, Quilp, and his machinations to procure with his lawyer accomplices, the Brasses, the false imprisonment of an honest Cockney servant boy, Kit Nubbles – is good early Dickens, painted in bold, unsubtle, but striking colours. Into it is inserted a more pastel sketch, sentimental-humorous in a true vein of late eighteenth-century humorous sentiment, of the redemption of a dissipated clerk, Dick Swiveller, by the devotion during his illness of an exploited, undersized maid of all work, the Marchioness. I have already suggested the possible biographical source of this in Dickens's childhood. It is well done, but with perhaps a slightly too conscious whimsy and pathos. The whole novel, indeed, comparatively short as it is, and written in weekly parts making for concision, shows up alarmingly to modern readers the degree of oddity then accepted in a supposedly realistic story – a devilish, fire-drinking dwarf, a little child, an undersized servant maid, a woman (Sally Brass), who is reported as having enlisted as a guardsman or gone down to the docks in male attire, a small boy who stands on his head in mudflats. It seems, to modern taste, a tale of the kind that we expect from the South (and the deep South too) – early Capote or Carson McCullers. We look for erotic overtones.

The Little Nell story is about death: 'The First Sense of Sorrow' by James Sant.

And here the first of our difficulties arises. The story of Little Nell is only connected to this other more conventional narrative by the fact that she is loved by the honest boy, Kit Nubbles, and brutally persecuted and pursued by the dwarf, Quilp, for her grandfather's supposed fortune. Let us take the love of Kit for Nelly first. It was a theme that Dickens delighted in; one of his later sketches revolves around the elopement of a small pair of ten-year-olds to Gretna Green. From late Victorian times in England, under public school (boarding school) domination, romantic attachments between boys and girls, whether children or even adolescents, were frowned upon or healthily laughed at as 'soppy', or 'unhealthy', or 'unmanly'. Calf love, like adolescent acne or the first fluff of beards, was tabu or a subject for crude teasing. American habits, like American education, were more natural in these matters. I can remember well when even something so conventional, not to say sentimental, as Andy Hardy's movie romances was an embarrassment to English parents, because they encouraged sloppy thoughts about 'boys' or 'girls' in the young of the opposite sex. Opinion would be more enlightened today, and we should be less embarrassed by childhood romance – but even so we should not exclude some physical thought. This would be completely to misunderstand the early Victorian attitude, particularly to misunderstand Little Nell. The love of Kit Nubbles for Little Nell is not really allowable, partly for class reasons, partly because Little Nell on her way to death passes out of the realm of any but the spiritual reverence of others; but even at the start, when Kit's admiration is admitted, it is seen as a sort of charming picture – like the many Victorian illustrations of children dressed in old-time clothes as lovers; they are not lovers in any emotional sense, merely endowed with an excess of childish charm for spectators by reason of their mutual attachment.

As to Quilp's feelings towards Nelly – they inevitably seem to us (especially when we know the degree to which children were prostituted for money in the nineteenth century) sensual, erotic, sadistic in a physical sense. What else can we make of his words to the old grandfather: 'Such a fresh, blooming, modest little bud, neighbour! . . . such a chubby, rosy, cosy little Nell . . . . She's so small, so compact, so beautifully modelled, so fair, with such blue veins and such a transparent skin, and such little feet.'? We may speculate upon the unconscious feelings of both Dickens and his readers, but consciously there is no horror attached to these words – their only horror comes in their blasphemy, that this is a true description of Nell spoken by an evil, misshapen, vile man. 'Whoso shall offend one of these little ones' – it is surely only in our century that these words of Christ have been seen solely in sexual terms. It is true that Quilp talks of making Nell his wife, if his present wife dies, but that is all in the future. In the end Quilp's persecution of Nelly, as of Kit Nubbles, comes out of a general hatred of good and innocent people – and appropriately, because Quilp, in both farce and horror, is the Devil himself. There is no physical way of connecting Nell and her winding pilgrim's progress through England to her death in the sleepy peaceful old village, with the life and characters of the London plot.

This is perhaps why critics since Chesterton have preferred to treat the novel as a fairy story, a legend. But this won't quite do. Legend is the skeleton framework of a great many novels, of almost all Dickens's; and among all his work the legendary structure sticks out most clearly in *The Old Curiosity Shop* (and, perhaps, *Dombey and Son*). But nevertheless the story has a framework of intended reality, is laid in the England of approximately its own time or a decade earlier. It is meant to be about real people with real social circumstances in real London. It would be truer to speak of it as a scene from that peculiarly English phenomenon, pantomime – where Dick Whittington may make jokes about the Beatles or devaluation, and Aladdin's mother, Widow Twankey, may appear in a mini-skirt. But it is hardly pantomime, for apart from the links that inadequately tie Little Nell to the Quilp-Kit plot, the Little Nell story is about death – not the meaning of death, but about the spectacle of death, the effect of death upon the mourners, particularly the effect of the death of a child. As such it is a very strange phenomenon for twentieth-century readers.

'Derby Day' by William Frith, 1858. 'She was one who sat alone in a handsome carriage and motioned away a gipsy-woman urgent to tell her fortune, saying that it was told already . . . but called the child towards her.' Little Nell at the racecourse in *The Old Curiosity Shop*.

The original readers of *The Old Curiosity Shop* did not know for many weeks or months that the novel would lead to Nell's death; and even as it approached they hoped that it would not end so – hence the cries to Dickens not to kill Nell. But that is part of the harrowing, of the sympathetic suffering. The book is shaped relentlessly from Little Nell in the old curiosity shop with its jumbled collection of what are now sometimes called 'bygones' – old dead things of a dead and past age – to Little Nell in the old village church with its jumbled collection of tombs and memorials. The room in the old curiosity shop where the child sleeps and the room in the old village house where she dies are alike in seeming to be theatre property rooms with their quaint objects and hangings. Like Mrs Jarley's waxworks, or Codlin and 'Short's' Punch and Judy, Cattermole's drawings of the child on her death bed, of the old grandfather at the tomb, the tailpiece of Nell winged to heaven by angels, these are all the show of Nell's death and the invitation to grief. Her adventures on the way with the various entertainers, against the background of the furnaces of the Black Country and the industrial riots there, are brilliant journalistic description, showing England in her many guises. They pass by the child like the old scenery that moved past a stationary car to give the effect of world travel in a fairground. For Nell's progress, save that it goes through Vanity Fair (the entertainment world) and the furnaces of hell, is that of the agonies, not so much of the dying human body, as of the relatives waiting round the sick bed: the high points are essentially collapse at the inn (we have known it must come), apparent recovery in the village (but if we notice that she makes her little garden by the tombstone we shall not allow our hopes to be deceived), and the final end. It is clear that for a public where child death (and in the home) was a common phenomenon the story struck endless chords of memory unstirred in us.

Twenty years later Dickens makes notes of the open grief discharged among bereaved members of the audience when he read 'Paul Dombey' aloud. But Nell's death is not, I believe, a model of dying, as is, say, the death of Clarissa ninety years earlier, where the accent is upon her victory over this world, as she goes with careful preparation of shroud and coffin selected by herself to greet her true bridegroom in Heaven. It is not, as with Clarissa, a deliberate baroque accent on the mortality of the flesh. To this great organ music of the preceding century Dickens was deaf. He praised a stage adaptation of *Clarissa* in Paris as being far better than the original: 'Richardson is no great favourite of mine, and never seems to me to take his top-boots off whatever he does.' The emphasis in Dickens's novel is upon those who are left behind: 'If there be any who have never known the blank that follows death – the weary void – the sense of desolation that will come upon the strongest minds, when something familiar and beloved is missed at every turn – the connection between inanimate and senseless things, and the object of recollection, when every household god becomes a monument and every room a grave . . . they can never faintly guess.' There were many to respond, judging by the novel's powerful effects on some readers. And those who knew this suffering were offered the consolation: 'When Death strikes down the innocent and young,

'Applicants for Admission to the Casual Ward' by Sir Luke Fildes, 1874. '"If they would rather die," said Scrooge, "they had better do it, and decrease the surplus population."' *A Christmas Carol.*

for every fragile form from which he lets the panting spirit flee, a hundred virtues rise, in shapes of mercy, charity and love, to walk the world, and bless it.'

Perhaps, as has been suggested, this indicates a certain desperation, a certain doubt about immortality in the sort of broad New Testament Christianity Dickens lived by. It may be so, but his assertions of belief in Heaven when, as rarely, he speaks of sacred things, ring true, if embarrassingly to our ears. And again, his impatience with excessive public mourning over Wellington and Prince Albert suggest that it is specifically a communication of his extraordinary grief at the ending of life in a young person, a symbol of all that is healthy and outgiving in life. May not an energetic, productive, materialistic society have wanted some assurance that the death of the young 'paid off', here and now, in an uplifting sense that comes upon the mourners? That 'a hundred virtues rise . . . to walk the world' from the vitality that appears to have been stilled. It is no more self-regarding than our determination to prove that all *sexual* activity must in some way be life-enhancing. The only fault with Little Nell is that, like Victorian funeral statuary, in order to establish her spirituality she is lifeless from the first pages of the book, whereas Clarissa Harlowe, like a baroque monument, is violently, almost frighteningly, alive. But 'blessed are they that mourn, for they shall be comforted'. We are in Wordsworth's world of the Little Maid in 'We are Seven', who takes her porringer and her knitting to the grave of her little brothers and sisters. Indeed, Sir David Wilkie in a letter of October 1839 says that Dickens spoke to him of his great admiration for this poem, adding that 'he deprecated what in some families occurred of never alluding to a near relation deceased; said he lately met with a severe loss, but took every pains to recall the person deceased to his family about him.' This conversation took place at a dinner to celebrate the completion of *Nicholas Nickleby*, the novel immediately before the story of Little Nell. And the last illustration to *Nicholas Nickleby* shows Nicholas's children at their cousin's grave.

Chapter IV
Away From It All and
Back Again 1840–50

t will seem strange to the majority of Dickens's admirers to open a chapter in the history of his world with the publication of *Barnaby Rudge*. It was not as successful as his previous novels when it appeared, and it has not been an outstanding favourite either with general readers or with critics since. It is not my intention to suggest that it is one of his four or five masterpieces, although I think that it is a very good novel indeed. It is, however, without any doubt, a considerable step forward in his artistic mastery of the fictional world that he saw in the real world around him; it is the first broad-based picture of English society persistent enough in narrative, and absolutely followed through in theme, to point forward to his later great parables of society. Like the later masterpieces, *Little Dorrit* and *Great Expectations*, its plot is not only weak through inherent melodrama but doubly weak by revolving around wicked deeds of violence performed long before the action of the book begins; we can see in *Barnaby Rudge* where Dickens will find the unity his great novels need, and where not. It does not force our wonder from us as does *Pickwick Papers* nor does it ever quite entrap us in a hilarious nightmare that seems to have been with us from our childhood as do the best Fagin or Dodger scenes in *Oliver Twist*; but by taking the author away from his own time (or from the time of his childhood) to a time thirty-odd years before he was born, and by dropping him plumb into the middle of a great historical public event – and an event of violence – it forced him out of the petty bourgeois world from which, save for the theatre world of the Crummleses, he had only made dream (Pickwick or the Fagin gang), or journalistic (Oliver's workhouse or Squeers's school) expeditions (at any rate with any success, for his Nickleby excursions into the wicked West End are hardly to be praised). With Mr (Sir John) Chester and Lord George Gordon we make a real ascent into the ruling classes; with Hugh the Ostler and Dennis the hangman we make a real descent into the underworld; and certainly in no previous novel are all classes welded together in one picture of society in conflict. I am not suggesting that a novelist, even a novelist with a firmly social surface, cannot say all that he wishes within a narrow group of charac-

ters, a narrow range of society. But for some – George Eliot, Dickens, D. H. Lawrence seem outstanding among English novelists – there is a drive to encompass a whole society without which their view of life cannot be fully illuminated.

Charles Dickens already knew enough of English society to make this translation a few years after *Pickwick*, but he needed to stand away in order to see it. That he was conscious, as soon as success came upon him, of a restricted range seems to me probable, although his biographers have not declared it. As early as 1837 he made his first visit to the Continent, to Belgium. It was a very short excursion and is usually treated as a holiday trip, since he went with Catherine. But it is notable that they took with them the young artist, Hablot Browne (Phiz), whose illustrations had been so successful in *Pickwick*. Shortly after this he took Phiz with him again, to Yorkshire, specifically to get ideas for the Squeers scenes in *Nickleby*; and a few months later again, to the Black Country, which was to provide some scenes for Little Nell's wanderings. It seems to me likely that, however immaturely journalistic the idea of getting 'foreign' scenes in a short excursion to Ghent and Brussles may be, this first expedition abroad was intended to feed his writing, else why should he take his illustrator with him? However that may be, he was soon to find travel abroad an absolute necessity to the development of his fiction world of England. But first, with *Barnaby Rudge*, he made a journey back in time.

Barnaby Rudge

Barnaby Rudge was the most fully matured of all his novels at any rate until his last completed novel, *Our Mutual Friend*. He designed it in 1836 for his first contracted publisher, Macrone. The enormous success of *Pickwick* led him in another direction. But with his changes of plan and of publishers (three in all), he carried with him the idea of this large historical novel. Originally it was to have been published in three volumes, after Scott's model, but at last it was forced out of him in weekly instalments in order to keep going *Master Humphrey's Clock* at the close of *The Old Curiosity Shop*. Because the question of this novel runs so persistently through all the accounts of his depressing troubles and quarrels with publishers in those years, in his letters and in his discussions with Forster, critics have too often presumed that it had gone dead on him before he began it. The first chapters, which were written two years before the rest of the book, are somewhat heavy with poor contemporary conventions of mystery setting, but even here the Maypole Inn is offered to us as a most ambiguous account of that great Dickensian institution, the cheerful domestic fireside. On the one hand we have the warm, cosy fireside feeling of an old English inn while the storm rages outside – what the Edwardian reader later took almost for the trademark of Dickens's writing – but on the other it is soon clear that John Willett, the innkeeper, is the most obstinate and stupid of tyrants, who is denying growth to his son, Joe, and laying down the law among his cronies with every sort of wrong-headed commonsense. The Maypole Inn is the very essence of old England, but in charge of it is an obstinate, domineering fool. He is the Alf Garnett of his day. We are off to an interesting start.

Barnaby Rudge is divided into two parts; the first lays the picture of England in 1775. When Dickens first conceived the novel in 1836 he must have been daringly looking to rival the great master Scott himself, although in the final version there is only a skeleton of Scott's world surviving: in the last part, the storming of Newgate Gaol by the rioters, which, despite critics' assertions, does not seem to me to owe more than outline to the taking of the Edinburgh Tolbooth in *The Heart of Midlothian*. The first section of *Barnaby Rudge*, save for the olde worlde language of the first uncertain pages, is lacking in the strong historical colour of Scott, or of the lesser Ainsworth and Lytton, though there are a few explanatory 'in those days', or 'at that time'; but I shall suggest that, in its characters, it wonderfully sets the whole late eighteenth-century conflict, at any rate as Dickens saw it. At the end of Chapter 32 we are then told 'and the world went on turning round, as usual, for five years, concerning which this Narrative is silent'. When Chapter 33 opens we are in 1780, the year in which, inflamed by the teachings of the Protestant Association and of its half crazy zealot leader, Lord George Gordon, a mob overwhelmed authority in London for some days, and, beginning with Roman Catholic chapels and private houses, ended by destroying, with burning and looting, large areas of private property. In the course of the riots that symbol of law, Newgate Gaol was destroyed and the prisoners released. When authority gained control again, retribution was brutal and often arbitrary. The second half tells, with gathering tension and pace, the story of this social explosion and its results. Having established authority in Part I, Dickens destroys it in Part II, and then sets it up again as the happy ending of the novel.

The first part of the book, dealing solely in the private affairs of the private characters, declares at once the ambiguity of his feelings. We see two tyrannical fathers denying life to their sons: John Willett, as I have said, is a dull-witted domestic tyrant; John Chester is far more sinister – an elegant, cold-hearted spendthrift man of the world, the embodiment of all that Dickens fancied to be the spirit of the eighteenth-century aristocracy, as it survived in the architecture which he detested. 'It was a house about the time of George II; as stiff, as cold, as formal, and in as bad taste, as could possibly be desired by the most loyal admirers of the whole quartet of Georges,' – artificial, unfeeling, imperturbable and completely unspiritual. The two representatives of eighteenth-century authority show reason in its worse guises. In John Willett good sense is merely a name for prejudice; in John Chester rationality is a cynical excuse for hard-hearted selfishness. The two rather characterless, good-natured, plain-spoken, warm young sons who are tyrannized over by these fathers, and who, under provocation, revolt from them and emigrate to America, are very sketchily drawn; but they emerge as honest, manly fellows near to Dickens's nineteenth-century version of the world of Tom Jones.

Yet, if Ned Chester and Joe Willett seem to argue for sons against excessive paternal authority, quite other is the lesson of the household of honest Gabriel Varden, the locksmith. This good old man – once to have given his name to the novel, and certainly, during the riots, the true hero by reason of his stolid bravery – has the greatest difficulty in keeping order in his home, because of domestic rebellion. Part of Mr Varden's difficulties comes from one of Dickens's hobbyhorses – a shrewish, domineering wife backed by what is worse, a soured, vain spinster, who is her personal maid. Mrs Varden and Miggs are, in fact, another of Dickens's easy, cheap jokes against women, but the humours in which the joke is clothed are, for once, good enough to dispel distaste. It is notable that both Mrs Varden and her maid, Miggs, are extreme Protestants; much of their disposition to set the house at odds arises from the influence of the Protestant Association, whose vaguely agitating talk eventually produces the horrible anarchy of the riots. Female domination of the home is clearly in Dickens's view one sign of general social dissolution.

An even more sinister manifestation is that of servant against master. Sim Tappertit, Mr Varden's young apprentice, is a member of one of the secret guilds of apprentices who are plotting to overthrow the rule of the masters. Dickens's treatment of these apprentices, their secret ceremonials and blood-thirsty oaths, is as violently hostile and as ruthlessly satirical as Conrad's treatment of political revolutionaries in *The Secret Agent* or *Under Western Eyes* or as Dostoevsky's of his plotters in *The Devils*. And, like Conrad and Dostoevsky, Dickens considers their absurd conspiratorial antics to be ulti-mately both serious and dangerous, for the apprentices play an important part in the riots, and Sim Tappertit, victim of physical vanity and hot-headed ideas, is both a dupe and a leader in the violence which ensues. The proceedings of the apprentices in their meetings after dark are clearly made to look forward to the French Revolution a decade later – 'Mark Gilbert, age nineteen. Bound to Thomas Curzon, hosier, Golden Fleece, Aldersgate. Loves Curzon's daughter. Cannot say that Curzon's daughter loves him. Should think it probable. Curzon pulled his ears last Tuesday week . . . . Write Curzon down, denounced.' The apprentices, like the lawyers' clerks (Mr Guppy of *Bleak House*), among whom Dickens had once unwillingly worked, are always ridi-culed for loving socially above themselves.

But if the apprentices, in general, are a comic but sinister pointer forward to the Terror, Sim Tappertit embodies a number of ideas associated with revolution which are suspect to Dickens: 'If I had been a corsair, or a pirate, a brigand, gen-teel highwayman or patriot – I should have been all right.' So Dickens quite unhistorically gets in a blow at one of his *bêtes noirs* – Lord Byron and that antisocial and amoral side of the Romantic rebellion. which was always abhorrent to him. Tappertit's general confusion of outlook, indeed, seems near to what its detractors charged upon the Romantic movement in general: 'I feel my soul getting into my head.' Indeed these suggestions of hostility to the excesses of Byronism and Wordsworthianism in *Barnaby Rudge* underline the need for a serious study of Dickens's relation to his Romantic predecessors; like most Victorian Romantics he fed upon and renounced them.

We are willing to accept that Sim Tappertit with his great belief in the power of the beauty of his own legs to conquer all the opposite sex is a ridiculous figure, even a great nuisance (though wonderful fun to read about); but the vindictive nature of his end – he loses his legs in the riots and marries a shrew who 'would retaliate by taking off his [wooden] legs, and leaving him exposed to the derision of those urchins who delight in mischief' – seems dispropor- tionate to his comic stature. It is clear that the rebellion of man against master (so very unlike Sam Weller's code) is hateful to Dickens, as we shall see later in his ambiguous attitude to Trade Unions. But any confusion that he may have sensed in *Barnaby Rudge* between his hostile attitude to paternal tyrants and his total allegiance to the tradesmen masters is satisfied for him by making the apprentices' movement an entirely reactionary affair. It is true, of course, that the eighteenth-century apprentices looked back to the medieval guilds for their rights. Most English revolutionaries have a tendency to find their charter for progress in the good old customs of the past. Dickens, indeed, is very unusual for an English radical in not looking back to a golden age; for him, English history was largely 'the bad old days'. He is thus saved from considering any justice that might be in the apprentices' rebellion by stressing its backward-looking nature: 'They [the apprentices] united therefore to resist all change, except such change as would restore those good old English customs by which they would stand or fall.'

In the first part of the novel the scene is well laid of an England in danger of revolt, and Dickens makes it clear that he has full sympathy neither with the forces of order nor with the forces of rebellion. In the second part, with the ride of the crazed, well-intentioned Lord George Gordon and his sinister adviser, Gashford, into London, we see the whole terrible violent episode, from its first rumblings in the mob's attempted assault on the Catholic gentle- man, Mr Harewood, to the streets literally running with burning spirits and the drunken rioters drowned in their own vomit. The private situation has swelled up and burst into public revolution. 'No Popery!' is the cry, but we are not surprised when one of the rioters, admonished for crying 'No property!' laughs the mistake off by crying, 'It's all the same thing'. On the dramatic level this change from private to public life is beautifully maintained by the burning of the Maypole Inn by the rioters, so that its glowing lights recall the first happy picture of the glowing light of the fireside that once proclaimed its happy, domestic warmth to the stormy world outside.

But the most remarkable, the most brilliant of all Dickens's successes in this novel is his organization of the riots under three leaders, two of whom have played some private role in the first part. Barnaby Rudge, the 'natural', is the most innocent of these, and he alone is reprieved from execution at the end. Barnaby is very much like the Idiot Boy and the many other simple- minded or 'natural' heroes of Wordsworth's *Lyrical Ballads*. One would expect that Dickens, with his cult of the heart and the imagination, would be wholly on the side of such a hero, and indeed he owes much to the ethics of the *Lyrical Ballads*. But there are important reservations to this. Certainly we are made to feel that Barnaby's fancies have a truth that the rational tyrants – Mr Chester and John Willett – cannot appreciate:

'Look down there. Do you mark how they whisper in each other's ears; then dance and leap, to make believe they are in sport? . . . See how they whirl and plunge . . . . What is it that they plot and hatch, do you know?' 'They are only clothes [says Mr Chester] . . . hanging on those lines to dry, and fluttering in the wind.' 'Clothes,' echoed Barnaby . . . . 'Haha! Why how much better to be silly, than as wise as you! You don't see shadowy people there, like those that live in sleep – not you. Nor eyes in the knotted panes of glass . . . . I lead a merrier life than you with all your cleverness.'

Mr Chester then comments on Barnaby: 'A strange creature, upon my word;' to which the dull-witted, dogmatic innkeeper answers: 'He wants imagination, that's what he wants!' It is fairly clear in this passage that Dickens is on the side of the 'natural' with the same divine gift of fancy as his own for making inanimate objects come to life. But at the last, Dickens's rational side wins the day, for although Barnaby takes part in the riots with the wierdest childish fancies of doing good, it is clear that the riots are evil and that fancy may therefore stray too far. I think it is clear that Barnaby represents the extreme freedom of fancy that in some aspects of Romanticism broke down the old eighteenth-century order; and that Dickens here expresses his fear of such total dismissal of the real world for the world of shadows, a fear strong, perhaps, because the dismissal of reality in so many of his moods was both dear and easy to him.

No less striking as an idea, and even more successful as a character – indeed, I think one of the most moving characters in Dickens, because unusually the author lends to him his own violent, humorous enjoyment of life – is Hugh, the ostler of the Maypole. Hugh is an illiterate man of great physical strength and a wild sort of gypsyish beauty; he has lived with the beasts and is treated like them. In fact, we learn that Hugh is the bastard son of the corrupt, elegant and cruel Mr Chester by a poor ruined girl, who is left to die on the gallows for thieving to keep her baby alive. Hugh, I think, is linked closely to a legendary figure familiar to Dickens from his childhood reading – familiar to most of Dickens's contemporaries, though hardly known to us. That figure is Orson of *Valentine and Orson* – the king's son, the wild man of the woods reared by a she-bear. But whereas Orson succeeds to kingdoms and to heroic enterprises, Hugh succeeds to leadership of the most violent part of the riots and ultimately to death on the gallows, like his mother. Once again Dickens's attitude to this character is mixed. As the victim of the selfishness and cruelty of Mr Chester and of the bullying of Mr Willett at the Maypole where he works he has Dickens's sympathy, although the satyr quality in his wildness is early reprehended when he makes advances to pretty Dolly Varden. There can be no doubt, as one reads, of Dickens's regard for the courage, the wild humour and the strange devotion to Barnaby of this half-savage, brutish man. But in the last resort he is condemned as one of the dangerous, anarchic forces that are released in the riot; whatever sympathy we may have for him must be measured because of his desperation. I think that in Hugh Dickens was portraying another of the concepts that did much to blow up the eighteenth-century system – the Rousseauistic concept of the noble savage. We shall see more than

once in Dickens's life how gravely he mistrusted such an idea, and how prejudiced, as a result, he was about missions to Africans, indeed almost comically
apprehensive of Africa as a continent.

A missionary preaching in Western Africa.

The last of the three leaders does not directly embody an idea. In part he is
also propaganda against public executions, for he is Dennis the public hangman, whose sadistic appetites see further delights in the outrages of the riots
and the subsequent actions of justice. But to read the passages in which Dennis
mixes authority so completely with anarchy in his gloating imaginings during
the riot is to see that he embodies the danger to any society that comes from
the brutalization of its own instruments. All the rioters, save Barnaby, however
the boisterous liveliness of Dickens's narrative of events carries them along,
give off the page a stench of filth and stale spirits and bloodlust; yet only Dennis
is physically repulsive in every movement he makes, every word he utters.
And that physical repulsion comes clearly from the long years of indulged
sadism he has known in his task on behalf of society as public hangman.
Thus here Dickens insists once more upon the rottenness of the threatened
society, at the heart of his attack upon the vileness of the rioters.

The whole trio of riot leaders constitutes a wonderful celebration and indictment of the forces of revolt; and the irony is the better preserved since none knows the others' motives. As a result the book is completely triumphant in its portrayal of the mob and of the riots. What is lacking is any good motivation. Dickens detested extreme Protestantism, and at the time of the publication of *Barnaby Rudge* this puritan, Exeter Hall wing of the Church was very vociferous. Even so, he never had any liking for Roman Catholicism and was soon to acquire a violent hatred for it. The whole religious division of the characters in the book seems lifeless and arbitrary. To have made this book his great novel about revolution, however ambiguous his attitude to it might have been, he would have needed some symbol for authority, some organization to represent the corruption of the forces of society; and this he did not yet have the power to create. He was to make a beginning with the invention of the bogus insurance company in his next novel, *Martin Chuzzlewit*. Meanwhile such symbol as there is lies in Newgate Gaol, which had fascinated and horrified him from boyhood; but ultimately the gaol cannot really stand for society – it has none of the political implications of the Bastille. In fact Dickens uses Newgate to dramatize another and rather irrelevant plot about Barnaby's father, who, as a fugitive murderer, is an obvious subject for Dickens's obsession.

In truth, the Gordon Riots historically had so little clear social cause (hostility to Catholic Irish immigrants by the London unemployed is given by modern historians, but was probably unknown to Dickens), and were so much a matter of incitement and pure riot that it seems almost as if Dickens chose them for the narrative of his novel in order to avoid the deeper issues posed by social revolution. As a result *Barnaby Rudge* is a very fine novel about individuals caught up in the horrors of mass activity. It never quite embodies the whole social tension that these dramatically portrayed individuals prepare us for. An anarchic mob let loose in pillage, rape, arson and self-destruction is answered by the courage of an elderly locksmith, an equally elderly vintner, and two young men returned from 'the Americas'. The proposition is demonstrably absurd. And, of course, there *are* bodies of horse, and posses of soldiers; and finally there are magistrates and summary executions and executions by proper forms of law – though Dickens dislikes all this almost as much as he does the rioters, save that in the retribution some evil people, like Dennis the hangman, are brought to justice, and that is always a good thing.

But in general Dickens does not care to examine the victorious forces of law and order too closely, for they demand a greater abstraction from the idea of individual benevolence as the key to morality than he cares to give. As a matter of fact Gabriel Varden as a good old man is a far more convincing figure than most of the good old men in the early Dickens novels, far more so than Oliver Twist's benefactor, or Nicholas Nickleby's twin benefactors, or Kit Nubbles's good master – but then they were not set up as the opposition to a riot, and even the very solid, likeable Gabriel Varden refusing to open the gates of Newgate cannot really convince one as an answer to the large social phenomenon of some days' violent riots that have paralyzed the life of a capital city. It is clear that to go further with his parable of society Dickens must stand further away from it, find symbols for society more meaningful than his own personal obsession with Newgate and judicial death.

America

No better way of so seeing one's own world can surely be devised than foreign travel, for in visiting foreign countries we must perforce generalize and concentrate upon abstractions, since we are without the particular individual knowledge that makes each of us in our home country an envelope of memory and particularity. Luckily Dickens's personal inclinations at this time were ardent for travel abroad. For us who are concerned with Dickens's fictional world, it will be no longer necessary to examine, as we have done in the previous chapters, any particular aspect of his private life in depth. The death of Mary Hogarth was perhaps the last of all the blows that came after Warren's blacking factory which so deeply affected him as to distort the world of his imagination. From now on we shall be concerned with his life as it gives immediate fresh material to his novels, as it widens his scope socially or geographically and as it illustrates the satisfaction or the frustrations, or, at last, the near exhaustion of those vast energies on which he depended in order to subject his teeming imagination to the discipline of art.

Broadstairs in Kent became their resort for summer months.

Dickens's social range, as we know, had expanded vastly since his first success, yet the yearly shape of his life was much that of the hard-pressed, successful, young professional man with a family. His new friend, John Forster, had relieved him from the nightmares of too many and too unprofitable contracts; John Forster, too, was someone with whom he could discuss his imagined world as it came to him; but John Forster could not do his work for him, or no more than proof reading. Dickens knew already that he was working too hard. By the time that his great predecessor, Scott, had been able to take enough from his creditors to visit Italy he had been a worn-out, ill man who could hardly taste all the joys he had dreamt of so long. Then again, as success followed success, but also as the near failure of *Barnaby Rudge* gave warning, Dickens lived in apprehension that he was driving his luck and his powers too hard, appearing before his beloved public too often and would tire them of his stories.

More than this, I believe, despite all his new friends – the honour of the regard of the great Carlyle, Forster, the theatre friends, Macready and Stanfield, Maclise, the artist and all the other friendships that were his overwhelming joy – daily life had changed too little. There was home now, it is true on a far larger scale than Doughty Street, where Mary had died; and there were now four children, two boys and two girls, He and Catherine took family holidays. Broadstairs in Kent became their resort for the summer months.

It so happens that we have a detailed account, written in old age, by a lady who was staying there as a girl in the summer of 1841 with some close friends of the Dickenses. It is unwise to make her picture – a lively and opinionated one – a sure picture of Dickens's life because, apart from anything else, she wrote after his separation from his wife and she was decidedly in Mrs Dickens's camp. But she does reveal the extraordinary degree to which his Broadstairs life was dominated by his relatives, parents, sisters and brothers.

Mrs Christian says, somewhat cattily, 'It was wonderful how the whole family had emancipated themselves from their antecedents, and contrived to fit easily into their improved position. They appeared to be less at ease with Charles than with anyone else, and seemed in fear of offending him.' When it is considered that they owed 'their improved position' to him, we may judge her view to be correct, especially as Dickens was to disclaim his father's debts in a newspaper advertisement a few months later. It is possible also that, not only for financial reasons, Charles, for many hours of the day, must have felt less at ease with them, for he was a successful married man of genius, aged nearly thirty – he should surely have grown away from such a very 'family' family holiday.

Pressure of work, fear of failure, perhaps a wish to put right his life with Kate, away from families; above all, I think, a longing to be rid of the past, must have made his natural desire to see other lands and ways of life a very strong pressure. In the June of 1841, some months before the seaside scene described by Mrs Christian, he had a short taste of what it could be like. His triumphant visit to Edinburgh had been followed by a tour of the Highlands

'Brighton and Back for 3/6d' by Charles Rossitor, 1859. 'Perhaps Brighton itself?' 'Upon my honour, Dombey, I don't think we could do better. It's on the spot you see, and a very cheerful place.' Mrs Skewton's funeral in *Dombey and Son*.

Overleaf. 'Manhood Suffrage Riots in Hyde Park' by Nathan Hughes, 1866. 'The crowd was the law, and never was the law held in greater dread.' *Barnaby Rudge*.

alone with Catherine, in stormy weather that satisfied to the full his conventional Victorian taste for dramatic mountain scenery. Now, with Forster once more as his advocate, Chapman & Hall, his publishers, agreed to generous terms by which he should be free from producing a novel for a year. He decided to leave for the United States early in 1842. He was away for six months. What was not expected, and what surely shows the depth of his need for a change of life, is that two years after his return he left for abroad again with his wife and children, and this time he was to live abroad on and off for three years.

The idea of a trip to America was not a wholly new one. Mrs Trollope, Captain Marryat and Miss Martineau were only the most notable among a rather mixed company of travel writers who had returned from there with largely unfavourable impressions to satisfy an interested English public. It was a sufficiently established joke to be included in *Pickwick Papers*. Tony Weller, devising the idea of rescuing Mr Pickwick from the Fleet prison in a hollow piano says:

> There ain't nothing in it. It 'ull hold him easy, with his hat and shoes on, and breathe through the legs vich his holler. Have a passage ready taken for 'Merriker. The 'Merrikin gov'ment will never give him up ven they hird as he's got money to spend, Sammy. Let the gov'ner stop there till Mrs Bardell's dead . . . and then let him come back and write a book about the 'Merrikins as'll pay all his expenses and more, if he blows 'em up enough.

Already it is clear that Dickens treats the anti-Americanism of his predecessors as something of a racket; but as an omen for the future it should be noted that he also accepts American concern for money as another part of the joke. On the face of it, however, it was reasonable for Dickens to believe that he, the young author, and the defender of the underdog, would be naturally more sympathetic to the young, vigorous, egalitarian republic, would return not to sneer or cavil, but to waken England with the story of the energy and the plain manliness with which things were done in the pioneer world. He had already heard from so distinguished an American author as Washington Irving that if he came to the United States his tour would be a triumphal one, and the popularity of his work in America (particularly *Pickwick)*, however little pecuniary profit might have resulted from it, gave every support to Irving's view. So America it must be.

Any thoughts of taking the children on so exhausting, indeed hazardous, a journey had to be put out of mind, even though the idea of parting from them was a considerable initial shock to Catherine. Luckily Macready, who had acted in New York with triumph, was very ardent for the Dickenses going there; he had a fatherly influence with Mrs Dickens, and he persuaded her that it was her duty to accompany Charles. As some recompense Maclise painted a portrait of the four children, which proved a great standby to both parents in their inevitable alarms and worries over the happenings of a family so far away. The large family home in Devonshire Terrace, Regent's Park,

'Ramsgate Sands' by William Frith, 1852–4. 'Running in with the waves, and then running back with the waves after them.' The Tuggses at Ramsgate in *Sketches by Boz*.

was let; and the children, with their young Uncle Fred, whose vitality and fun delighted them, were housed in Osnaburgh Street. The Macreadys, with children of their own, agreed to keep a watchful eye on them.

So, in the rather unfortunately chosen month of January 1842, Dickens and his wife set off for Boston by the first Cunard steamship, the *Britannia*, whose maiden voyage had been in 1840. They took with them Catherine's maid, Anne Brown, who was to remain associated with the family until after Dickens's death, and who was close enough to be a confidante during the last year of his cohabitation with his wife. She proved invaluable on the American trip and indeed later in Italy, Switzerland and France – imperturbable and totally uninterested. Her conduct did much to confirm Dickens in his view that the English working classes had an inbuilt inability to learn anything new, although this was somewhat modified by their English cook in Genoa, who proved immediately adaptable to foreigners and their ways.

The cabin was cupboard-like (in a nice, Dickensian extravagant fancy, 'portmanteaus . . . could now no more be got in at the door, not to say stowed away, than a giraffe could be persuaded or forced into a flowerpot'); the ship overcrowded; the weather terrible; the voyage a nightmare of plungings and swayings and sickness. Even Charles Dickens seems to have been daunted. His description of the little party who gathered together in the ladies' cabin, when comparative lulls made it possible, is curiously lifeless and flat. He determined to return by sailing ship. The first call was at Nova Scotia, where Dickens was led in triumph to hear the local parliament in session. He began to sense the extraordinary ovations that he was about to receive: 'I wish you could have seen the crowds cheering the Inimitable in the streets.'

What happened? And why did it all go wrong? We have three accounts of the trip from Dickens himself – in his private letters to England; in *American Notes*, the essays on his tour, already commissioned by his publishers, that he published after he returned home, and in the American scenes that he interpolated into *Martin Chuzzlewit*, probably with the hope of improving the disastrous sales figures that at first met the serial publication of that novel. I start with the last first. It may be said that the American chapters of *Chuzzlewit* are good, often inspired journalism, although somewhat repetitious. Of their value to the novel I shall try to judge when we arrive at an estimation of that book. But to some extent the ills and horrors of America are exaggerated here because they are specifically to be the time of testing of the hero, Martin, from which he emerges less selfish. Nevertheless, apart from an immigrant family of co-sufferers with the hero in the pestilential swamp of Eden, one friendly Negro and the liberal-minded, cultivated Mr Bevan of New York, who lends Martin and Mark Tapley their return fares from Eden, there is not a pleasant person in the American chapters of the novel. Boasting, brawling, greed, sharp dealing, prudery, snobbery, lack of hygiene, cultural pretension, bullying violence – all of these are at one time or another shown in American action; and over it all a naïve, ignorant, self-flattering chauvinism that on the whole disgusts more than it amuses. Here is Mr Chollop: 'He always introduced himself to strangers as a worshipper of Freedom; was the consistent advocate of lynch law, and slavery; and invariably recommended, both in print and speech, the "tarring and feathering" of any unpopular person who differed from himself. He called this "planting the standard of civilization in the wilder gardens of My Country".' He is the frontiersman. And here is the Honourable Elijah Pogram, representative of greater cultivation, of oratory and politics, discouraging upon Mr Chollop:

Our fellow countryman is a model of a man, quite fresh from Nature's mould! He is true-born child of this free hemisphere! Verdant as the mountains of our country; bright and flowing as our mineral licks, unspiled by withering conventionalities as air our broad and boundless Perearers. Rough he may be. So air our Burrs. Wild he may be. So air our Buffalers. But he is a Child of Natur', and a child of Freedom; and his boastful answer to the Despot and the Tyrant is, that his bright home is in the Settin' Sun.

'Our broad and boundless Perearers . . . our [wild] Buffalers.'

It is all good stuff, if a trifle heavy-handed, and it convinces. The only trouble is that Chollop and Elijah Pogram are repeated again and again in the chapters under other names. One feels sure that a lot of Americans then, perhaps the majority, were like this; but unlike the humours of, say, Mrs Gamp or Mr Pecksniff in the same novel, behind which reverberate whole scales of social and cultural overtones that Dickens knew by heart, here the tune comes brightly off the surface only. And it is very repetitious. America had a small population and no doubt there *was* much repetition; but surely not as much as the novel's limited range suggests. One feels that it comes from a man who had travelled too quickly and too crowdedly to get more than a very brilliant impression. And after a bit it palls, as the endlessly loquacious, repetitious, boasting American co-voyagers of Dickens bored him. Only one piece of fooling in the *Chuzzlewit* American chapters is up to his very highest best, the dialogue of the Transcendentalist lady in the wig: 'Mind and Matter glide swift into the vortex of immensity. Howls the sublime, and softly sleeps the calm Ideal, in the whispering chambers of Imagination. To hear it, sweet it is. But then outlaughs the stern philosopher, and saith to the grotesque, "What ho! Arrest for me that Agency. Go bring it here!" and so the vision fadeth.' I know of no better mockery of cultural pretension in literature, though perhaps Dickens need not have crossed the Atlantic to eavesdrop on Emerson's disciples; something similar might have come to him if he could have listened to some admirers of Carlyle without too much reverence.

American Notes, the commissioned result of his voyage, is an altogether more sober account of things. Although it, too, infuriated the Americans, who had no idea that their late fêted guest had come away with such hostile impressions, it is much toned down from Dickens's immediate feelings: a narrative as sober as the need to entertain his readers allowed, and an account of institutions more measured than is usual for him, for he was peculiarly anxious to show that he was a journalist of careful responsibility and exact documentation, as indeed throughout his life he largely was. But, despite its good sales in England, it must be said that *American Notes* makes pretty dull reading – and, indeed, something of the initial collapse of the sales of *Martin Chuzzlewit* which followed may have been due to the dreary impression left by these essays. To avoid personalities, too, Dickens dwells more even than his philanthropic interests would seem to make necessary upon institutions he visited – so that a careless reader could not be blamed if he thought that the American nation consisted mainly of convicts, with a sprinkling of the destitute, lunatics, blind people and the deaf and dumb. To get a full idea of Dickens's six months in the States it is necessary to read his published tour along with his surviving letters.

His initial impression when he landed in Boston was of Utopia, more perfect than he had imagined: 'There is no man in this town, or in this State of New England, who has not a blazing fire and a meat dinner every day of his life. A flaming sword in the air would not attract so much attention as a beggar in the streets.' And the reception given to him overwhelmed him. He reported to his friend Forster that Dr Channing, the famous New England Unitarian minister, had told him, 'It is no nonsense, and no common feeling. It is all heart. There never was, and never will be such a triumph.' Such utterances and Dickens's reception of them make one see how on occasions Victorian rhetoric could have the same damaging effect as Admass has in our own days. For Dickens, to whom 'the heart' spoke for the deeper values, to suppose that it could be manifested in a few days in public noise is to make nonsense of the meaning of his life's work. But it was, without any doubt, a triumphal reception of a young man, on a scale that America had offered to no other visitor since Lafayette.

What is more, in these first days in Boston, it was a reception, like the granting of the freedom of Edinburgh, in which some of the most distinguished and cultivated people in the United States played a large part – Prescott, the historian of the Incas; the great Longfellow; Dana of *Two Years Before the Mast*. It is significant that the most lasting friend Dickens made in these days in Boston was Cornelius Felton, a Professor of Greek, with whom he was soon in that one-note, chaffing relationship (in this case about Felton's love of oysters) that must claim anyone before he could enter the charmed circle of Dickens's friendship. I cannot but think that the cultivated tone of his New England reception misled Dickens. He was a genuine enemy of gentility, and a violent opponent of all class patronage, but he had only just emancipated himself from a narrow, innately vulgar, petty bourgeois background, he was revelling in the spreading of his social wings in England, and now here in New England he seemed to step into an even more accomplished, cultured milieu: acquaintance with professors of Greek; later a visit to Harvard with Longfellow, and later still, on the way to New York, being serenaded by the students of Yale; Early Victorian Oxford and Cambridge had no such place for journalists turned author, however large the monthly or weekly sales of their novels.

All this, indeed, and freedom and social decency too. Perhaps the most pleasant moment in the whole of this visit of Charles Dickens to America was his visit to the new factory town at Lowell. There he discovered that the factory girls, who lived in what we should now call hostels, enjoyed a civilized, ladylike existence in which they were not ashamed to produce their own magazine, to subscribe to a circulating library, to play the piano. When Dickens had thought of the United States with hope and admiration, exactly this had been his picture – everyone raised up by his or her own effort. But after he left Boston he increasingly began to feel that everything had been pulled down.

Of course he, too, the newly risen young author, with his pretty looks, his

Yale College and State House, Newhaven, Connecticut.

flowing locks, his brightly coloured waistcoats and dandyish clothes, was a bit of facer for some New England worthies. They seem to have found excuse for it in the vagaries of his own fiction – Longfellow saw Dick Swiveller's harmless, lovable pseudogent in him. Mrs Dickens was sometimes judged better bred (last triumph of the poor Hogarths' once vaunted social superiority). On the whole, Boston and New England were sophisticated enough to make allowances for any discrepancy between what a noble author should be and the young ringleted Boz. The good impression on both sides was comprehended by that useful Victorian portmanteau word 'manly': Dickens left a manly impression on them, and for him the Americans were noble, manly fellows.

The first rifts, as is well known, appeared when Dickens referred publicly to the question of International Copyright. He, and indeed many other English writers, felt bitterly about this. Their works were regularly printed in the United States; Dickens's novels sold in millions, for which he got not one halfpenny. To him this was of special importance, because upon an author's power to enjoy the fruits of his labour, to be paid for the pleasure he gave to his great public, rested the independence of the profession, its raised and deserved social status, its freedom from arrogant patronage. Surely America of all places, where he had seen the happy, independent, respected, well-turned-out factory girls, would realize that an author, like other labourers, was worthy of his hire. At the first great dinner in Boston he referred to the grievance in his speech. The newspaper attack upon him the next morning was indignant. When he returned to the matter a little later at a dinner in Hartford, Connecticut, he was more assertive, for he was shocked to find that the cultivated writers of America, many of whom he knew to be sympathetic, did not dare to speak. The press following this was far more violent, and he received many abusive, anonymous letters.

To Dickens this press hostility seemed sheer self-interest and greed; and to a large extent he was right, for the newspapers stood to gain hugely by serial use of books for which they paid nothing. But the feelings of his hosts are interesting too. America was, as he gradually began to see, a money-conscious, acquisitive society, but it was also a society (like Dickens) in pursuit of a more cultivated way of life (even if for the major part of his audiences this was but the most superficial culture). Dickens had made them laugh with *Pickwick*, and more important still perhaps, cry for Little Nell. And now he talked in public of money and, what was more sordid, his own rights to it. It was not for this that they spent hard-earned dollars on banquets (and expensive ones too; the tickets for the Boston dinners were £3 a head); it was not for this that the ladies (those emblems of all that was pure and delicate – for, in its estimate of women, American convention was close to Dickens) put on their pretty frocks. Thus does the older public react nowadays when a pop star talks about Vietnam. It was all very hypocritical and sordid, as Dickens saw, but his behaviour had struck at the heart of the pretences of America, and the Americans would not give way. Dickens, it is true, tried to disengage a little, he determined that he would accept only two public invitations in New York. But this, like his determination to pay his hotels wherever he went, can have seemed only a rudeness to his hospitably determined hosts. For the rest he was adamant – he would speak out on copyright whenever he felt right. As he hardened, so did the Americans – if he would talk of money, then they would show him a tough philistinism, and often, I think, they pulled his leg and, in his fury, he didn't see it. I am sure that he didn't behave as they thought a gentleman should, and they treated him, therefore, more than ever as a public entertainment. Two powerful forces moving rapidly in the same social direction upwards had collided.

As a result, when he reached New York, despite his delight at meeting Washington Irving, everything began to go wrong. Both he and poor Catherine became worn out. 'I can do nothing that I want to do, go nowhere where I want to go, and see nothing that I want to see. If I turn into the street, I am followed by a multitude. If I stay at home, the house becomes, with callers, like a fair,' and so on and so on. A great part of this is a complaint far more familiar to us now than then, coming from public figures who have, like the goat in Grimm's fairy story, 'more than enough of this nice green stuff'. But much of

Broadway, New York.

'The Tombs' he thought a hell on earth.

it must have been exceedingly offensive. 'Then by every post letters on letters arrive, all about nothing, and all demanding an immediate answer. This man is offended because I won't live in his house; and that man thoroughly disgusted because I won't go out more than four times in one evening. I have no rest or peace, and am in a perpetual worry.' Under the weight of all this, English sensitivities became lacerated. The overheating of the rooms: 'their effect upon an Englishman is very easily told. He is always very sick and very faint; and has an intolerable headache morning, noon and night.' And, judging by his emphasis upon American speech rhythms in dialogue in *Martin Chuzzlewit*, I suspect that he suffered as the tour went on, not only as he thought, an excess or bores, but, as few Englishmen will admit, the realization, when confronted with boring American men or women, that American accents and stresses to an Englishman can seem like a relentless machine.

When they left New York by a combination of long train and ship journeys for Philadelphia and Washington, other horrors began to press upon Dickens's

Slavery in that time horrified him.

nerves – the constant spitting, so that at a later point on a Mississippi riverboat Catherine's dress was covered in spittle carried by the wind from a man in the front seat; the food that they did not like, set down in great masses and gobbled up rapidly and noisily by the diners at one long table in the hotels; their Philadelphia landlord, admitting thousands of paying visitors to see them, each of whom demanded a handshake, and then presenting Dickens with an enormous bill on departure; the realization that party politics, that *bête noir* of Dickens, was the ruling passion of the lives of most American men. By the time they had reached Washington Dickens's disillusion was complete. Even the public institutions he had admired at first now seemed to him much inferior to those at home. The local prison house, 'The Tombs', in New York, he thought a hell on earth, and the vaunted separate system prison in Philadelphia was to become one of his chief hatreds (though in England for opposite reasons to the high-minded, unintentional cruelty that horrified him in the States, where criminals could remain for long numbers of years without any human contact at all). Much of all this Miss Martineau and Mrs Trollope and Captain Marryat had already written about, to the anger of America. More than all they had said was in Dickens's mind, but his hosts did not know it. It is not surprising that, when he did eventually publish, their fury was so great.

He had intended to go as far as Charleston. But, with the hot weather and the swampy fevers, he was advised at Washington to go no further than Rich- mond, Virginia. What he saw of slavery in that time horrified him as much as he expected. He could see clearly that the Southerners were hostile to the English. It was an unfortunate moment, for the English Navy had just released at Nassau slaves from a Southern ship, the *Creole*, on its way to New Orleans.

He returned to Baltimore and then set out to see the Far West. Here perhaps he could find something of the hoped-for vision, for, as he wrote to Macready,

A journey in confined paddle steamers on the Mississippi – a river whose muddy surface and stagnant banks Dickens came to loathe.

'This is not the republic I came to see; this is not the republic of my imagination. I infinitely prefer a liberal monarchy – even with its sickening accompaniments of court circulars – to such a government as this.' But, at least, he told Forster: 'There are some very noble specimens . . . out of the West. Splendid men to look at, hard to deceive, prompt to act, lions in energy, Crichtons in varied accomplishment, Indians in quickness of eye and gesture, Americans in affectionate and generous impulse. It would be difficult to exaggerate the nobility of some of these glorious fellows.'

But, alas, the voyage to the West proved it all too easy. It was a hard and exhausting journey over rough roads or in confined paddle steamers on the Ohio and the Mississippi – a river whose muddy surface and stagnant banks Dickens came to loathe with intensity. Catherine showed a propensity for

Niagara was all he had hoped.

falling and hurting herself, although, on the whole, he recognized that she had faced difficult circumstances bravely – he called her 'a brick'. They were both lucky in having the young American secretary, Putnam, whom they had hired at Boston to look after them. He was naïve and at times very boring – the patronizing comments of both Mr and Mrs Dickens about him shock one, as surely do all comments on people who have no idea of the effect they are making. But they recognized that he revered them highly and kept them from a vast amount of discomfort. Even so, the squalors and hardships of the journey were bad enough – the difference of views on hygiene between the Americans and Dickens became intense when bottled up for nights in small ships. At the end of it, when Dickens, leaving Catherine at St Louis, made an expedition to Looking Glass Prairie to see the far distances of the Great West, he was, as anyone who knew his Victorian taste for Scottish Highland scenery could have predicted, bored by the vast flatness before him.

Niagara was all that he had hoped – 'when I felt how near to my Creator I was standing'.– especially from the Canadian side, although his susceptibilities were upset by the visitors' book, 'scrawled all over with the vilest and the filthiest ribaldry that ever human hogs delighted in . . . among men, brutes so obscure and worthless, that they can delight in laying their miserable profanations upon the very steps of Nature's great altar'. But in general Canada was, after the disappointment of the States, a very pleasant surprise. True, things were occasionally a little too Tory. But young Lord Mulgrave, who had travelled over on the boat with them, was with the garrison, and Dickens was asked to produce and play in three plays – augury of the future! And Catherine played in them too, 'devilish well, I assure you'.

'Canada has held, and always will retain, a foremost place in my remembrance. Few Englishmen are prepared to find it what it is. Advancing quietly . . . nothing of flush or fever in its system, but health and vigour throbbing in its steady pulse: it is full of hope and promise.' When one considers how he now transferred his hopes for emigration as a great answer to Britain's social ills from the United States to Australia; how he subsequently sent his sons to find a life for themselves in Australia and India; how stoutly he defended British rule during the Indian Mutiny and the 1865 revolt in the West Indies; when we consider some aspects of the changed interests of his unfinished novel, *Edwin Drood*, we may wonder, I think, whether, if he had lived on into the latter part of the century, he would not at last have found in Radical Imperialism a political cause that he could espouse. But for the moment Canada pleased mainly because it reminded of England and the children, and because in any case home was drawing closer. They returned in a delightful voyage on a sailing ship, and were reunited with the children by midsummer.

Martin Chuzzlewit

The homecoming was good for both the Dickenses. For both of them there was the excitement of the children, pleased to return to a nursery world a little

The Lord Mayor's Dinner at Guildhall. 'The majority of the guests were like the plate, and included several heavy articles weighing ever so much.' Mr Podsnap's dinner-party in *Our Mutual Friend*.

less strict than the Macready's. For Charles there was also a wonderful slap-up dinner at Greenwich, the traditional reunion with his men friends. Only one domestic change that followed their return from America needs noting; but that had incalculable consequences for Charles's and Catherine's private life and played an important role in the population of his fictional world. During their absence the children had learned to appreciate the friendliness, the kindliness, the natural orderliness of their aunt, Catherine's sister, Georgina. Now she was rewarded by an invitation to a long stay at Devonshire Terrace – a stay which turned almost unnoticed into a life-long visit.

Georgina Hogarth was now sixteen – much the age that Mary had been when she kept house with the newly married Dickenses. Georgina – Georgy as she was to become, and eventually, the matriarch of the family, Aunty – early conceived an admiration for her brother-in-law that was absolute. For an intelligent, steadfast, shrewd and lively girl the Dickens household was certainly a world of extraordinary interest, a life far beyond that of most Victorian women. Georgy set herself to be worthy of it, and she succeeded totally. Putting behind her her own bohemian Hogarth home, she gradually brought that order and efficiency, smooth and happy running of the house that Dickens so desperately wanted in his home life: the atmosphere that Catherine, for whatever reason, failed to provide. And, as Charles and Catherine produced more and more children (to his declared chagrin), Georgy, who had a marvellous power with children, made the expanded home that was needed for the newcomers. It is neither profitable nor possible to say whether her entry into the Dickens household helped or harmed the incompatibility of Charles and Catherine. Without Georgy everything might have slid down-hill far more rapidly; with her, Catherine's maternal instincts and house-keeping powers no doubt atrophied for want of use; she became more indolent. There must have been for her some humiliation; but, it would appear, no jealousy. She became jealous of some other women, but never of her younger sister – and rightly, for Dickens loved Georgy dearly but he was never sexually attracted to her. To Mrs Hogarth he declared that Georgy reminded him every day more of the dead Mary – certainly her youthful portrait gives her splendid looks with a well-structured, rather Scots head – but his feelings for her were never like those for Mary. As time went by he expressed occasionally to correspondents a doubt that she would ever marry – a doubt in which a rather tiresome masculine complacency is mixed with genuine concern, for there is no doubt that he had the very greatest affection for his sister-in-law based upon a gratitude for all the decency and order that she brought to his life, and for her unshakeable loyalty to him.

My feeling is that Georgy's effect upon the *dramatis personae* of his fiction was less happy. There was no reason at all why he should not have wanted a woman to order his household, but to have found one who gave him this service out of deep emotional attachment and asked (or certainly received) no such depth in return, only added to Dickens's power to deceive himself about women. There appears in *Martin Chuzzlewit* Ruth Pinch, the first of the little house-

'A London Street Scene' by John Parry, 1835. 'To shuffle through the streets ... in utter darkness ... to see people read ... and not to have the least idea of all that language.' Jo in *Bleak House*.

keeper heroines, whose existence as human beings (let alone as physical, sexual beings) is all subordinated or indeed forgotten in admiration for their qualities as man's helpmeet. As Georgina was still only a visitor of sixteen years when *Martin Chuzzlewit* was written, it seems likely that Ruth Pinch is Dickens's ideal into which Georgy trained herself to grow, rather than the other way round. But in three major works of the next decade – in the figures of Agnes in *David Copperfield*, of Esther in *Bleak House*, and to a much less degree, of Little Dorrit – this ideal of the passive, obedient, bright helpmeet, who gives man spiritual and physical support in life's journey while asking nothing in return, is a serious blemish in works of genius.

Georgina Hogarth, eventually the
matriarch of the family.

Martin Chuzzlewit, on which he worked once *American Notes* had been offered to the public, is an advance on earlier novels in Dickens's determination from the first to maintain a complete unity of theme. The subject is selfishness – particularly selfishness as shown in the relations of a family. He felt that his previous novels had suffered, through their serial method of presentation, from insufficient unity, and that this should not happen again. Unfortunately events were against him. The sales of the book were poor from the start (probably because neither *Barnaby Rudge* nor *American Notes* had much pleased the public), and for Dickens, returned from six months of non-earning to an expensive family household, the prospect was alarming. Taking, as he always did in financial crises, rapid and firm measures, he introduced America into the story as the place where the hero, Martin, learns to be less selfish. No arguments convince me that this does not change *Martin Chuzzlewit* from what could have been a major Dickens novel to a very original but very uneven work. Not only are the American scenes, as I have said, no more than good journalism (certainly quite shallow beside the rest of the book), but the hero, as a result, is, more than previous heroes of his novels, cut off from the book's life and meaning.

It is a solid compensation that in the Anglo-Bengalee Disinterested Life Insurance Company Dickens invented his first fully realized fraudulent institution – the company of Dombey and Son, the Court of Chancery, the Circumlocution Office, Mr Merdle's enterprises, are others – which provides a central element to symbolize the rotten society he is attacking. It is notable that the two other great nineteenth-century social novelists who investigated society in the same manner, by interdependent plots, mysteries and prolifera-

The reunion with his men friends: Dickens, Forster, Stanfield and Maclise on holiday in Cornwall, sketched by Thackeray.

tions of characters, Balzac and Dostoevsky, both invented similar semi-conspiratorial symbols of society's corruption. Balzac gave us the arch-criminal, Vautrin; Dostoevsky used his 'scandals' – the governesses' benevolent fête, the arrival of the revolutionary youths at Prince Myshkin's summer villa, the visit of the Karamazov family at the monastery – to suggest that the foundations of social order were being eaten away.

Everything connected with Dickens's brilliant and simple fraudulent design of Montague Tigg is excellent. While the company flourishes, characters are transformed: Bailey, the wretched, undersized boots at Mrs Todger's boarding house, becomes the rollicking, dandyish tiger, cutting errand boys with his whip and threatening old ladies with annihilation; Dr Jobling, whom we had previously seen as a mean, shabby little doctor attending on the mean, shabby death of old Anthony Chuzzlewit, becomes the witty, wining-and-dining doctor of the Company, with the latest story of a West End client on his lips. But it *is* all a fraud – this company and the transformation. And it points up to us the fact that everything and everybody in the book (save the good few) is a fraud. On this level Dickens succeeds in his new unity admirably.

In the development of the brilliantly drawn Jonas Chuzzlewit, under the stress of blackmail, from a vulgar, money-grabbing brute into a murderer with a dark and complicated life of inner terrors and superstitions that would have done credit to Dostoevsky, Dickens adds a whole dimension to the book that makes the last quarter (from Jonas's enforced return when trying to flee to Antwerp) one of the most sheerly exciting of all his stories. These two parts of the novel – the social symbolism of the Company and the gothic nightmare of Jonas the murderer – work together admirably, and, sufficiently anchored to them not completely to sail away, are the two giant balloons of the book, Mr Pecksniff and Mrs Gamp. I am inclined to suppose that even if these two monsters took off, they would be sufficient creations in themselves, as satires or satirical mosaics of aspects of Victorian thought and feeling, to allow us to regard their sabotage of the novel as an act of artistic creation in itself. But it is not necessary to do battle with more strict believers in the novel's form over this, for they do not, in fact, ever quite leave the novel they are in, and, staying with it, they undoubtedly enhance and enrich it greatly.

Martin Chuzzlewit: 'Mr Pecksniff on his Mission'; 'Mrs Gamp proposes a Toast' by Phiz.

What is it that Mr Pecksniff tells us about the age he lives in? I think, mostly, that the highly developed conscience, which was one of the finest products of Victorian ethic – a man living twenty-four hours of the day with a full consciousness that his every word and deed had absolute moral meaning and effect – could also, by its very minute nature, its concern with the small, hourly routines of life, be easily degraded into a parody of itself. Mr Pecksniff trades upon a world that mistakes scruple for Truth, and concern with morality for Morality. He is able to impose a mean, petty, cruel life upon those around him, because he talks in the way that a good man of deep conscience would talk, and people generally are too frightened of the slender basis of their own conscientious lives to question him. He always does his duty, however painful to others; and he does so in a way which satisfies society that he is carrying out an unpleasant duty. Again, he has no real concern for words except a love of creating the right total effect – 'Playful – playful warbler,' he calls his daughter, Mercy; and Dickens comments: 'It may be observed in connexion with his calling his daughter "a warbler" that she was not at all vocal, but that Mr Pecksniff was in the frequent habit of using any word that occurred to him as having a good sound, and rounding a sentence well, without much care for its meaning . . . . A strong trustfulness in sounds and forms was the master-key to Mr Pecksniff's character.' And within these empty forms he always cares so much about Truth, exactitude: 'Is it not enough, sir, that you come into my house like a thief in the night, or I should rather say, for we can never be too particular on the subject of Truth, like a thief in the daytime?' There is an aura of scripture about his speech, yet it somehow remains, though highly spiritual, secular. He is not, like Mr Stiggins or Mr Chadband, a vulgar religious fraud. Mr Pecksniff is the Victorian concern for morality overblown, gone to seed, run rampant.

Mrs Gamp's dialogue is a triumph, perhaps the greatest triumph in literature of verbal collage. The male verbal maniacs in Dickens, Pecksniff, Micawber and others, deal in abstractions, in empty rhetoric as befits man's education. But the women of the species pour out the folklore of their age in concrete images that form a visual mosaic. Mrs Nickleby's is a mosaic of the folklore of gentility, Flora Finching's of romanticism, Mrs Gamp's of the lives of the poor. Being a midwife as well as a general nurse, she is close to birth and death, and, what is more, to death in birth. And since birth is the result of sexual union she is close to that unspoken mystery too. Her wonderful reminiscences of the fictional Mrs Harris (a very small number of pages in the book, in fact, compared to the impression they create) give us that strange mixture of popular religion and other superstition by which the poor lent sweetness and sentiment and excitement and an aura of mystery to a coming and a going which were as brutal as life itself. The squalor, the greed and the brutality of Mrs Gamp are woven as closely into all the tag ends of religiosity, folk wisdom, macabrerie, coy salaciousness and sickly sentiment that make up her speech, as the brutality of the lives of the Victorian poor was blended with all their desperate attempts to evade it. It is only fitting, then, that Mrs Gamp 'was by this time in the doorway, curtseying . . . . At the same moment a peculiar fragrance was borne upon the breeze, as if a passing fairy had hiccoughed, and had previously been to a wine vaults'. Nor, for all her sycophancy towards her better-off clients, does Mrs Gamp ever associate herself with any but the poor she maltreats and cheats: 'Rich folks may ride on camels, but it ain't so easy for 'em to see out of a needle's eye. That's my comfort, and I hope I knows it.' Mrs Gamp is always a 'woman of the people'. And finally, all scripture, all feminine coyness, all gross appetite put aside, she remains, deep down, the repository of female learning, of the secret knowledge shared together by which Victorian women, and especially Victorian poor women, claimed some sacred position in a society made by men to their abasement:

> 'But,' says Mrs Harris, the tears a fillin' in her eyes, 'you knows much betterer than me, with your experienge, how little puts us out. A Punch's show,' she says, 'a chimbley sweep, a newfundlandog, or a drunken man a-comin' round the corner sharp, may do it.' 'So it may . . .' said Mrs Gamp, 'there's no deniging of it; and though my books is clear for a full week, I takes a anxious art along with me, I do assure you, sir.'

It is a large picture of society, then, that is composed around the fraudulent farce of Mr Tigg Montague's Anglo Bengalee Insurance Company. It lacks any real penetration into the upper reaches, such as Dickens had attempted in *Barnaby Rudge*, but it is in itself a good enough assemblage for what he requires. What finally prevents *Martin Chuzzlewit* from being one of his greatest novels is the injection into the book of three quite different and much feebler forms of art. The first is the American journalism I have named. The second is poor drama – the story of old Martin Chuzzlewit's dissembling his real feelings so that he may expose the hypocrisies of Mr Pecksniff. All parts of this are stagey; its denouement especially so – including all the pairing off, which is exactly like that of the stage finale of some inferior company, as when Mark Tapley declares his intention of wedding Mrs Lupin: 'Why, sir!' said Mr Tapley, *retiring with a bow towards the buxom hostess*, 'her opinion is the name isn't a change for the better, but the individgle may be.' In Phiz's illustration of this scene we see a copy of *Tartuffe* among the books that have fallen around Pecksniff's head as he cowers on the floor away from old Martin's avenging stick; and the whole of this part of the book is indeed what some hack in Mr Crummle's touring company might have produced if he had been told to translate and adapt Molière's play for the company over a weekend. But the book finally ends on an even less felicitous scene – this, of all irrelevant themes for the close, is Charity Pecksniff's fainting away before her wedding when Augustus, her beloved, sends the note that says he is 'unalterably, never yours'. The whole of Todgers's boarding house where this scene is laid (save for the admirably unsentimental but sympathetic Mrs Todgers herself) is, with its crude pen portraits of the commercial gentleman and their weakness for Cupid's darts, out of the most coy, facetious stuff in *Sketches by Boz*. The 'there was I waiting at the church' joke against the old maid, Charity, is a fitting culmination to this feeble section, but it is the most unfortunate ending, in irrelevance and in inferiority of tone, to this rich novel.

Whatever its merits as a work of art, *Martin Chuzzlewit*, although it was soon to be classed among his most popular novels, had come near to commercial failure in serial form; there had been some damage to his relations with Chapman & Hall, his publishers. His visit to the United States, which had begun with such warm adulation, had ended by making his name hated there; he decided not to see Macready off from Liverpool on the start of an American theatrical tour lest the association of their names in the press might bring hostile audiences. The problems and anxieties of 1840, in fact, had not been solved by the hoped-for device of getting 'away from it all'. The fading of the great flow that, beginning with the miracle of *Pickwick*, had reached its height at the death of Little Nell, continued.

He had arrived so suddenly and so completely that it was perhaps inevitable that he should be apprehensive of losing his audience as suddenly as it had come. This would seem to be the immediate explanation of the tensions, frequent changes of plan and constant changes of ground, which form the pattern of his life in these years up to 1850. After he took over the editorship of *Household Words* in 1850 he had found a regular occupation, compatible with authorship, which gave him a steady, regular income and kept him in a steady, regular relationship with his public. But even after that date, throughout his life, there was to be a continuous restlessness – a moving in and out of London, in and out of England, attempts at closer or different relationships with his public, a multitude of different schemes for putting his social and political ideas into practice and, despite his extraordinary loyalty to friends, the formation of a new circle of near disciples, 'Dickens's young men'. Later, towards the year of his separation from Catherine, he attributed much of this restlessness to the failure of his marriage, to a search for peace, for a happiness which he could not find in the home.

Yet it is not easy to imagine Dickens as a man of retired life, producing from the obscurity of well-regulated domestic bliss his series of masterpieces. It is mainly not easy for the self-evident reason (too often forgotten by speculative biographers) that we can only judge the fitness of a man's actions by the life he actually lived. Even so, with the most compatible wife in the world, with a compatible family, and compatible in-laws, there were certain pulls to change and restlessness that, I think, would still have operated in Dickens's life. To begin with, as he developed his art – and he did so all the time – he was constantly forced into a wider, more complete picture of life, in which it was less and less possible to propose partial hopes or remedies for human ills; or, as it is usually put, Dickens became socially more pessimistic. This is true of the underlying statement of his books, but, given his active, energetic nature and his positive, Christian, humanistic view of life, he was bound to engage in a series of philanthropic social tasks in his daily life in order to counteract his increasing pessimism. Then this social pessimism of his novels attached to *English* life, which was the very source of his creation. The intense love-hate of his own country – his revulsion from it, his entire creative dependence upon it – must inevitably have produced the restless moving abroad and back again that we find in these years. And, as with England, so with London.

But most important, I think, in estimating the endless restlessness of Dickens's life, acute from 1840 to 1850, endemic from 1850 to the end – is the plain fact itself that he was a novelist, whose art was continually advancing, changing, maturing. The very personal colouring of his world, above all the extravagance of its humour and melodrama, have led readers, until the last thirty years or so, to see only its homogeneity. And this is real. 'Dickensian' has significance as an adjective – though it is a portmanteau word so stuffed with meanings that it would be unwise to examine it too closely, lest the mass of contents overwhelm the enquirer. To this extent, the old statement that *A Tale of Two Cities* was a very un-Dickensian book had a certain sense. But the concept of Dickens's world as something apart and completely consistent takes no account of the enormous progress he made in shaping, enlarging, defining and therefore, in the last resort, successfully expressing his vision. It is only in the last decades that this remarkable artistic development has been realized. This means that he could never be fully sure of the reception of his next book, for he was aware how different it would be from the last. I do not mean that he was always faithful to his artistic conception; he frequently made changes, sometimes major changes, to maintain his link with his readers. Even so, his novels developed so greatly that he must always have feared getting out of touch with his public – and although he never did so, although he remained a best-seller, there is a certain sense in which the late Dickens was in the main not so popular as the early, as well as being more strongly attacked by contemporary critics.

In all the last thirty years of his life he wandered restlessly in and out of England, in and out of London, in and out of public activity. Occasionally in the course of his wanderings he was hit violently by a sudden, romantic *schwärmerei* for a young girl, but in the main he relied emotionally upon whipping up ever more heartily the many hundred friendships that his charm and energy had created. Above all, he sought by various means to forge new links with his public – links that could withstand changes in his own creative form, changes in public taste, sudden exhaustions of creative powers; links that would remove from his novels, to some other sphere of life, his desire for the immediate gratification of an audience; links that would remove into another sphere some of the labile improvisation that the serial medium he had chosen for publication introduced into his novels. He found these outlets first in the Christmas Books, in theatricals, then most substantially in editing, at last in public readings. His conscious motives were seldom the artistic ones I have listed, usually they were the immediate needs for money or for social activity; nor were these activities ever quite separate from each other or from his novel writing. But only one of these activities – the Christmas Books – belongs *directly* to his fictional world.

The Christmas Books

The idea of the first Christmas Book, *A Christmas Carol*, came to Dickens at a great Manchester meeting where, sharing a platform with Disraeli and others, he propounded his growing conviction that education was the answer to England's social problems. He composed it as he walked about the streets of London at night during the writing of *Martin Chuzzlewit*. It was designed specifically to regain the readers lost by the disappointment of that novel. He published it at Christmas 1843 in a beautiful edition with illustrations by the well known Punch artist, John Leech, a good friend of his. The success of the venture, the great wave of personal, direct emotion that came to him from readers, decided him to repeat the idea. The following year he produced *The Chimes*, with illustrations by many of his artist friends. Then, with one year of failure in 1847 due to the pressure of the writing of *Dombey and Son*, he produced a Christmas Book each year: *The Cricket on the Hearth, The Battle of Life* and *The Haunted Man*, until 1848. Subsequently, from the time of his becoming editor of *Household Words* until his death, he usually included a special story (though decreasingly as the years went by one specifically connected with the festive season) for the Christmas number.

These later Christmas stories include many with interesting biographical details, like *The Christmas Tree,* with which I began this book; others were famous in his own day, like *The Seven Poor Travellers*, *Mrs Lirriper's Lodgings*, *Doctor Marigold*, *Mugby Junction* and, with Wilkie Collins, the sophisticated thriller *No Thoroughfare*. But in general Dickens's genius was not suited to short stories – the humour truncated becomes whimsy, the pathos removed from a wider social context becomes sentimentality, all those overtones of meaning which accrue to the great novels from the thematic patterns are lacking, the resulting stories seldom seem more than vapid magazine pieces, without, save in the last where Collins collaborated, even the suspense and lively action that mark the best Victorian magazine stories.

Nor do I think that the Christmas Books, save one, are much better. The *novella* length hardly suits Dickens more than the short story. *The Battle of Life* and *The Haunted Man* were deservedly less successful in their own time and have only the interest now of being quarries in their rather peculiar stories for autobiographical obsessions. *The Cricket on the Hearth* enjoyed great popularity at the time; it is interesting as foreshadowing the pathos about a child-wife that is central to *David Copperfield* and it has much of Dickens's strange animism about masks and faces and pictures in the burning coals; but it is an empty piece of aimless pathos. *The Chimes*, perhaps, was the most successful of all; it is of great interest to the student of Dickens's social ideas and shows him unusually on the brink of straight political satire; but as an imaginative creation the story of Trotty Veck's adventures with Alderman Cute and the other more well-intentioned representatives of a wicked social order never comes to life. Its chief interest, for the student of Dickens's fictional world, is the way in which its total analysis of the evils of society and their interdependence points forward to the overall pictures of his later great novels: the relatively good intentions of the villains of *The Chimes* (Alderman Cute and the others) is the start of thinking which leads to the original title devised for *Little Dorrit – Nobody's Fault*. The only one of these Christmas ventures that has retained popularity is the first, *A Christmas Carol*, and rightly so, for it has a vigour, a directness of dialogue and story, which profit from the abbreviated form. It is just as much a compendium of the social obsessions that pressed upon Dickens so fiercely at this time, but they are incorporated into one of the myths that had grown with him from childhood, and the result is extraordinarily vivid, like some sermon acted out in a dream.

In *Martin Chuzzlewit* he had tried consciously to describe the dream world that unconsciously informs all his novels. Jonas Chuzzlewit, just before he murders Montague Tigg, dreams of Judgment Day, a curious, panoramic, confused city scene, in which the dreamer looks down upon a hurrying multitude of people, faces half remembered, half strange, spread before him in an elusive survey of his life. Such a form of dreams fits geographically with the Arabian legend I described in the first chapter, in which, either seated on a magic carpet or borne on the wings of a fabulous bird, the hero flies over all the scenes of the world. Used as it was by Le Sage in the book to which Dickens refers in *American Notes*, *Le Diable Boiteux*, the vision becomes a social and moral one, in which all the many contrasts of human life – riches and misery, vice and innocence, age and childhood, death and birth, are laid out before one.

In *A Christmas Carol*, the story of Scrooge's visions, these two themes are combined – the world in all its contrasts is put before him and so is the picture of his own past life, the story of the loss of his childhood and his innocence. And deep in the heart of this vision Dickens, through Scrooge, sees the contrast that had been with him ever since the last days of Warren's blacking factory – out from the warm bedchamber we fly into the terrible darkness, out from the warm fireside over the desolate, storm-swept plains and seas, out from the festive Christmas table to the lost children – 'This Boy is Ignorance, this Girl is Want'.

Dickens at this time was possessed by the belief that all the crime, the misery, the inequality, the violence that he so hated and feared in contemporary society were the result of lack of education. He believed always in education (a man who wishes to have some faith in the future has to); yet his views on methods were to change considerably. But these years after his return from America seem to have been the moment of crystallization of his sense, that only education could change evils so deep-seated as he now began to think were the ills of a society organized on the false and cruel principle of man as an economic unit.

This is the theme of his first two Christmas Books, but whereas in *The Chimes* he treats it directly as a satirical political issue, in *A Christmas Carol*, by incorporating it into Scrooge's terrible vision of the two children, Ignorance and Want, he involves in it his deepest personal apprehensions. Scrooge, in a sense, is the last of those personal conversions, of the good, benevolent men, who can change society by individual charity and generosity. But there is a difference, for Scrooge is part of a formal ghost story; the story is a Christmas story, a particular myth of redemption and goodness that belongs to that season of good tidings. We are not to take Scrooge for a real merchant, like the Cheerybles. Like Mr Pickwick, Scrooge goes through the refining fires of the knowledge of the world's misery, but this is brought home to him by the recapturing of his own childhood, by the present childhood of Tiny Tim and by the general childhood of the Spectres of Want and Ignorance. We are shown how, just as in the midst of life we are in death ('Christmas time . . . when men and women . . . think of people below them as if they really were fellow-passengers to the grave, and not another race of creatures bound on other journeys'), so in childhood we are on the edge of loss: in his vision his own childhood fades into the death of his heart; in his vision Tiny Tim dies; in his vision it is the children, Ignorance and Want, who turn to something worse: 'Beware this boy, for on his brow I see that written which is Doom.' Everything is precarious in the nightmares of Scrooge, just as it is mere chance whether we are born the child seated by the festive fireside or the one of whom Tiny Tim, 'who had a plaintive little voice', 'sang . . . very well indeed' – 'the child lost in the snow'.

A Christmas Carol: 'Scrooge and Bob Cratchit'; 'Mr Fezziwig's Ball' by Leech.

There is no attempt in *A Christmas Carol*, as in *The Chimes*, to give a coherent account of the evils of the social system nor to propound any remedy other than a redemption through the grace of the Spirit; but by means of a nightmare vision we feel the intense precariousness of life, the extraordinary momentary possibility of joy, the vague but inescapable sense that this joy connects with something long buried in our childhood – and all this is connected with Dickens's Christianity; 'it is good to be children sometimes, and never better than at Christmas, when its mighty Founder was a child himself'. *A Christmas Carol*, in fact, is Dickens at his most muddled, but since this muddle is given a very simple story form, clothed in a legend that comes from Dickens's earliest reading and embodying most of his deepest obsessions, it has an emotional impact as strong as any of his work and is, like *Oliver Twist*, a 'pop' classic.

Italy

The impact of *A Christmas Carol* on readers was overwhelming. It brought Dickens a flood of personal reaction. As Thackeray put it: 'To every man or woman who reads it [you have done] a personal kindness.' Unfortunately, owing to the lavish production Dickens had insisted upon, his profit from the vast sales was far lower than he had anticipated. His alarm and disappointment brought his quarrel with Chapman & Hall, smouldering since the unhappy start of *Martin Chuzzlewit*, to a head. With no definite novel in mind almost for the first time since *Pickwick*, Dickens decided to seek once more in foreign scenes the perspective to give artistic form to his growing social vision. He had already been learning Italian. He would take the whole family to live in Italy. He cut off from Chapman & Hall, made a new contract with the printers, Bradbury and Evans, hired an enormous old coach, and with Catherine, Georgy, Anne Brown and a number of other English servants, a courier, Roche, who was to become a beloved associate, and his five children (the last, Frank, a small baby) he set out on 2 July for a rented palazzo in Genoa.

Genoa, from The Heights.

The palazzo Bella Vista proved to be a dilapidated, dirty, old, pink house at Albaro, a suburb on the hill outside the city walls. From Dickens's letters, it sounds suspiciously like one of those houses for rent that only the most guileless travellers get saddled with. But the negotiations had been made in haste and through a friend. The chief disadvantage was a plague of fleas (but these were a regular hazard of foreign travel well into modern times). The view was magnificent, and, despite the general squalor of the streets of Genoa, Dickens found a great deal to fascinate him in wandering there, especially the marionette theatres. There was obviously something about toy and marionette theatres that especially appealed to him – the manual dexterity, no doubt, akin to his own competent conjuring so much in demand at the children's Christmas parties, but also the simplicity of the performance, and the absurdity of it too. In his visits to Italy and France Dickens was an ardent theatregoer – very enthusiastic about the best in the Paris theatre, but, as in England, almost as happy to be entertained by what was bad. He seems never to have tired of the absurdity of foreigners pronouncing English names wrongly or getting details of English titles muddled. It is a clue, I think, to the degree which his finally so sophisticated extravagant humour owed its origin to an almost childish aural delight in verbal eccentricity of any kind.

The unwonted heat, the fleas, the discomfort, the non-arrival of his books sent by boat, all these gave Dickens's restlessness an excuse for not settling down to writing. Then he went to Marseilles to fetch, for a short visit, his brother Fred – still his favourite family companion, but soon, with a rash marriage, to start on a steady downhill career of debt. There was swimming and walking and exploring Genoa, and some social life in the city. Yet Dickens was impatient to start his Christmas story. After Fred's departure the family removed to the vast *plano nobile* in a real palazzo, the Peschiere, elegant, with huge, painted, stuccoed and mirrored rooms. He had his books now, and his desk, and a noble salon for a study; but he missed the London streets to tramp for inspiration, and the bells of Genoa maddened him. It was a difficult time, of old spasmodic kidney pains and irritated nerves not helped by the continuous pouring rain of an unusually stormy autumn. However, despite all these trials, he completed *The Chimes*.

It was a new experience to have written something he thought so good, and to have only himself and his womenfolk to appreciate it. True enough, now, as in all his later stays abroad, he consulted continually by letter with Forster about the details of his work; but this was not the same as the comments and tributes of friends to mark the end of a hard task performed. He decided that he would return to England for a short visit to see the new book through the press and to read it aloud to a select circle of friends. The journey, detailed both in his letters and in *Pictures from Italy*, is extraordinarily characteristic of Dickens and strikes deep into the dilemmas of his life. He began with two weeks' tour of relaxation after the tensions of writing. He travelled with Roche, his beloved and very individual courier, who did battle with every customs officer on the many crossings of frontiers they made through the small states of Northern Italy. It was a typical journey of jogging night-time coach rides, early starts, Dickens walking in the morning ahead of the equipage, energy, curiosity and a determination to miss nothing. At Modena the waiter was annoyingly full of Milor Bearon; at Verona the geography seemed at cross purposes with Dickens's mental picture of *Romeo and Juliet*; the gloom of Mantua appalled him. But Venice had been so magnificent in its fabulous, *Arabian Nights* splendour that all else paled beside. By the time that he had reached Milan, where Catherine and Georgy met him to speed him on his journey back to England, he had found the ordinary Italian people delightful (he must have been happy to find his own Italian better than Roche's); the paintings often magnificent as long as one kept one's head, knew what one

'Venice, the Salute and Doge's Palace from the Giudecca' by Turner, 1840.

liked, and refused to be abashed by the art connoisseurs' 'humbug', and the flavour of despotism and priestcraft disturbing. Then, away over the Alps in a hard journey through passes that were only just negotiable, and on, through mud-thick French roads to Paris. And, hey presto, he was at Cuttriss's Hotel on 30 November, one day before he had said that he would arrive – as he said to Forster, 'You know my punctiwality'.

The journey as described in *Pictures from Italy* is a model of those strange, jolting, half-dream coach journeys into which odd passengers, beautifully described, obtrude through the shaking, creaking night – a world of flashing, passing lights and sharp-aired morning breakfasts and half-sleep and drowsy meditation that made coach journeys so significant for Dickens. This one has, I think, a special meaning, because here the wanderer is going from 'home' (his children, his wife, his loved ones) in a foreign land to 'home' (London, friends, admiration, talk of his book and talk of the latest important happening). Real ties of love hold him to the first, from which also grumbling doubts about his married life drive him away; in this Genoese home he has amid his loved ones the tranquillity he so much needs for his work and also the absence from the stimulating talk of the town, a monotony which makes work impossible. In the 'home' (London) to which he is going there is care, responsibility, all the tension of his fame, his security, his reputation, all the consideration of whether and how he should buttress his life with other activities, literary or social; and there is also the stimulation of friendship, gossip, humour, talk both professional and political (for at this moment of isolation in far off Italy, Dickens's social concerns had never taken him closer to involvement in English politics, as *The Chimes* shows). The fireside glow, the lighted window of 'home' had at each end its comforts, its attractions, and its claustrophobic gloom. To be eaten up by a world of children and ill-regulated household affairs, though it spelt tranquillity, spelt also despair; to be eaten up by London meant the stimulation of competition, of worldly activity, and the possible submerging of his art beneath a load of worldly cares. To the wanderer through the snow, through the storm and the rain there must have been much attraction in the sheer hardship of the journey itself, in the energy needed to keep going, in the freedom of abandonment and of isolation. In that strange Dickens world of the lost, of a forsaken child trudging through the cruel night towards the distant fireside glow of the homestead, there was always a strong pull away from home, a morbid attraction towards wandering desperation.

However, there could not have been a better reception to make him feel he had come home than his friends prepared for him in London. At Forster's chambers in Lincoln's Inn Fields on 3 December he read *The Chimes* aloud to a distinguished circle including close friends – Douglas Jerrold, Carlyle, his brother Fred, Stanfield, Forster himself and Maclise, who sketched the scene. It was a triumphant success. He also read it to Macready: 'If you had seen Macready last night, undisguisedly sobbing, and crying on the sofa as I read, you would have felt, as I did, what a thing it is to have power.' It was a power that he was to taste more fully over a decade later, a power that was to grow into an addiction, a slowly killing drug.

On 2 December he read *The Chimes* aloud to a distinguished circle, drawn by Maclise.

He returned to Genoa through Paris, where Macready was starting a theatrical season; and now for three days he first tasted that well-mannered adulation of artists that regularly turns the head of successful English writers in France. He met for the first time on equal, honoured terms great European literary lions like Hugo and Dumas and Théophile Gautier, Michelet the historian, Delacroix, and perhaps most impressively of all, De Vigny. Everything conspired, indeed, to soothe his sense of being a great writer, for at Marseilles he got on to the wrong boat for Genoa, and, despite the annoyance of many American passengers, his own steamer was delayed for over an hour until his arrival on board.

Back with the family at Genoa he still found himself unable to write, but there was another and unusual call upon his powers. In Genoese society he had made friends with a Swiss banker, De La Rue, and his wife. Madame De La Rue suffered from a nervous tic and, as it came out in more intimate friendship, recurrent nightmares, particularly of a mysterious and evil stranger who threatened to enter her real life. As far back as 1838 Dickens had become friendly with Dr Elliotson who, as President of the Phrenological Society, had been one of the first in England to use mesmerism in the relief of pain. Dickens had found by practising upon his wife and sister-in-law (on one occasion to the alarm of Macready) that he had mesmeric powers. Indeed he had much alleviated Catherine's headaches in this way. As in most such matters that seemed to go beyond the material explanation, he approached mesmerism with scepticism; but already in 1844 in Boston he had written, 'I should be untrue to myself if I shrunk for a moment from saying that I am a believer against all my preconceived opinions and impressions.' Now, after treating Madame De La Rue, he had reason to believe more strongly, for her nervous troubles demonstrably decreased.

The episode, apart from the unfortunate fact that Dickens's obsession with Madame De La Rue roused his wife's annoyance, has a chief interest for the way in which it shows Dickens moving in a Balzacian atmosphere, partly compounded of careful, though to us somewhat ludicrous, medical discussions of nervous magnetism, and partly of a sort of personal heroic fight against the phantom: 'I see afar off, how essential it is that this phantom should not regain its power for an instant.' Alas, the story which he eventually wrote from the whole incident has no Balzacian force, none of that intense immediate obsession of the creative artist with these nightmares that Dickens many years later, when he reprovingly recalled to his wife her former anxieties, claimed to have been his.

The mesmeric treatment had temporarily to be suspended, for Dickens took Catherine for a tour with all the attendant Salvator-Rosa-like hazards of storms and *banditti*, through Florence and Siena to Rome in carnival time, and on to Naples where Georgy joined them by boat. From here they went as far as Paestum, taking in Pompeii and Herculaneum. But the high point of the journey was a visit to Vesuvius. They made the ascent in a party of thirty including guides, but the only ladies were Catherine and Georgy, borne in litters. Sunset and moonrise both passed before they reached the platform on

Florence from below San Miniato al Monte by Signorini; outside Rome by Rebell.

the mountain-top – 'the region of Fire'. 'What words can paint the gloom and grandeur of this scene – the broken ground; the smoke; the sense of suffocation from the sulphur, the fear of falling down through the crevices in the yawning ground . . . .' But for Dickens himself there was 'something in the fire and roar that generates an irresistible desire to get nearer to it', and, despite all warnings, he and two others climbed further to look down into the crater's mouth. In fact, it was the descent that proved more perilous. The ladies were taken from their litters and almost carried down, supported on each side, and with a third man preventing them falling by holding on to their skirts. The precautions, too, were not excessive, for two men of the party and a boy guide fell headlong into the darkness before them and, although not killed, were sadly damaged. From Vesuvius he and his two lady companions returned unharmed, if somewhat tattered.

On their way back through Rome they were rejoined by the De La Rues, and the mesmeric sessions were recommenced until, by the time they regained Genoa, Catherine's jealousy had burst forth in open refusal to speak to these intrusive friends. However, any challenge that his wife's remonstrances might have made to Dickens's obstinacy was luckily stillborn, for their time in Italy was at an end.

In July 1845 the whole family returned to England, once more in a huge coach, over the Alps. *Pictures from Italy* was published the following spring.

Vesuvius, ascent and descent: in fact, it was the descent that proved more perilous.

Decorated with some very pleasing poplars and vines and glimpses of palazzi by Samuel Palmer, the book is a rather ordinary account of the customs and beauties of Italy, with what seems to me the splendid description of the coach trip through Northern Italy I have already described, and a very few passages of excellent, characteristic humour. As a liberal Englishman, already acquainted with some of the exiled Italian revolutionaries, and expecting the despotic police states that he found, Dickens suffered far less distress and disappointment in Italy than he did in the United States. He lived in Italy as a tourist, relaxed as a tourist, and wrote a tourist's book which, unlike *American Notes*, is not so very different from the private comments he makes in his letters.

The stay in Italy, though unproductive of creative fiction, comes through his writings as one of the really enjoyed periods of his life – a time for that kind of energetic relaxation which was the only sort he could ever know. He liked the friendliness, the manners and the gaiety of the ordinary Italian people as much as he disliked the temperament and manners of the ordinary Americans. His English servants soon made easy relations with the Italian servants, despite the language barrier; indeed before the Dickenses left Genoa the English cook married a foreign man and remained behind. As always in his life where his fancy and his heart were touched, Dickens took great pains to see that the simple Englishwoman settling in a foreign land should get all the legal and financial protection he could obtain for her before he left her behind. A sense of responsibility for others, so long as he did not feel himself threatened by them, was developed in him to an almost incredible degree. Out of this incident, I think, comes one of the least sentimental, most genuinely feeling depictions of working people in all his novels – the befriending of the lively, happy Italian working man, Cavaletto, by Mrs Plornish of Bleeding Heart Yard in *Little Dorrit*. Certainly her method of interpreting to the Italian – 'E please', 'E glad get money', 'E 'ope you leg well soon' – must come from Dickens's memory of the discourses between the English and Italian servants that he remarks on in his letters. Cavaletto is the only Italian in his novels. He is not an outstanding character but he does not suffer as do Dickens's French characters from a disastrously mistaken idea of literal translation of French syntax as a means of conveying the speech of the French. This suggests, I think, that Dickens's Italian, though very adequate to his conversational purposes as a visitor, had not, like his French, reached a stage where the syntactical shape of the language was foremost in his mind.

The Italian story, however, is really of chief interest for the light it throws on Dickens's views upon the fine arts and upon history – two subjects which inevitably dominate the tourist's life. Dickens's taste in painting has been made famous by his attack in 1850 on Millais's *The Carpenter's Shop*, the painting of the young Jesus with his parents and family, that was hung in the Royal Academy of that year. His attitude to this painting is quite consistent with the many comments he makes on the paintings and sculptures he saw in Italy, and, I think, closely connects with his very dogmatic, violent views

'The Street of the Tombs: Pompeii' by Samuel Palmer, from *Pictures from Italy*.

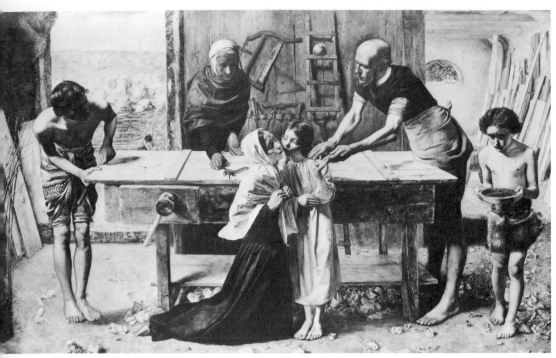

'The Carpenter's Shop' by Millais; 'Lux Mundi' by Holman Hunt.

about the past. Despite certain vague attachments to 'old things' and 'old buildings', such as mark the end of *Nicholas Nickleby* or the description of Master Humphrey's room – 'Its worm-eaten doors, and low ceilings crossed by clumsy beams . . . its very dust and dulness, are all dear to me' – Dickens was always suspicious of reverence for the past; but his distaste for such reverence grew greatly in the forties and the fifties when he was confronted with many movements in England that seemed to him reactionary and obscurantist. Whereas when he wrote *Barnaby Rudge* in 1841 the extreme Protestantism of Exeter Hall had still been a menace, it was now Tractarianism with all its suggestion of Roman Catholic peril that was in the air. The Young England Toryism of Disraeli, too, which he had wished to satirize in *The Chimes*, reposed in great degree upon the assertion of a golden pre-industrial age of social harmony. A whole character is written into *The Chimes* to show how wrong it is to praise the 'good old days'.

What he attacked now was not the harmless medievalry of Scott's influence or of the famous revived Chivalric Tournament at Eglinton in 1839; there were serious social and political overtones to this new love of the past that had to be fought. Such was certainly in his mind when he wrote his *Child's History of England*.

As early as 1843 he spoke of this project as a means of protecting his eldest boy, Charley, aged six, 'I don't know what I should do if he were to get hold of any Conservative or High Church notions,' and he suggests it again to

Charley's godmother, Miss Burdett Coutts, that 'he [Charley] may not fix his affections on wrong heroes or see the bright side of Glory's sword and know nothing of the rusty one'. This little book he eventually published in instalments in *Household Words* in 1851, 1852 and 1853. Indeed, he must have been working on the history at the time of his attack on Millais's picture. In both and indeed also in his writings about paintings and buildings in Italy, he adopts an absolute and total rejection of any pleas, artistic or scholarly, that may condone the wrongdoing and tyranny of the past. In all English history only those heroes of the Victorian radical, King Alfred and Oliver Cromwell, are

In all English history only King Alfred and Oliver Cromwell are allowed any real moral stature.

allowed any real moral stature. (Given a Carlylean need for heroes, they seem to me an excellent choice.) Praise or admiration for all the rest – medieval kings, barons or prelates, Tudor and Stuart monarchs alike – is humbug and cant, speciously denying morality under some plea of historical relativism or some false assertion of the picturesque. In *Dombey and Son* Mrs Skewton's falsity and affectation is clearly illustrated on her visit to Warwick Castle: 'That inestimable Queen Bess! . . . Dear Creature! . . .She was all Heart! And that charming father of hers! . . . so bluff . . . so burly . . . with his dear little peepy eyes and his benevolent chin.' Dickens shoots all this down in the history with: 'Henry the Eighth has been favoured by some Protestant writers, because the Reformation was achieved in his time. But the mighty merit of it lies with other men . . . and it can be rendered none the worse by this monster's crimes, and none the better by any defence of them. The plain truth is, that he was a most intolerable ruffian, a disgrace to human nature, and a blot of blood and grease upon the History of England.' And as for good Queen Bess, 'She had a great deal too much of her father in her, to please me.'

Of course this is for children, but it is the same knock-down, no-nonsense tone of the passages in *Pictures from Italy* which dispose of the picturesque dungeons and fortresses of the past. And, indeed, of the paintings and sculptures that he feels to have been falsely praised. In part Dickens's reaction here is a conventional aesthetic one. His ideal of a painter was a very literary or perhaps more theatrical artist like his friend Maclise – as he writes of Maclise's Hamlet in 1842,

> What an extraordinary fellow he must be who so manages the lights in this picture, that on the scene behind, is an enormous shadow of this group – as if the real murder were being done again by phantoms. And what a carrying out of the prevailing idea, it is, to paint the very proscenium of the little stage with stories of Sin and Blood – the first temptation – Cain and Abel – and such like subjects – crying for murder! from the very walls.

Such theatrical repetition of theme was a commonplace of Victorian narrative painting; and Phiz always provided the same symbolism in his illustrations for Dickens's novels, where, if examined under a magnifying glass, every picture or statue represented in any scene tells the story all over again. The theatricality had to be realistic – the baroque rhythms of Bernini appeared to him merely ludicrous – 'the most detestable class of productions in the wide world . . . breezy maniacs . . . whose hair is like a nest of lively snakes'. But it had also to be elevated, noble, if not sublime: 'the exquisite grace and beauty of Canova's statues,' and as he says of works 'by Titian, Guido, Domenichino, and Carlo Dolci . . . Correggio, and Murillo, and Raphael, and Salvator Rosa, and Spagnoletto . . . their noble elevation, purity and beauty!' It will be seen at once from the names that a good part of this taste is purely the convention of his time. But when he attacks the appearance of everyday models in sacred subjects – one supposes that he refers to Caravaggio and his pupils – it is at first sight more surprising: 'I freely acknowledge that when I see a Jolly young Waterman representing a cherubim [sic] or a Barclay and Perkin's Drayman depicted as an Evangelist, I see nothing to commend or admire in the performance, however great its reputed painter,' for surely a practising Unitarian as he was at this time would welcome such emphasis on the Man in Christ, on the Human in the Sacred.

To say this, however, is to mistake the degree of elevation which, even in this Unitarian period of his life, Dickens demanded from religion. Our Saviour appears regularly to illustrate by his life and teaching our duty here on earth; but he is always Our Saviour with a capital O and S. This surely accounts for Dickens's horror at Millais's depiction of the young Jesus with a hand cut in the ordinary course of work in the carpenter's shop.

> You will have the goodness to discharge from your minds all post-Raphael ideas, all religious aspirations, all elevating thoughts, all tender, awful, sorrowful, ennobling, sacred, graceful, or beautiful associations: and to prepare yourselves as befits such a subject – pre-Raphaelly considered – for the lowest depths of what is mean, odious, repulsive, and revolting . . . . Such men as the carpenters might be undressed in any hospital where dirty drunkards, in a high state of varicose veins, are received.

Such transports of disgust might seem to accord ill with the New Testament regard for the poor and the sick, which marks the defender of Jo the sweeping boy and Martha the Magdalen of *David Copperfield*. But Millais had offended

Dickens agreed with his publishers to the founding of a new, liberal daily newspaper, the *Daily News*.

not only against beauty and nobility, he had also tried to defend his error by reference to the past, to the painting before Raphael. It may be that Dickens knew that the German Nazarene masters of the Pre-Raphaelites had gone over to Rome. At any rate, the whole backward-looking movement was suspect, as the rest of the essay makes clear; he goes on to attack imaginary obscurantisms of a scientific Pre-Newtonian Brotherhood in literature, and so on. Neither the chronicles of the past, nor the art of the past, must be allowed to prevent the bettering of the world for future generations; particularly are history and art connoisseurship dangerous humbugs, for they may infect education and hence the minds of the young. As he specifically wrote to Forster from Venice on his second tour of Italy in 1853:

> Your guide book, representing the general swarming of humbugs . . . directs you, on pain of being broke for want of gentility in appreciation, to go into ecstasies with things that have neither imagination, nature, proportion, possibility, nor anything else in them. You immediately obey, and tell your son to obey. He tells his son, and he tells his, and so the world gets at three-fourths of its frauds and miseries.

But, whatever the humbugs of history, one aspect of England's past was sacrosanct. In his *Child's History of England* he writes: 'The names of Bacon, Spenser, and Shakespeare, will always be remembered with pride and veneration by the civilized world.' And surely to these he would have added many of the Jacobean dramatists, whose black violence and whose humours are so alive in his own works. In humours none more so than Ben Jonson. It is therefore highly appropriate that shortly after his return to England he should have begun the long series of amateur dramatic performances of his adult life by playing the braggadocio bully, Captain Bobadil, in Ben Jonson's *Every Man in His Humour*. The performance was given to a distinguished audience: Carlyle, Tennyson, specially come up from the Isle of Wight, Macready, old Lady Holland; and at a second performance given for the benefit of a new nursing home, Prince Albert, the Duke of Cambridge, Wellington and old Lord Melbourne. There were some sharp comments, and the distinguished audience was said to have been difficult to unfreeze, but there was also a great deal of praise, enough to lead Dickens on over the next decade to a series of performances in what was to be one of his most complete and satisfactory distractions.

But a more important enterprise awaited him in London than amateur acting. The episode of the *Daily News* is, perhaps, in the speed with which it all happened and the extent of the commitment he so happily assumed, outstanding even in Dickens's life, in which sudden enterprises were a constant feature. On his return from America he had sounded out the possibility of founding a new liberal newspaper; although he was rebuffed, the idea did not die in him. An ever more pressing sense of England's social ills as being systematic rather than piecemeal inclined him towards the need of some political pressure to secure reform – particularly, no doubt, educational reform. A doubt about committing himself only to fiction as a means of livelihood in view of

'The Coliseum' by Sir Charles Eastlake, 1822. 'God be thanked: a ruin!' *Pictures from Italy*.

the cost of his ever growing family and, I suppose, a slackening pace of inspiration as he ploughed beneath the accumulated soil of his youth and largely unconsciously reached for a richer, more unified level of material; a feeling that if he were to find a second string for the material dependence of his life, it had best be done now rather than later, and a knowledge that he had proved himself a good journalist – all these led him into agreeing with his publishers, Bradbury and Evans, to the founding of a new, liberal daily newspaper, the *Daily News*.

He entered into the enterprise with his usual vast energy, despite the advice of Forster (and Macready), who saw in such work no aid to his fame or his genius, and some loss of position through involvement in party politics. He surrounded himself with an able staff, many talented old friends like Forster, Jerrold, Mark Lemon, his father-in-law and his father. From the start there was some difficulty about the financial backers – most of these were northern industrial magnates (can Mr Bounderby have been among them?) and, what was to prove the immediate cause of Dickens's withdrawal, there was a strong element of railway interest. There was also Paxton, the Duke of Devonshire's former gardener, on his way to the highest fame in a few years' time as the designer of the Crystal Palace. Such a coming together of two men so formidably climbing the Victorian ladder of self-help was unpromising, and in fact Dickens was soon quarrelling with Paxton. However, the first number appeared on 21 January 1846. Although the success was not overwhelming – its circulation never approached that of *The Times* – the paper was by no means a failure. But Dickens found his subordinate position to the owners quite intolerable and after nineteen days, on 9 February, he resigned leaving Forster as editor. Once released from the editor's desk, his relations remained amicable – his *Pictures from Italy* appeared in the *Daily News* and he contributed important letters on capital punishment, describing in detail the psychology of murderers to suggest that their vanity and egotism was only fed by the drama of hanging, particularly of public hanging.

No doubt the experience of being subordinate was the chief cause of the quick end of this odd episode, for he never again accepted work on a periodical in which he did not have some financial proprietorship. But he must surely, too, have quickly seen that such a daily task was incompatible with novel writing. Indeed, he now had some clear ideas about *Dombey and Son*. From my own experience, I should suggest that the very realization of the hopeless step he had taken probably stimulated his imagination to work again. At any rate the whole feeling of the unpleasantness (and, it must be said, the failure) of this *Daily News* episode made him feel that he could not write in London. Once more he left for abroad.

Switzerland

This time, influenced by Catherine's distaste for Genoa and the De La Rues, he rented the villa Rosemont at Lausanne, overlooking the Lake of Geneva.

'The Val d'Aosta' by John Brett, 1858. 'I have visions of living . . . in all sorts of inaccessible places . . . a floating idea of going up above the snow-line.' Letter to Forster, 1854.

Taking the whole family and the servants and Roche again, he went by steamer down the Rhine, where he was gratified to find that his works were well known. Life at Lausanne began with a plague of flies, as life at Genoa had with a plague of fleas; but the Swiss stay, which lasted from June until October 1846, was a considerable success. In composing *Dombey* he missed once more the London streets. There were perhaps almost too many English friends passing through Switzerland. Yet he clearly enjoyed being host in a foreign country and the society of Lausanne itself proved peculiarly congenial; indeed, it was the pleasure and success of reading *Dombey* episodes aloud in a salon there that led him to make the first as yet somewhat facetious reference to embarking on regular public readings. Here he and Catherine and Georgy made friends with the Watsons, a young, wealthy English county couple, the owners of Rockingham Castle in Northamptonshire, a place that was to be the scene of many of Dickens's most happy amateur theatrical ventures and the model for Chesney Wold. Together they all climbed to the Great Saint Bernard – like Venice, to be used as a prison symbol in Mr Dorrit's prosperity. Yet the awful sublimity of Swiss mountain scenery made a strong appeal to Dickens, as to most Victorians. He visited the Swiss Alps again with Wilkie Collins in 1853; and they were to be the scene of the dramatic finale of one of his last Christmas Stories, written with Collins, *No Thoroughfare* (1867).

In general Switzerland aspired loftily, like its sublime peaks, to freedom and

Together they all climbed up the Great Saint Bernard.

progress. The superiority of the Protestant to the Catholic parts of the country reinforced what he had seen in Italy:

> I should like to show you the people as they are here, or in the Canton de Vaud – their wonderful education – splendid schools – comfortable homes – great intelligence and noble independence of character. It is the fashion amongst the English to decry them because they are not servile. I can only say that if the first quarter of a century of the best general education would rear such a peasantry in Devonshire as exists about here or about Lausanne, it would do what I can hardly hope in my most sanguine moods to take effect in four times that period.

But it was not only to the English that the Swiss could teach a lesson: 'They are genuine people, these Swiss. There is better metal in them than in all the stars and stripes of all the fustian banners of the so called and falsely called, U-nited States. They are a thorn in the side of European despots, and a good wholesome people to live near Jesuit-ridden Kings on the brighter side of the mountains.' So much for his late hosts, the Americans and the Italians.

Despite his liking for Switzerland, he found writing *Dombey and Son* slow going, especially when by autumn he had to prepare his new Christmas Book as well. Attributing the slow progress to the lack of animation, he moved first to Geneva and then for a three-month stay to Paris, in a very ornately furnished house in the rue de Courcelles.

'The Swiss are . . . a good wholesome people to live near Jesuit-ridden Kings.'

France

Since France was to play so important a part in the relaxation of Dickens's life the moment of this first residence in Paris is perhaps appropriate to outline his relation to that country. During the next decade (the fifties), which was the time of his masterpieces and of his greatest personal distress and greatest social despair, he sought refuge increasingly from England, and it was France that he chose as that refuge. Apart from short visits to Paris with old friends like Maclise or new ones like Wilkie Collins, he established his family at Boulogne during the summers of 1853, 1854 and 1856, long enough to complain of English trippers; and he rented a large apartment in the Champs Elysées from October 1855 to April 1856. In the sixties, when the crisis of his marital unhappiness had passed and his energies were increasingly given to the public readings, his

Dickens established his family at Boulogne.

restlessness took him in the main all over England itself, but even so he was in France, mainly Paris, for short visits each year from 1862 to 1865, and again in 1868 and there seems some evidence of a French hideout in the last, more secret, years of his life.

The United States showed him in hostile, disappointed mood; Italy revealed his prejudices; Switzerland his enthusiasm; but it may truly be said that, although he was never more than an Englishman in France, he was greatly enlarged in his cultural, moral and habitual life by his love of Paris and of French life. Francophilism among English people of influence was not so common in the nineteenth century that Dickens's love of France should not be welcomed as an enlightening, anti-insular force telling against Podsnappery, for Dickens's greatest influence was exactly among those middle classes who were most self-satisfiedly xenophobic. The Christmas Stories which had a

He loved the Paris food and drink: 'interior of des Trois Frere Provanceaux'.

peculiar appeal to his conventional readers contained many special tributes to France, 'the dear old France of my affections' – notably 'His Boots' in *Somebody's Luggage* (1862) and the whole of *Mrs Lirriper's Legacy* of 1864.

It is not to be supposed that Dickens's knowledge of France was either wide or deep. He was entertained lavishly; *Martin Chuzzlewit* was being serialized and generally talked about while he lived in Paris in 1856; he felt lionized and liked it; he spoke French well enough to feel that he could communicate; he loved the Paris theatre, the contrasts of its night life, its food and its drink and with characteristic morbid interest, its Morgue. He came to know the more

. . . and with characteristic morbid interest, its morgue.

established of the main figures in Paris in the world of the arts, but I know of no evidence that he was touched by the new movements that were transforming the novel or painting in France in the sixties, although he greatly influenced Alphonse Daudet. He remained in great degree the visiting Englishman, speaking French fluently with a strong English accent, with a firm foot in the British Embassy, where indeed he gave one of his most successful readings to a smart French audience in 1863. Hugo and even more Lamartine, whom he tried to popularize in England, commended themselves to him not only on literary but on political grounds. He looked with great hope to the 1848 revolution in France, where he thought his friend Lamartine would build a true radical democracy. All through the main period of his sojourn in France in the fifties, Napoleon III held sway. Dickens had not disliked Louis Napoleon when he met him in exile in London at Lady Blessington's Gore House, but he mistrusted him greatly as Emperor. Nevertheless, when the Crimean War broke out he welcomed it warmly, in part because it made England and France allies. A special incident is written into his Christmas Story, *Seven Poor Travellers*, of 1854, to make this point. He speaks most admiringly of the Empress Eugénie, whom he saw reviewing troops at Boulogne. As the war went on he came for many reasons to be its bitter opponent, but he always regarded its bringing France and England together as an unmixed blessing.

The crowd chanting '*mourir pour la Patrie*'.

However much he distrusted Napoleon III, I think that he would have been ardently pro-French had he lived the few months more necessary to have known the Franco-Prussian War.

France, and especially Paris, served as a standard to set up against England, and especially London, which all through the fifties he was coming more and more to dislike, more and more to despair of. It is in this light that we see his praise, for example, of the Paris Salon in 1855:

> It is of no use disguising the fact that what we know to be wanting in the men [the English painters] is wanting in their works – character, fire, purpose, and the want of using the vehicle and the model as mere means to an end. There is a horrid respectability about most of the best of them – a little finite, systematic routine in them, strangely expressive to me of the state of England itself . . . . There are no end of bad pictures among the French, but Lord! the goodness also! the fearlessness of them; the bold drawing; the dashing conception; the passion and action in them! . . . Don't think it a part of my despondency about public affairs, and my fear that our national glory is on the decline, when I say that mere form and conventionalities usurp, in English art, as in English government, and social relations, the place of living force and truth.

Yet it was not just as a counterpoise to Podsnappery or a relief from the limitations upon art and living by Mrs Grundy that he liked France. He could be critical. He was no lover of libertinism. He laughed at Wilkie Collins on their 1853 tour of Italy on this ground: 'he occasionally expounds a code of morals taken from French novels, which I instantly and with becoming gravity smash.' He saw the French insularity, ridiculing perhaps too easily their attempts to portray English life on the stage, although one of the funniest things in his letters is a long account of the absurdity of a Paris production of *As You Like It*. But he was also, I think, positive in finding there a concern for form in art, for ideas, for freedom from a devouring moralism, that he rather wistfully envied.

Dombey and Son

It was by walking the streets of Paris at night that Dickens released himself from the pent-up emotions he experienced in writing of little Paul Dombey's death. The first numbers of *Dombey and Son* had been published while he was still living in Switzerland and the last was written in March 1848 when he had been back from France nearly a year. The book was a tremendous success from the start; its sales were prodigious. Indeed from this time, though often feeling himself hard pressed by the cost of his dependants and the need to provide for many of them after his death, Dickens was never again in financial difficulties.

The success was richly deserved, for *Dombey and Son* surely represents a great advance in his art. With Paul Dombey Dickens begins that extraordinary study of the child's view of life, which is one of his great achievements in fiction. For all his concern with his own sufferings as a child, his early studies of children have much of that eighteenth-century treatment of them as puppets, mere creatures acted upon. Oliver Twist, the retarded Smike, the little dying boys of both *Oliver Twist* and *The Old Curiosity Shop* are all purely passive figures who never make a positive claim to our recognition. Young Bailey really only comes to life when his promotion to 'tiger' for Montague Tigg gives him a raffish adult existence like that of the Dodger, another real character who has never been a child. As for Little Nell – 'the child' as she is always called – she is far too peculiar a compound of emotions set up in the author and demanded from the reader to be a real child. With Paul Dombey a new reality begins. It is notable that one of Paul's persecutors, Mrs Pipchin, was drawn from Mrs Roylance, the woman to whom Dickens himself had been consigned in the worst days of the blacking factory. Working on *Dombey and Son* undoubtedly woke Dickens up to that recall of his own childhood that culminated in the next novel, *David Copperfield*. Dickens's long line of living children are the victims of two views of life – the Benthamite, economic treatment of the young as units of memory and of learning, a sort of sponge to absorb facts in order that they may take their useful place in a money-organized society; or secondly, as the victims of the Calvinist view of children as limbs of Satan, as unregenerate small mommets. Both views surely have their roots in the eighteenth century. Both deny the Dickensian world of love and imagination. Paul Dombey and the young Gradgrinds of *Hard Times* are victims of the money system view of children; Esther Summerson, the heroine of *Bleak House*, Pip of *Great Expectations* and Jo the crossing sweeper are victims of the limbs of Satan view; above all, David Copperfield suffers from this at the hands of the Murdstones. 'The gloomy theology of the Murdstones made all children out to be little vipers (though there *was* a child once set in the midst of the Disciples) and held that they contaminated one another.'

The first part of *Dombey and Son* is a superb attack upon the treatment of a child as a potential economic unit, even though, as Mr Dombey's son and heir to his great trading house, Paul's potential is for a status of wealth and power. The story of the education of Paul, first at Mrs Pipchin's and then at Dr Blimber's Academy, is a model of humour, compassion, and economy of narration. There is hardly a spare word in this first quarter of the book. For those to whom right education is the key to social decency, this first part of *Dombey* along with *Hard Times*, must be accounted the most important books that Dickens ever wrote, for they are certainly among the most efficient parables of false education and its results that have ever been written. It was also a master-stroke to make Paul 'an old-fashioned' child, for in this way he is quite naturally able to assert his own identity and so to free Dickens from that negative, passive quality by which he had previously tried to suggest the innocence of children. Paul is innocent but he is also devastating: ' "Well, sir," said Mrs Pipchin to Paul, "how do you think you shall like me?" "I don't think I shall like you at all," replied Paul, "I want to go away. This isn't my house." "No, it's mine," retorted Mrs Pipchin. "It's a very nasty one," said Paul.'

If *Dombey and Son* had ended with Paul's death it would have been, like *Hard Times*, a remarkable sketch about the killing of the human soul by the destruction of children's feelings; but Dickens's concern in the novel was far larger; it was with the education of a deadened, proud and spiritually maimed man through his experience of life so that he could learn to love; and this education was to be conveyed in a total survey of English society showing the forces of death that had control in every sphere of power and the forces of love that lay hidden in less eminent positions, among the absurd, the meek and the simple. To say that he totally succeeds in this vast New Testament parable would be untrue, although undoubtedly it is a parable extolling the New Testament over the old, as we see when we are told on the same page that the eccentric but loving Captain Cuttle 'always read for himself, before going to bed, a certain Divine Sermon once delivered on a Mount', and that Rob the Grinder, the boy corrupted by the cruelties and hypocrisies of the charity school, 'had been developed by the perpetual bruising of his intellectual shins against all the proper names of all the tribes of Judah'. Compared with his later masterpieces there are many faults in *Dombey and Son*, chiefly because he was exploring for the first time new devices and ways of expressing his view of life, which are sometimes used with less skill than he later developed.

But the first part, the story of Paul, cannot be divorced from the rest of the book without a destruction of the whole. The true theme of the book – Mr Dombey's relation to his loving, neglected daughter, Florence, is carefully led up to as early as the masterly chapter IV where at the end Walter Gay toasts: 'So here's to Dombey – and Son – and Daughter.' The first part of *Dombey and Son*, telling of the childhood and death of Mr Dombey's first heir, is in fact wonderfully closely united with the second part telling of the failure of Mr Dombey's search for a second heir in his disastrous, bought second marriage to Edith Grainger; together they form a total novel that is concerned with the discovery by Mr Dombey, in the failure of all his hopes, that love in the person of his daughter has been beside him all the time unnoticed and despised. A small example of this unity must suffice to illustrate the beautiful, detailed control of Dickens's grasp. In the first part Mrs Pipchin appears as one of the false educators of little Paul – a comic character but also a hard, embittered, selfish woman grieving over her late husband's rash investments in Peruvian mines, she conveys her plight to little Paul and his sister. In this capacity she tells the powerful Mr Dombey, 'There is a great deal of nonsense – and worse – talked about young people not being pressed too hard at first, and being tempted on, and all the rest of it, Sir. It never was thought of in my time, and it has no business to be thought of now. My opinion is "Keep 'em at it".' Years later Mrs Pipchin is brought by Mr Dombey as housekeeper into his mansion in order to teach his second wife that he does not think her fit to command his great establishment. But when that wife runs away from him and his business fails he is brought almost to second childhood. Mrs Pipchin then echoes her old no-nonsense sentiments, but this time about the great man himself:

'Hoity! Toity!' said Mrs Pipchin, rubbing her nose. 'There's a great fuss, I think, about it. It an't so wonderful a case. People have had misfortunes before now, and been obliged to part with their furniture. I'm sure I have! . . . It's a pity he didn't have a little more to do with mines. They'd have tried his temper for him.'

But before I suggest the many devices of this kind by which Dickens, some-times more, sometimes less successfully, strengthens his narrative, it is well to say that in *Dombey and Son* he first achieves that complete social panorama towards which he seems to have been moving from the beginning of his career. For the first time, and with one stroke, he introduces the upper classes with complete success into this novel; and, what is more, makes their representatives stand for that very conflict of values which are the novel's total concern.

Dombey and Son: 'Major Bagstock is delighted to
have that opportunity' by Phiz.

In Mrs Skewton and Major Bagstock, Dickens produced the funniest, the most violent and the most frightening attack upon worldly values embodied in Regency manners, in the whole of his work. We can tell that Major Bagstock is a man who will toady to anyone who will gratify his appetite for the good things of life and his snobbish desire to be in the right set, as soon as he tells Mr Dombey, indicating little Paul, '" My little friend here, Sir, will certify for Joseph Bagstock that he is a thorough-going, downright, plain spoken Old Trump, Sir, and nothing more. That boy, Sir," in a lower tone "will live in history. That boy, Sir, is not a common production. Take care of him, Mr Dombey." ' These are the perfect humours of the falseness of the world.

But a greater achievement – and very unexpected in Dickens as he had shown himself up to that time – is the production of two other equally fashionable men, who embody the innocence and goodness of life as effectively and movingly as any of his more socially humble characters. To show the unworldly in a garb of an absurd parody of worldliness is a remarkable achievement. Cousin Feenix, the debilitated, impoverished peer, has only a few feeble jokes about the House in his day and Mr Pitt, and a few sporting stories about Regency boxers as his stock in trade; yet in his conduct as well as in his sentiments he succeeds wholly in convincing us that the human heart can survive a vast deal of Clubman aimlessness. Mr Toots is perhaps the finest of all Dickens's divine idiots, but who would have expected Dickens to clothe goodness in the shape of a young man of money, whose highest ambition is to be seen in the company of that splendid, though parasitical representative of the Fancy, 'The Game Chicken'? Mr Toots and Cousin Feenix are a very important step forward in Dickens's embodiment in fiction of his belief in the greater importance of the heart than of the head. With them he succeeds entirely where Dostoevsky was less secure – in making us respect persons whose every utterance is totally ludicrous; indeed in making us respect them *for* this, because their absurdity sets them off against the calculating, mean society which the author is attacking.

In *Dombey and Son*, with Mr Toodles the engine driver and his wet nurse wife, Dickens for the first time embodies a working class (neither criminal nor faithful servants), independent, performing a meaningful function, good, and equally respectably absurd. All classes, in fact, are represented in this novel, and none are treated with that innate petty bourgeois prejudice which had lingered in his humour from his *Sketches by Boz* days. The mark of this, indeed, is the understanding and compassion shown for Miss Tox, the genteel spinster with her foolish illusions about Mr Dombey's regard for her – such a person would have been a stock joke in his earlier novels. This proper concern for people as human and not as units in a journalistic joke is reflected in the formal writing of the book; for the first time every character is fully related to the theme of the novel.

In the great house of Dombey, the importing firm, Dickens has found a centre for the organization of the society he is portraying. The picture he gives of the working of the firm is somewhat vague, more so than that of the Anglo-Bengalee Disinterested Life Insurance Company in *Martin Chuzzlewit*. Indeed Dickens was never to bring alive the functions of an organization as Zola did in his novels. However, he uses other devices, less journalistic, less detailedly realistic than the sort of treatment Zola provided for department stores or mines. In the first place, the business house of Mr Dombey is closely connected with his great private household. Whenever events of importance happen – little Paul's christening, Mr Dombey's second marriage, his homecoming after the honeymoon, Edith's flight, the failure of the business – all these are orchestrated by two choruses, the reactions of the clerks at the business, and the reactions of the servants at the house. And in Mr Perch, the office messenger, whose wife is often below stairs in the Dombey private household, we have a perfect link between the two.

Into these brilliant passages, which punctuate the fortunes of Mr Dombey, Dickens for the first time also lets loose a timely, controlled stream of imagery. The christening feast will suffice to show his powers:

> 'Mr John,' said Mr Dombey, 'will you take the bottom of the table, if you please? What have you got there, Mr John?' 'I have got a cold fillet of veal here, Sir. What have *you* got there, Sir?' 'This,' returned Mr Dombey, 'is some cold preparation of calf's head, I think. I see cold fowls – ham – patties – salad – lobster. Miss Tox will do me the honour of taking some wine? Champagne to Miss Tox.' There was a toothache in everything. The wine was so bitter cold that it forced a little scream from Miss Tox, which she had great difficulty in turning into a 'Hem!' The veal had come from such an airy pantry that the first taste of it had struck a sensation as of cold lead into Mr Chick's extremities. Mr Dombey alone remained unmoved. He might have been hung up for sale at a Russian fair as a specimen of a frozen gentleman.

For the first time Dickens's poetry is not only diffused throughout the novel, instead of being presented in chunks of sudden 'poetic language', but it is also made strictly to serve the author's intentions.

I do not think that the symbolic devices of the novel work so well. Unlike the fog of *Bleak House* or the prisons of *Little Dorrit*, the image of the sea which speaks for death and the hope for immortality is too wide and vague. We can accept its force when the dying little Paul asks, 'What are the wild waves saying?'; we can see how it has no message for the paralyzed, dying, worldly Mrs Skewton: 'She lies and listens to it by the hour; but its speech is dark and gloomy to her, and a dread is on her face, and when her eyes wander over the expanse, they see but a broad stretch of desolation between earth and heaven.' But the ending of the same chapter that tells of Mrs Skewton's death tries to extend the sea's symbolisms to the dead, bitter future that lies before her daughter, Edith, the second Mrs Dombey of the loveless marriage, and at once Dickens falls into an inflation that is on the edge of the ridiculous: 'Edith standing there alone and listening to its waves, has dank weed cast up at her feet, to strew her path in life withal.'

The symbolism of the railway that also runs through the book is more successful than the sea. To begin with, it absolutely fits into the social theme of the book: Mr Dombey, the proud individualistic merchant, belongs to the past and the railway speaks to him only of death; he fears it as do the inhabitants of Stagg's Gardens whose houses stand in the way of the new northern line. But Dickens shows how the lives of these same people are benefited by the progress they feared. Up to this point the symbolism is clear – the railway is progress and Dickens is on its side. But with the dramatic death of Mr Carker, the villainous manager and would-be seducer of Edith Dombey, broken in pieces by an express train, the railway seems to become normal vengeance rather than progress. With the fog of *Bleak House* four years later Dickens showed that he had learned to use symbolism that was simple and coherent, to give extra dimension to the novel instead of the vague and muddled symbols of *Dombey and Son*.

Yet *Dombey and Son* could be counted not only a brilliant novel but a fully successful work of art if it were not for the two main women, Florence and Edith Dombey. If only they were treated with that mixture of compassion and ridicule that Mr Dombey is given, they would have life. Mr Dombey (brilliantly reinforced by Phiz's drawings) is surely one of the best, most fully rounded of Dickens's obsessed characters, an unique presentation of a humour seen from all sides. But then Mr Dombey is a man and can be accorded the human treatment and respect of being laughed at. Edith Dombey is a beautiful woman, she can therefore not be exposed to the full compassion that may be given to ordinary humanity, the dignity of being occasionally ridiculed, the charm of being absurd. With Lady Dedlock Dickens did better in *Bleak House*; but it was very late in his career, if ever, that he could do his heroines the justice of bestowing upon them his greatest gift, his mockery.

David Copperfield

Dombey and Son, as I have said, has echoes of Dickens's childhood. It was appropriately finished in March 1848 at Brighton, scene of little Paul's dialogue with the waves and of Mrs Skewton's grisly death. Already the Christmas Book for 1847, *The Haunted Man*, had shown overtones of his bitterness about his childhood. A little before this he had written the autobiographical fragment on which our knowledge of his months at Warren's is based, but the misery of his recall of the failure of his romantic love for Maria Beadnell had proved too great for him to go on with these memoirs. In February 1849, also at Brighton, he began *David Copperfield*, the novel which incorporates more of his own life more openly than any of his other novels: 'I really think I have done it ingeniously and with a very complicated interweaving of truth and fiction.' It ran with enormous success until October 1850, and signifies, whatever other merits or demerits it possesses, a full and powerfully reinforced return to himself after the flight first into the historic past of the Gordon riots and then abroad.

Other more immediate experiences played a part in the making of this famous novel. From the time of his residence in Switzerland Dickens had been actively discussing with Miss Coutts a project for establishing a house for fallen women. After very careful planning and selection of suitable candidates (many the inmates of a prison) Urania Cottage in Shepherd's Bush was opened in November 1847. This was one of Dickens's most successful and most persistent social works. He continued some active supervision of the home until his separation from his wife in 1858 caused a coolness between him and Miss Coutts. His individual charities were not generally known; indeed his philanthropy in general was not advertised to the public. It is necessary to stress this, for our information of his constant social services from his letters may lead us to forget that these were private. His article in *Household Words* in 1853, 'Home for Homeless Women', describing Urania Cottage, was, like the major part of the contributions to that periodical, anonymous. The home, run on New Testament teaching only, was a model of shrewd discipline and friendly, sympathetic, unpuritanical treatment. Many of the inmates were assisted to emigrate, married and prospered. The language of the 'Appeal to Fallen Women' (1846), which Dickens addressed to women prisoners in seeking suitable inmates, has a strangely emotional, rhetorical note:

> There is a lady in the town [Miss Coutts] who, from the windows of her house [in Piccadilly] has seen such as you going past at night and has felt her heart bleed at the sight. She is what is called a great lady; but she has looked after you with compassion, as being of her own sex and nature, and the lot of such fallen women has troubled her in bed. She has resolved to open, at her own expense, a place of refuge very near London, for a small number of females who without such help are lost forever; and to make it a HOME for them.

That a man who, from his letters, we see to have administered this home with humour, good sense and understanding, should have sought to open it with such an appeal makes us perhaps less surprised at the conventional, unreal, Magdalen treatment of Martha, the fallen woman of *David Copperfield*. But we can only regret that his admirable social work should have coincided with the novel to provide it with a character so little required. His preoccupation with emigration to Australia as a social benefit is not happy in its effect on the ending of the novel. These purely journalistic intrusions are the more odd as *David Copperfield* is a metaphysical rather than a social novel. Even more obtrusive and unnecessary to the novel is the whole chapter towards the end of the book where David as a well-known author visits a model prison in which Littimer and Uriah Heep are shown to prosper hypocritically under the separate system of imprisonment, which had by now become Dickens's penological King Charles's head.

More striking is an indication of the way in which the immediate and the long digested combine together in his fiction. In January 1849, only a month before he started writing *David Copperfield*, he made an expedition with his *Punch* friends, Leech and Mark Lemon, to Norfolk. The occasion was a very Dickensian one – to see Stanfield Hall near Norwich, scene of the recent Rush murder. But the murderous associations proved disappointing and the party went on to Yarmouth. They stayed there two days, on one of which they walked over to Lowestoft. Here Dickens must have seen a signpost to Blunderstone, though it is unlikely that he visited the village. From this casual contact came the birthplace of David Copperfield a month later, concealing its association with his own life. From it too came all the Peggotty scenes at Yarmouth and the magnificent storm scene in which Ham and Steerforth die. The reality of the East Anglian setting of that shipwreck shows that his quick journalistic eye for scene could be as fruitful for his fiction as his sudden journalistic social concerns could be digressive and weakening.

David Copperfield was, not surprisingly, Dickens's own favourite novel: 'I don't mind confiding to you, that I can never approach the book with perfect composure, it had such perfect possession of me when I wrote it,' he told a correspondent some years later. Although its immediate serial sales were not so high as those of *Dombey and Son*, it soon acquired great popularity and

Emigration to Australia: 'Second Class – the Parting' by Abraham Solomon.

fame both in England and abroad. Dostoevsky a few years later, emerging from the first incarcerated stage of his Siberian exile and permitted to read books, asked for this new Dickens before any other. Its influence on his work was considerable.

David Copperfield had still, forty years ago when I was a boy, a sort of 'classical' status that perhaps no other of Dickens's novels enjoyed. If critics were asked to name an English novel worthy to stand among the great fiction of all time – *War and Peace* and so on – *David Copperfield* was very likely to be their choice. This great reputation had been handed down from Victorian times. It still remains a highly esteemed and very popular novel, but I doubt if most critics now would rank it quite so highly either among world fiction or among Dickens's own works. Told in the first person, it is Dickens's great

The separate system, Pentonville chapel; the silent system, Millbank workshop.

internal – what used to be called 'psychological' – novel, a Proustian novel of the shaping of life through the echoes and prophesies of memory. As such, it is beautifully told. We are always conscious of David looking back and asking himself when this happened or that happened, did I have any intuition of where it was leading me? And when he decides now and again that, yes, there were intimations, overtones that had led him to feel apprehensive, or restless, or sad, so beautifully is the book constructed that we forget altogether that it is an artefact, made up by Dickens, and we consider only the reliability of David Copperfield as a guide to the meaning of his own past life; and usually we are convinced, so balanced and careful and real is the sense of remembered things, that David is a valuable guide, that this is how it happened. In this sense *David Copperfield*, the least socially integrated of Dickens's novels, the most internal, is paradoxically the most 'real'. In part, as with Proust's Marcel, this is because with D. C. (David Copperfield) we are so close to the reality of C. D. (Charles Dickens). But it is so even more because of Dickens's superb artistry in the management of the narratives, of the echoes and the overtones of memory. In this one respect *David Copperfield* seems to me quite the artistic equal of *A la Recherche du Temps Perdu*.

The book is admirably constructed in another way, for this recall of the past is also David's lesson of life. From the shape of his past he learns that we cannot live in dreams, that, in the popular Victorian quotation from Longfellow, 'life is real, life is earnest'; he learns to strengthen his will; he finds achievement through discipline and duty; he learns, in short, 'true happiness'.

Above all, he learns that romantic love (the sort of love that had so cruelly hurt Dickens in the collapse of his hopes for Maria Beadnell), a love that distorts and falsifies our view of the loved one, can bring only unhappiness and regret. This is splendidly shown in David's own life, where we see that the little, spoilt child-wife, who was his mother, is absolutely repeated in his choice of a little, spoilt child-wife, Dora (modelled upon Maria Beadnell). But Dickens was not content with that; and one of the glories of the novel is the way in

HORRID MURDER,
Committed by a young Man on a young Woman.

The scene of a recent murder.

which the theme is repeated again and again in a series of different relationships: David's worship of his friend, Steerforth, already made trivial and false by the worship given him by *his* mother; old Dan Peggotty's worship and spoiling of his niece, Emily; Doctor Strong's blind worship of *his* child-wife, Annie; Aunt Betsy's romantic, ruined marriage; Mr Wickfield's blind concern for his daughter, Agnes, which ruins not her but himself. So subtly are these told that they seem (often to modern critics disconcertingly) like a series of unconnected stories; yet after one has closed the book, the repetition of theme is what leaves a strong impact. All this, and the complete mastery of scene and character (the Micawbers, Heep, Steerforth, Rosa Dartle, the Murdstones, all for the price of one book!) and narrative certainly make *David Copperfield* a sort of masterpiece. And yet at the end of it, I think, there is a disagreeable sense that this most inner of Dickens's novels is the most shallow, the most smoothly running, the most complacent – indeed, in the pejorative use of that word, the most Victorian.

The reasons for this are in part social and in part something deeper. David learns the lessons of life, and through hard work and the acquirement of a steady will, he becomes a famous novelist: 'I had advanced in fame and fortune, my domestic joy was perfect,' is what he tells us of himself. 'Having some foundation for believing, by this time, that nature and accident had made me an author, I pursued my vocation with confidence. Without such assurance I should certainly have left it alone, and bestowed my energy on some other endeavour. I should have tried to find out what nature and accident had really made me, and to be that, and nothing else.' And again, 'the more praise I got, the more I tried to deserve.' There is nothing wrong with all this; Dickens did work hard at his craft to improve the great powers that nature had given him. There are many letters to aspiring writers over his whole career, stressing this point. For those who liked to dwell on the sober, hardworking, competent, efficient, commonsensical side of Dickens, which, as I said in an earlier chapter, is certainly a great part of him, *David Copperfield* will be a very sympathetic book. But although the demonic, driven side of Dickens may have been exaggerated, it *is* there and it constitutes a great deal of the unique side of his genius. There is nothing of it in David.

But, it may well be objected, David Copperfield is not Charles Dickens; to demand this is to impose our knowledge of biographical background on a work of fiction. Very well, but I think one still asks in a book which tells us of an author's genesis some indication greater than an assertion of natural capacity improved by hard work, and this without demanding of Dickens any aesthetic view of the purpose of life such as we get from Proust. David Copperfield as a writer (and it is to this that his story brings us) is too much like Trollope as he tells us he was in his autobiography. In the long run, by making art so much a matter of moral duty, Dickens diminishes it as he criticized Thackeray for doing, although in a different way.

But this sort of philistine, bourgeois, complacent view of his powers as a writer only reflects the social and ethical whole of the book. No novel of Dickens is so bounded by middle-class horizons. Once or twice in the novel – at the Waterbrooks's dinner party, and when considering Mr Spenlow's complacent view of the machinery of the law – Dickens the social critic peeps out through David. But for the rest it seems as though David's battle to emerge from the pains and the illusions of his childhood and youth have left him exhausted, fit only for the comfortable domestic fireside with his good angel, Agnes, and the round of good works that she suggests his fame demands of him.

When David returns from his healing travels after the deaths of Dora and Steerforth, Agnes asks, 'Have you any intention of going away again?' 'What does my sister say to that?' 'I hope now . . . I think you ought not, since you ask me. Your growing reputation and success enlarge your power of doing good; and if *I* could spare my brother, perhaps the time could not.' Dickens in this philanthropic and Unitarian phase of his life may have thought that his literary genius was intended solely to make him powerful in 'doing good', but we cannot. And we know that an author who could see society and its evil so wholly as he had done in *Dombey and Son* will not find 'good work' enough as a solution. Indeed in the next chapter we shall see that he did not. *David Copperfield* on this social level is the epitome of Victorian bourgeois morality. But its insufficiency is deeper than purely social. David's life of good works must be seen in a Christian context, but it is exactly here that the novel, and with it Dickens's very sincere Christian beliefs, seem inadequate to give meaning to life. He has mocked at romantic love, at the distorting power of passion, and he makes his case; yet the complacent domestic fireside of Agnes seems an empty thing to put in its place. He has inveighed against the cruel Calvinist creed of the Murdstones and he more than makes his case; yet a Christianity of 'doing good' seems somehow as empty without grace as his wonderful social observation does when denied the total view of society which he had glimpsed in *Dombey and Son* and was to see whole in his next novel, *Bleak House*. This is perhaps why Dickens, in compensation, gives one of the finest portrayals in fiction of that secular semblance of grace, called charm, in the marvellously living character of Steerforth.

Chapter V
England, Home and Beauty 1850–8

o Charles Dickens like David Copperfield (but hardly so permanently) came home. Though not without hesitations. In 1847 he wrote to a friend: 'If you should have any commands for Australia after *Dombey* is finished, I think of making a little excursion there. I shall come home by way of China.' And throughout the fifties private and public life so pressed upon him that over and above the foreign jaunts with friends and the lengthy family stays in France, in 1854 he speaks of:

> Dreadful thoughts of getting away somewhere by myself . . . the Pyrenees . . . . I have visions for living half a year or so in all sorts of inaccessible places. A floating idea of going up above the snow-line in Switzerland, and living in some astonishing convent, hovers about me . . . . Restlessness, you will say. Whatever it is, it is always driving me, and I cannot help it. I have rested nine or ten weeks, and sometimes feel as if it had been a year – though I had the strangest nervous miseries before I stopped. If I couldn't walk fast and far, I should just explode and perish.

Nevertheless there was, as Agnes told David, the urgent fact that his growing reputation and success enlarged his power of doing good in England and there were many other positive reasons for being at home beside. But much though Dickens relied on Paris or Boulogne as a refuge from the growing tensions of his life in England during the fifties, it is impossible to imagine him as an expatriate – at any rate, in the bohemian way of life that had been laid down for the expatriate artist since the days of Shelley and Byron. The literary-journalistic world in which Dickens moved in England was not without its irregularities, whether high-minded like the union of George Lewes and George Eliot, or the lifetime of separated marriage of one of the chief contributors to his magazine, Mrs Lynn Linton, or the curious half-submerged ménages of his younger friend, Wilkie Collins; but all these were woven into patterns of regular work and/or social devotion.

The sort of lives that expatriates often tended to lead were eccentric and undisciplined in a way that was abhorrent to Dickens, who loathed all things

untidy and messy. There is the account of the Thompson regime that he wrote
to Catherine during his 1853 visit to Italy:

> Coming upon them unawares, I found Thompson with a pointed beard, smoking a
> great German pipe, in a pair of slippers – the two little girls [one was the future poet,
> Alice Meynell, who wrote decades later the only really good analysis of Dickens's
> style of writing] very pale and faint from the climate, in a singularly untidy state
> – one (Heaven knows why) without stockings – and both with their little short hair
> cropped in a manner never before beheld, and a little bow stuck on the top of it.
> Christiana said that she had invented this head gear as a picturesque thing – adding
> that perhaps it was and perhaps it wasn't . . . . We had disturbed her at her painting
> in oils; and I rather received an impression that what with that, and what with the
> music, the household affairs went a little to the wall. Thompson was teaching the
> two little girls the multiplications, in a disorderly old billiard room with all manner
> of messes in it.

In that year he had already shown in *Bleak House*, with Mrs Jellyby, that
attention to foreign missions could lead a woman away from her true domestic
role; now there was Christiana Thompson and art to drive the lesson home to
Catherine.

For the next decade, with the refreshment of the foreign visits mentioned in
the last chapter, he gave himself up to hard work, to artistic and social duty,
to vigorous exercise, absorbed relaxation, and to maintaining his household
in the same cheerful discipline as himself; the really tragic irony was that by
the decade's end he was caught in a domestic situation more sadly messy than
any expatriate's, if only because it was alien to all he respected in life.

Household Words and social views

First in importance, now that he was settled at home again (by 1851 in a grand
family mansion, Tavistock House in Tavistock Square) was to find a regular
centre for his ideas and energies. As early as 1845 he had hankered after editing
a weekly magazine, 'price three halfpence, if possible; partly original, partly
select, notices of books, notices of theatres, notices of all good things, notices
of all bad ones; Carol philosophy, cheerful views, sharp anatomization of
humbug, jolly good temper; papers always in season, pat to the time of the year,
and a vein of glowing, hearty, generous, mirthful, beaming reference in everything to Home and fireside . . . .' But a month later the idea had turned into
the Christmas Book, *A Cricket on the Hearth*. Then had come the disaster of the
Daily News. But with *David Copperfield* well in train, with his return home
sure in every sense, the idea pressed upon him again, and in March 1850
appeared the first number of *Household Words*. From that date until his death
twenty years later he was an active editor of such a periodical, although a
quarrel with his publishers, Bradbury and Evans, at the time of his separation
from Catherine, led to the foundation of his own magazine, *All the Year Round*,
in 1859. The enterprise had certain attractions for him purely on grounds of
financial certainty; for editing *Household Words* he received not only £500 a

year but was part-owner of the enterprise. But the greatest value to him was the close relation it gave him to his readers, both for expression of his social and ethical views, and for the publication of fiction of the kind that he thought good and wanted by the public. The first number announced: 'We aspire to live in the Household affections and be numbered among the Household thoughts of our readers . . . to be associated with the harmless laughter and gentle tears of many hearts.'

He had at the start two sub-editors. One of these, the erratic, somewhat dubious Horne, went a little later to Australia, a lucky event for it left Dickens with W. H. Wills as his chief assistant. I have indicated how precious his friendships were to Dickens; and if they are to be measured by the degree that they lightened and helped his work, and so made his overburdened life a happier one, Wills must stand very high in the list. To have found a competent man to sit in the office each day, a man to undertake all the donkey work and yet to be subject to Dickens's close scrutiny even from abroad, a man to be open to continuous order and counter-order, was a piece of marvellous luck for an editor of Dickens's temperament and determination, for he knew that he was a first-rate editor and he did not intend his sub-editor to usurp any of the finally deciding functions.

The intimacy of Dickens's correspondence, especially over his separation from Catherine, with John Forster, the old friend who had fought all his early publishers' battles for him and had been his ever ready confidant in the writing

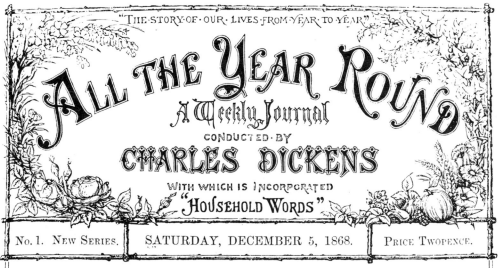

Title page of *All the Year Round*, incorporating *Household Words*, 1868.

of his novels, shows that their close friendship did not, as is sometimes said, lapse with the years. But Forster, although his marriage in middle age inevitably prevented him from being Dickens's constantly available adviser, resented Wills, as he did also Dickens's new literary and playtime companion, Wilkie Collins, the younger novelist. In 1856 Forster who had been part-proprietor of *Household Words*, withdrew from the paper and Dickens immediately gave his shares to Wills. Wilkie Collins was a frequent and most successful contributor to this magazine and its successor, and during 1856 a sort of third editor. But important though Collins was (with some other young journalists and writers) in giving Dickens in these last two decades a sense of being in touch with the young, much though he loosened Dickens's view of pleasure, and valuable though he was in stimulating Dickens's general ideas about writing, he was primarily a novelist, and no novelist could give over a long period the time or concern that Dickens required. Forster, then, and Wills, of all that extraordinary array of talented men and women whose friendship Dickens commanded, were closest to his work. It is moving to note that they were the two people who had the courage to batter, however unsuccessfully, against Dickens's determination to go on his last reading tour to America, which probably did much to shorten his life. And it is a sign of his respect and affection for them that he listened to their objections with gratitude, though without giving way.

Household Words and its successor *All the Year Round* are important to the study of the world of Dickens's novels in three ways: firstly, on three different occasions the need to maintain the high circulation of these magazines forced from him novels whose shape and length are much conditioned by appearing first as weekly serials; secondly, in his letters to contributors we have a collection of his views on the writing of fiction that up to a point illuminates his own practice – the craftsmanship, rather than the deeper aspects of his art; thirdly, and most interestingly, the magazines were the forum for his ideas upon every sort of social question – poverty, crime, education, factory conditions, the position of women, divorce, foreign missions, housing, hygiene and sanitation, trade unions, administrative reform. These views are closely connected with his treatment of the themes in his novels and with his private views put forward in his letters; but the three are by no means always in agreement, and from the differences we can see much of the pressures and strains that often made Dickens in the last twenty years of his life a seemingly divided, contradictory man.

So much has been said in recent years of the contradictory nature of Dickens's views of English society, so much to suggest that he was muddle-headed, that it needs to be said straight away that in one thing he was absolutely consistent – his respect for and trust in the English working class. He was implacable in his condemnation of criminals of every class, but one of the reasons for this severity was his belief that sentimentality or misplaced romanticism was securing benefits for criminals that were being denied to the decent poor. By temperament, indeed, and by the hardness he had imposed upon himself in gaining his success and independence as a writer, he was a

'The Bottle', plate V: Cold, misery and want destroy their youngest child.

paternalistic, masterful man – as inclined to domineer in his lively, happy, exuberant moods as in his angry, despondent, impatient ones. Perhaps the underlying irony of his life is that a man who believed so deeply in the New Testament virtues, in the Sermon on the Mount, in humanity, forgiveness and mercy, who hated so much the angry God of the Old Testament, should have had so much of Jehovah in him (of the benevolent Jehovah as well as the fierce one) – but then so did Jesus. And again, despite all his histrionics, his indulgence in emotion, he was so often a very tender, loving man. This conflict did cause some inconsistency in his view of the society he lived in, particularly in his expression of that view; but it did far more harm, as we shall see, where he himself suffered most, in his relations with his own children. The truth is that if he did not always see very clearly, he saw very deeply into the world he lived in; perhaps indeed not clearly because so deeply.

This is the real reason why he sometimes (but not so often as some critics have implied) parted company with intellectuals and experts, people who could think clearly or who knew the facts. In part – and it is the bad part of him – it was that he had not been very well educated, and he maintained many of the philistine prejudices of the class he had been born into; but very much more it was that he thought many answers of intellectuals and experts on matters which concerned human beings to be too clear, too simple; that they left out feeling (in this, at least, he was the unambiguous heir of the Romantics, and gave a moral shape to his master, Laurence Sterne), or pretended that people were numbers, or adopted the easy sort of false realism that could eliminate or reduce to permanent misery a few thousand human beings in the name of economic laws, or of efficiency, or of a more rational, clear view of a better future.

He was not dismissive of intellect or reason, but only of what he thought monstrous or absurd perversions of it. One of his most moving accounts of the horrors of the destitute, one of his finest tributes to the generosity of spirit of the very poor, 'A Night Scene in London' of 1856, makes this clear in its ending. He refuses, he says, to join 'with the unreasonable disciples of a reasonable school', who say that these things ought to be in order to maintain the health of the economy:

> Without disparaging these indispensable sciences in their sanity, I utterly renounce and abominate them in their insanity; and I address people with a respect for the New Testament, who do mind such things, and who think them infamous in our streets.

So much has been said of his determination from the blacking factory days to leave common men and boys behind him, that it sometimes seems as though modern critics had forgotten what Victorians did not, that he recompensed for this all his life by making the welfare of common boys and men, and women and girls, the object of a very great part of his time, of his extraordinary energies and of his fierce affections. And his respect increased over the years

'Letter from Papa' by Frederick Goodall, c. 1855. 'God bless you my darling – I long to be back with you again, and to see the sweet Babs.' Letter to his wife, Catherine, 1838.

as we may see from comparing two letters about working-class readers of his works. The first, written in 1844 of the *Christmas Carol*: 'I assure you it would have given me heartfelt satisfaction to have been in your place when you read my little Carol to the Poor in your neighbourhood. I have great faith in the Poor; to the best of my ability I always try to present them in a favourable light to the Rich; and I shall never cease . . . to advocate their being made as happy and wise as the circumstances of their condition in its utmost improvement, will admit of their becoming.' The second, written of a Birmingham audience in 1853, says: 'I never saw . . . such an interesting sight as the working people's night. There were two thousand five hundred of them here, and a more delicately observant audience it is impossible to imagine. They lost nothing, misinterpreted nothing . . . and animated me to that extent that I felt as if we were going up into the clouds together.'

This appreciation of the working people as an audience is only an extension of his constant concern, from *Sketches by Boz* onwards, to protect the relaxations and pleasures of the poor from incursions by moralists, Sabbatarians, or cultural snobs. As he said in those early sketches: 'The occasional foolery of working boys is more tolerable than whiskered dandyism.' There is an element of paternalism in this as in most of his actions. He was stern against rowdyism. Nevertheless this sense of the positive, happy quality of the lives of the people, when for a second the crushing burden of work or of material misery was lifted from them, prevents him from presenting the poor as a dramatic tableau of horror and distress, as much as it does from labelling them as anonymous statistics in a blueprint for greater efficiency or future utopia, or indeed as figures in a moral fable. He was, for example, well aware of the degree to which cheap drink and the resultant drunkenness was a barrier to the betterment of the lives of working people – the brickmakers' home in *Bleak House*, Stephen's drunken wife in *Hard Times*, the drunkard father of the Doll's Dressmaker in *Our Mutual Friend* bring the lesson home in his fiction; in his own experience his faithful servant John, who fell to pilfering at the magazine office, was pestered by a drunken wife. But he knew at once that Cruikshank's fanatical pictures of workers and their wives dragged down into disaster by a single indulgence in a drink with their Christmas goose was a story that treated them as automatons, not as living beings. Drink, he insisted, was in the main the result of misery, not misery of drink.

This appreciation of the good life of the poor – of the Plornishes, the Nubbles, the Toodles – is the more admirable because it is never sentimentalized; never, as sometimes seems the case with, say, Orwell, treated as the best life, or even the warmest, richest life; there is no compounding with the horrors of the slums. It is also the more remarkable in that the larger part of Dickens's knowledge of the life of the poor was for a variety of reasons – reformist, journalistic, emotional, sensational, obsessive and genuinely compassionate – a knowledge of misery, of workhouses and ragged schools, of down-and-outs and prostitutes, of asylums and orphanages and poor people's hospitals, of prisons and criminals' dens. From this knowledge, desultorily at first, then

'The Great Exhibition' by Thomas Colman Dibden, 1851. 'I have always had an instinctive feeling against the Exhibition.' Letter to Wills, 1851.

more concentratedly connecting poverty, ignorance, slums and crime as in *Oliver Twist*, he had been led on to stating his priorities: first and immediately slum clearance, decent housing; second and more permanently some education. To these all other concerns – prison reform, women's rights, foreign missions – must be subordinated. Without these two the shameful blot on England would remain; without them there could be no proper hope for civil order; without them there was always the infection of crime and of disease to make nonsense of the domestic happiness of the better off, of the bourgeois wedding bells that gave happy endings to his own novels; without them the Sermon on the Mount was gibberish to the vast, illiterate masses like Jo and a hypocrisy for all the 'decent' folk above him, who professed to follow it.

His realization that these were the two key approaches to social decency had come gradually. The importance of slum clearance and better housing is implicit in the warrens where Fagin and the other vermin scuttle, but any serious concern for rebuilding came from his friendship with Thomas South-wood Smith. He had first known this reformer and medical man when Smith was Commissioner on the Employment of Young People way back in the early forties. The Commission's reports of the atrocities small children suffered in mines and factories had roused Dickens's horror. A few years later Southwood Smith had shown him 'the dreadful hours of labour which at this time prevail'. Yet once again here his immediate feelings for what being poor meant prevented him from taking the longer view, 'the necessity of a mighty change I see, yet I cannot reconcile it to myself to reduce the earnings of any family – their means of existence being so very scant and spare'. Indeed, it was the realization of conflicts of feeling of this kind that forced him on beyond charity or even single reforms to a more total view of society's evils. It was Southwood Smith's expert information about insanitary conditions, however, that led him to see decent housing as the first step. From that time (1843) on he held to this priority. The cholera outbreak of 1850 did much to underline his view. In 1852 he had the opportunity to advise Miss Coutts on one of the most important slum clearance and rehousing schemes of Victorian London – eventually Columbia square model flats. But a far worse cholera epidemic in 1854 producing no serious reaction from the government provoked from Dickens an article in *Household Words*, 'To Working Men', which alarmed many of his friends, including Miss Coutts, by what seemed its revolutionary tone. The working class, he insists, must help itself. Never was the time riper, for the middle classes,

> newly smitten with a sense of self-reproach (far more potent with it, we fully believe, than the lower motives of self-defence and fear) is ready to join them. The utmost power of the press is eager to assist them .... Let the working people, in the metropolis, and in any one great town, but turn their intelligence, their energy, their numbers, their power of union, their patience, their perseverance in this straight direction in earnest – and by Christmas, they shall find a government in Downing Street and a House of Commons within hail of it, possessing not the faintest family resemblance to the Indifferents and Incapables last heard of in that slumbrous neighbourhood.

Cholera: 'The "silent highway"-man. "Your money or your life."'

Such was the challenge he seemed to be throwing down to the incompetent government of Lord Aberdeen (guyed in *Household Words* as John Bull's ancient housekeeper in a state of somnambulism, Abigail Dean, called for short Abbie Dean).

'By Christmas', and it was already October; by their 'energy and numbers'; it was no wonder that readers found his article perplexing and suspected revolution, for the working classes whom he addressed had no vote and therefore no constitutional power of influencing Parliamentary democracy. But, as he made clear, no revolutionary aim was intended. It was simply an expression of the frustration to which his aims at social reform had brought him in a petrified, indifferent social order.

The appeal to self-help by the workers was a typical expression of a self-made man's belief. More than once he told working people who applied to him for leadership that they must help themselves; he especially commended in charity such organizations as the Warehousemen and Clerks' Schools or the Artists' Benevolent Fund, where some contribution, however small, was made by the beneficiaries' families. He mistrusted most of the workers' leaders (whether Chartist or trade union), as he did the leaders of the two national parties, as incompetent or self-seeking (in many cases he had very good grounds for his mistrust); but it left him with a hope for some sort of spontaneous action by the masses, assisted by the benevolent middle classes, which was certainly not to be revolutionary. The answer is vague; the perception of the dilemma profound; the frustration enormous.

If the working classes must seek their own salvation without the violence that could break the public order which he so revered, for it alone stood against the eruption of crime and mob appetites and unleashed human evil of which he always was so aware, then clearly education was really the most hopeful reform. Here again his labours were hardly less frustrating for an impatient, warm-hearted man.

Schools play a large part in his novels, although the main part are variations of middle-class private schools and these are outside the consideration of which I am writing – of education as the key to the social evils of England, to the securing of a working class able to ensure its own freedom from desperate poverty.

For the children who begged in the street, or loafed, or sold what little goods they could to earn a penny, there were only the Ragged Schools. And these, because they touched the very poor, mattered most to Dickens. They had been started to give a few hours of instruction to the young flotsam of the streets by a few devoted, mostly self-educated young men in the 1820s. In 1843 Dickens first visited one of these run voluntarily near Holborn by a lawyer's clerk.

From that time, despite some misgivings about an excess of sectarian religion, he propagandized for the Ragged Schools through thick and thin, getting Miss Coutts to give money in 1843, writing a powerful letter on their behalf of the *Daily News* in 1846, rising to be a height of invective in his own *Household Words* in 'A December Vision' of 1850:

> I saw a Minister of State, sitting in his closet; and round about him, rising from the country which he governed, up to the Eternal Heavens, was a low dull Howl of Ignorance. . . . I saw 30,000 children hunted, flogged, imprisoned, but not taught, all joined in this cry . . . the Minister said, 'Hearken to this cry. What shall we do to stay it?' Some voices tell him one thing, and some another, but a whisper in his ear says, 'Correct this for thyself! Be Bold!' But in the end, the Minister shrugged his shoulder and replied, 'It is a great wrong, but it will last my time.'

Some of the 30,000 Dickens describes in his account of a visit to the Saffron Hill Ragged School in March 1852, when it had acquired rough dormitories in which the down-and-out children and others slept after the hours of teaching. He describes an old drunk who is being taken off to the workhouse to die, and then he adds:

> Beside this wreck, but all unconnected with it and with the whole world, was an orphan boy with burning cheeks and great gaunt eager eyes, who was in pressing peril of death, too, and who had no possession under the broad sky but a bottle of physic or a scrap of writing. He brought both from the house-surgeon of a Hospital that was too full to admit him, and stood giddily staggering in one of the little pathways while the Chief Samaritan read, in hasty characters underlined, how momentous his necessities were. He held the bottle of physic in his claw of a hand, and stood, apparently unconscious of it, staggering and staring with his bright glazed eyes, a creature surely as forlorn and desolate as Mother Earth can have supported on her breast that night.

Surely here we have the embodiment of Jo, Dickens's greatest blow at social inhumanity, perhaps the greatest blow against social wickedness that any novelist has ever struck; Jo, the foundation, because the lowest level, of his great social novel, *Bleak House*, which had begun serial publication the previous November 1851, the year in which *Bleak House* first appeared, was the year of the glorious success of the Great Exhibition in Hyde Park, the triumph of England's technological and mercantile glory. Despite its popular and educative nature, the Great Exhibition received little notice in *Household Words*: 'I have always had an instinctive feeling against the Exhibition, of a faint, inexplicable sort,' Dickens wrote to his assistant Wills. When we think that it was in this year that he was cogitating *Bleak House*, with its total indictment of England's social order, we may understand the instinct.

Bleak House, and its successors, *Little Dorrit* and *Great Expectations*, after

A ragged school in Whitechapel: '30,000 children hunted, flogged, imprisoned, but not taught.'

The atrocities small children suffered in mines and factories.

fifty or so years of comparative neglect (they were by no means favourites of the Dickensians of the late Victorian and Edwardian eras), have, with the recent growth of Dickens's reputation, and in an age more sympathetic to his increasing pessimism, become the centre of critical admiration in our time.

With so much written about these later novels, with such successful discovery of novelty and of greater depth in them, a short account can only hope to suggest something of their extraordinary power and quality.

Bleak House

Seldom did his journalist's concern with a topic of the day serve his artistic purposes better than in *Bleak House*, although, as so often, he laid the book's action some decades earlier. The Chancery Court, whose reform was being actively discussed in the early fifties (though long delayed by exactly the corruptions and ineptitudes of government that Dickens charges against the English party system of his time) was the perfect institution around which to organize a novel that would describe the evils of the English social system. Dickens had known of its evils from his youthful law days and had attacked its cruel delays in the story of the Chancery prisoner of *Pickwick Papers*; but it probably came to him now because it was 'in the news'.

Chancery was outdated, ramshackle, complacent and parasitical in the number of legal functionaries of all levels living upon the delays, obscurities and costs of litigation; by a slow and cruel process it destroyed the souls and bodies of those who became involved (often through no more active intent than by being named as beneficiaries in contested wills) in its machinery. Exactly such was the state of England's government, as Dickens saw it, with two interchangeable political parties contesting for office, neither concerned with anything but the avoidance of seeing the evils they chose not to reform. Jarndyce v. Jarndyce, the long lasting Chancery case in which so many of the characters are involved, is paralleled by the coming in and going out of the governments of Boodle and Coodle (the system of aristocratic party government which is controlled and faithfully believed in by Sir Leicester Dedlock, the obstinate, outdated squire of Chesney Wold in Lincolnshire). From these two strands, which are interlocked because Lady Dedlock is one of the claimants in Jarndyce v. Jarndyce, is formed a great web of characters covering every class (and, it almost seems, every profession) of English life.

Perhaps Dickens's greatest achievement in this vast social network is that he never allows the reader to forget that, however wide the tapestry, it is a vertical web with the Lord Chancellor on his woolsack and Sir Leicester Dedlock in his country mansion at the top of a heavy structure all borne in misery at the bottom on the bony, filthy shoulders of Jo, the road-sweeping boy, in his rags and fever and ignorance. Yet by a terrible revenge the air and the poisoned sewage flow back again from Jo's hideous rookery of down-and-outs and penny-a-nighters in Tom All Alone's to infect the cosy snuggeries of the middle classes – even the paragon of domestic goodness. Dickens's heroine, Esther, is infected by Jo's smallpox. From the first chapter the London world of Chancery is shrouded in fog; from the second chapter Chesney Wold, that stately country home where cabinets are made, Coodle brought in and Boodle turned out, is dank with watery mist. There are no crudities in this social indictment. The Lord Chancellor is a kindly man, as we see in his notice of poor Miss Flite, the suitor driven mad by legal delays, and his fatherly friendly interviews with the Chancery Wards, Ada and Richard. As for Sir Leicester Dedlock, stiff-backed and wrong-headed, he is one of the most touching characters in all Dickens's work in his honourable concern for those who depend on him, his almost romantic old husband's chivalrous loyalty to his beautiful wife when her dishonour becomes public. And there are so many reasons for not abolishing Chancery, not altering the system, which Sir Leicester believes given to England by God. For example, who will support the solicitor Mr Vhole's aged father in Devonshire and his three daughters if he is not able to destroy his client, Richard Carstone, slowly by the endless expensive fees of legal delay? And what would happen to Cousin Volumnia, poor, wretched, rouged old Regency leftover, with her pearls and her girlish screams, if Sir Leicester, whose benevolence she depends on, were no longer to be patron in chief of England's social system?

Yet Dickens powerfully suggests, though he never says it, that the system which allows one weak human being, Jo, to die of want and neglect, is the more dreadful because other weak human beings depend upon it for their survival. There surely enters here a distaste for the whole relationship of patronage and dependence which had always surrounded him in his own family since his success, and which was to increase to dreadful proportions in his last fifteen years. To call Chancery and Chesney Wold symbols of fog and mist is confusing, for it recalls such vaguely infused symbols as the sea in *Dombey and Son* or the rivers in *Our Mutual Friend*. The wonderful thing about Chancery and the fog is that they do stand for England but they are also absolutely and concretely themselves. The structure, the symbols, the narration of *Bleak House* (everything indeed except the plot) are so successful because, however complex, they work in a simple, direct manner. And at the last Jarndyce v. Jarndyce is wound up when a definite will is discovered and nothing is gained because all the estate has gone in costs; Sir Leicester's proud world comes to dust in his wife's shame and death; Mr Krook, the dealer

'A November Fog in London' by W. Small; Miss Sarah Whitehead, Chancery claimant.

in scrap, who is the kind of mock Lord Chancellor of the world of rags, hunger and plague, is brought by his drinking to a spontaneous combustion that leaves only charred bones and a seeping yellow oil. A society, rotten from top to bottom, moves its whole course through this extraordinary novel.

This is no place to describe in detail the vast *dramatis personae* of all classes through whom the story makes its shape; but it must be said that in general they create and recreate little knots of self-regarding and therefore trivial-minded individuals, each neglecting the family or persons dependent upon him, as the ruling classes do the people of England. Mr Turveydrop, the fat, sur-viving admirer of the Prince Regent, thinks only of his deportment; Grandpa Smallweed and his grandchildren, who have never been young, think only of scrabbling for gain; Mr Chadband, the itinerant preacher, thinks only of his own voice; Mrs Pardiggle, bullying her small children into giving their pocket-money to good causes, thinks only of her own right-mindedness in taking her High Church tracts into cottages where the need is for food; Mrs Jellyby, neglecting her children altogether, is disappointed in African missions and turns to women's rights (both *bêtes noires* of Dickens while the social situation is so critical). Best of all, Mr Skimpole, that enchanting, boyish prattler, with his sponging and his pretty turn of cynical phrase, never tires of explaining artlessly how he thinks only of himself. They are like little groups of children dotted over the nation's face, playing out their self-absorbed, immature games, while hunger and disease spread unregarded.

As to Jo, the symbol of the victim, it seems to me that he is almost completely successful. No heavy pathos, not even the dramatic recital of the Lord's Prayer over his death-bed, can destroy the impression his bewildered, animal-like ignorance gives, of a human being neglected, chivvied, driven to death. Jo is the great triumph of Dickens's image of the lost, wandering child. There is nothing genteel or romantic about him, nothing in his favour except that he suggests the possibility of a natural decency that survives all corruption. In a book which specifically refuses virtue to the savage Africans he is (with Hugh the Ostler) Dickens's one concession to the idea of the noble savage. More telling than any of Dickens's other tributes to the poor and ignorant is the scene where the Snagsbys' orphan servant girl, Guster (the lowest form of Victorian domestic life), watches with surprise and compassion the interro-gation of Jo, a form of life unguessed at by her, something lower even than herself, and then – generosity of the poor to the poor – befriends him: ' "Here's something to eat, poor boy," says Guster. "Thankee mum," says Jo. "Are you hungry?" "Jist," says Jo. "What's gone of your father and mother, eh?" Jo stops in the middle of a bite, and looks petrified. For this orphan charge of the Christian saint, whose shrine was at Tooting, has patted him on the shoulder; and it is the first time in his life that any decent hand has been so laid upon him. "I never know'd nothink about 'em," says Jo. "No more didn't I of mine," cries Guster.' The faint parody of the lady bountiful in Guster's 'poor boy' seems to me to prove how Dickens at his best can achieve pathos and sentiment in the highest degree and with the greatest histrionics, without toppling over the edge into the maudlin.

Most modern readers of *Bleak House*, however, will probably object to this account of the novel as ignoring completely what is often thought now a central defect – the character of the heroine, Esther Summerson. Esther is an orphan, unknown until half way through the book to be the illegitimate child of Lady Dedlock. Adopted by Mr Jarndyce, she shares the life of the young claimants to the estate. Dickens boldly decided on giving half the narrative to Esther in the first person. The decision, I think, was a good one, for only so can the reader participate with the victims of society part of the time, and in the other chapters, when the author describes from afar, see the victimization as a whole. Esther, too – especially in one of Dickens's most successful scenes of action, the search for her mother, Lady Dedlock, after her secret has been discovered – does emerge as a competent, courageous heroine; she has the guts and the wits to tell Mr Skimpole and Mr Vholes what corrupt men they are – quite something for a timorous, feminine, Dickens heroine. But, alas, Dickens feels unsure of whether we will recognize her virtues, the typical Dickensian ones of a household order, thrift and busyness, unless she reports to us, with an almost intolerable coyness, all the praises that others give her. It is a blemish, perhaps inherent in the idea of an intelligent girl, who, having to conform to Dickensian ideals of womanhood, must be absolutely modest in every word she says.

A more serious defect in my opinion also stems from this falsity about women, for the plan, so logical and complete, by which the Jarndyce lawsuit corrupts all who touch it (save Mr Jarndyce, a nonsuch) is quite upset when we discover that Lady Dedlock's fall from virtue has nothing to do with her being a claimant in the case. The fault is the more glaring because Miss Flite, the little, mad suitor at law, specifically tells how her own sister went to the bad as a result of the misery brought to the family by their legal involvement. But then Miss Flite's sister is never seen, her fall is hinted at in a veiled sentence; Lady Dedlock's sin is central to the book, she is a beautiful woman. Of such a sin, in Dickens's finally unreal treatment of women's sexuality, there must be no analysis, no clear explanation, however integral to the book's shape. Even so, Esther is a far more admirable, real girl than busy, efficient, little Ruth Pinch; Lady Dedlock, whose fashionable boredom is mocked, has as a result some greater reality than that other proud beauty, Edith Dombey. Even in his Achilles' heel Dickens has improved in this otherwise superb indictment of society.

And what is his solution? At the end of the book we are left with few positive social groups. Perhaps the most outstanding is the world of Mr Rouncewell, the self-made Yorkshire iron-master, where factories and forges alike speak of a lively, active, prosperous world of work, of progress to set against the mouldering world of Chesney Wold where Sir Leicester lies half-paralyzed. And it is to Yorkshire that Esther goes to her husband Alan Woodcourt, the busy G.P., who brings medical attention and care, something more positive than the vague charitable good will of Dickens's earlier novels.

Yet ironically it is exactly against this self-made, northern industrial world of Victorian capitalist progress that Dickens aimed his next fierce onslaught in *Hard Times*, the novel that followed in 1854.

When the publication of *Bleak House* was complete he set off on the trip to Italy with his young friends, Wilkie Collins and the painter, Egg. Despite the occasional irritations of his young companions (not a little, it must be said, because they were poorer than he and wouldn't set about their economies in the way he felt decorous) the holiday was a gay, carefree remove from England, work, and family life.

On his return he made the first truly public reading of his life – further augury of the next decade – at Birmingham, to a paying audience; the proceeds went to a new Mechanics' Institute for Birmingham and the Midlands. His wife and his sister-in-law heard him read on three evenings to acclaiming crowds. Yet for the moment he resisted a rush of further invitations to read elsewhere. How long this period of rest might have continued without the usual consequent depression of his spirits it is impossible to know, for a crisis in the sales of *Household Words* forced a new work from him, or rather – for he announced himself gripped by a new idea – forced that idea into the shape of a weekly serial. It seems likely that his appalled vision of the blast furnaces of the Midlands, which had been anticipated by the Chamber of Horrors scene of infernal forges and maddened, rioting workers glimpsed by Little Nell, may have been revived by his recent visit to Birmingham. And to sharpen this vision his journalist's instinct was aroused by a long-drawn-out battle of strike and lockout that had been fought in Preston between owners and workers in the cotton mills for twenty-three weeks. In January 1854 he made a visit to Lancashire to see the battle for himself. In April appeared the first number of *Hard Times*. Its success triumphantly put *Household Words* back onto the rails of material profit.

Hard Times

Hard Times is of the utmost importance in the extension and sharpening of Dickens's attitude to Victorian society. In it he comes out strongly against Victorian progress as it was viewed by the materialist, laissez-faire capitalists. From the days of *Oliver Twist* he had consistently attacked that aspect of Benthamism which treated human beings as cyphers; he had for long detested education which destroyed imagination in its blind worship of fact; he had constantly championed the poor and the submerged; he had held to his belief in the honesty and industry of the working people of England. What is new, however, in *Hard Times* is his rejection of the virtues of self-help, of the heroism of the man who by hard work and self-denial reaches the top. It is true that this rejection of the Victorian capitalist virtues is slightly hedged by the fact that Mr Bounderby the manufacturer-bully's boasting of having raised himself from the gutter turns out to be something of a fraud – he had been helped and assisted by loving, humble parents. Nevertheless he is a self-made man, who has risen by hard work, material self-denial, and ambition – yet none of this avails him in the final judgment because of the exploiting, soulless system of which he is a leading member.

The hands (the employees) of Mr Rouncewell, the iron-master of *Bleak House* 'are very sinewy and strong'. For all its imperfections – they are 'a little sooty, too' – Mr Rouncewell's self-made Yorkshire world promises the health of progress at the end of that novel. Mr Bounderby's self-made world brings misery and death to all around. In this novel, in fact, Dickens gives up one of his last active hopes – the ideal of self-help, of ambition, of social striving. It was the essence of his own career; but it had been increasingly at odds with his social views. All the early, benevolent, old boys had been of the self-made kind – Pickwick, the Cheerybles, Scrooge reformed, Garland, old Martin Chuzzlewit as he really was. Now Mr Bounderby banishes them forever. Henceforth most ambition of a worldly kind will be sour grapes in the mouth, the only answer to social despair will be a withdrawal, a quietism, a Christian resignation, a very private life of limited good works.

Not, certainly, revolt. *Hard Times* is a fierce book, but it is certainly not the socialist tract it was sometimes thought to be in its own day. The strikers are good men misled by the self-interested, sly agitator, Slackbridge. Left-wing critics drawn to Dickens's indictment of capitalism have always been dismayed by the crude, ill-drawn picture of the strike leader. Certainly it is at variance with his picture of the strikers at Preston, contributed to *Household Words* on his return to London in early February 1854, only two months before the novel began to appear. He shows here that his visit to a meeting of the strikers (he seems, indeed, to have attended only one) gave him a high opinion of its efficiency, orderliness and honesty: 'If the Assembly, in respect of quietness and order, were put in comparison with the House of Commons, the Right Honourable The Speaker himself would decide for Preston.' He also specifically notes that the strike committee decided not to hear a deputation of Manchester delegates from the Labour Parliament, when they found that these delegates wished not to speak of the strike at issue but to defend the Labour Parliament's political principles in general. This immediacy, moderation and order find no place in the ranting demagogy he portrays in *Hard Times*.

Yet I do not think left-wing readers of Dickens should be so surprised at this contrast. In that very article, 'On Strike', it is true that Dickens recounts how he defended the strikers on his railway journey from a fierce old gentleman who declared that: 'They wanted to be ground . . . to bring 'em to their senses.' But it is notable that Dickens's defence of the strikers is only against the lockout behaviour of the employers, not actively for their strike, except that he finds it understandable.

Three years earlier, at the time of a railway strike, he had not even felt this. He wished for no reprisals against the strikers, but he counselled them to return to work at once, objecting that they had no right to use their power against the public, nor, indeed, against the railway companies who had invested capital to give them work: 'What the Directors might have conceded to temperate remonstrance, it is easy to understand they may see it culpable to yield to so alarming a combination against the public service and safety.'

Even so, between the caricature of the strike leader in the novel and the favourable picture he gives in his Preston article there is a great gulf. Was Dickens guilty of bad faith in order to please his middle-class readers? But

Preston Moors: the strikers 'wanted to be ground ... to bring 'em to their senses.'

they were in great degree the same readers as those who read the article. It seems to me more probable that the novel called forth a heightened picture all round, and in writing about the strike meeting he had only to draw upon that part of himself which had (with some reason) despised the more violent leaders of the chartists, that feared so desperately mob rule, to find himself in tune with the middle class who could take so much concern for social reform in *Household Words*.

Where does *Hard Times* stand in the canon of his art? Despite its immediate success it has not been a favourite novel with the general public. It has, however, had its great admirers: for instance Bernard Shaw, whose own work owed so much to Dickens, and in recent decades, owing to the advocacy of F. R. Leavis, it has been much praised in some academic circles not otherwise favourable to Dickens's work. In so far as such advocacy has led readers to a neglected, interesting novel it is to be welcomed; in so far as it has kept them away from Dickens's masterpieces it is to be deplored. The claim for *Hard Times* to be considered among Dickens's masterpieces can hardly be sustained. The claim is based upon its conciseness, the clarity of its moral statement, the lack of complication of plot or of elaboration of characters, of humorous dialogue, or of subplots. All this brevity is due to the discipline of weekly serial publication which, as he had not used it since *Barnaby Rudge* over twelve years before, and then not in such tight episodes, Dickens found 'crushing'. Neither the mechanism that compelled him to write so briefly nor the fact that he found it a strain need have prevented the result from being a masterpiece; indeed they might have had exactly that effect. But surely it is not so.

The moral fable is clearly stated in the first two chapters, where in Mr Grad-grind's Benthamite school the circus girl, Cissie Jupe, disgusts by failing to define a horse, and Bitzer, the model pupil, at once gives the right answer: 'Quadruped. Graminivorous. Forty teeth, namely twenty-four grinders,' etc. The contrast between Mr Gradgrind's dead world of fact and Sleary's circus world of imagination is well established. And seldom in Dickens does so simple a plot serve, after the stage is set, to expound the fable proposed. Yet this is almost where the novel's virtues end – the rest is very good stuff (so good that it well repays reading) spoiled for lack of elbow room – and the other social question with which Dickens was probably even more concerned, the harshness of English divorce laws, is so wedged in as to be hardly noticeable.

This is unfortunate because in this novel – particularly in the heroine, Louisa Bounderby, potentially one of Dickens's most successful women – he is moving into new depths. Louisa Gradgrind, as she is born, is a girl deadened by her father's education of fact, forced on too early to a vision of life at once priggish and materialistic, marrying a coarse brute at her father's dictation and for her brother's material advancement, but more still because she has no awakened response to life, almost succumbing at the last to an empty, witty London seducer because in his cynicism she thinks that she finds for the first time an honest statement of the meaninglessness of life as she sees it. Here is a character and a theme worthy of George Eliot. In his succeeding novels, Dickens in his own way works out exactly such psychological depths. But here, just where he needs room for reflection and analysis as never before, he has to abbreviate and truncate so that Louisa's story is only a sketch for a more profound study. And the young circus girl, Cissie Jupe, whose naturally clear moral vision and loving imagination intervenes at the right moment to save Louisa, has (even in a very short book) been off stage so long that we have no knowledge of her spiritual growth and no belief in it.

And all this is played in a northern industrial town where Dickens is not at home. For a journalist's article Coketown would serve very well. Even in his novels Dickens could use a place he knew little, where it was only incidental. For example, from his many journeys through France he was able in a short paragraph or two to give us the feel of Chalons-sur-Saône in *Little Dorrit,* but then the town is only there as a voyager's vision, the place where the acquitted murderer, Rigaud, halts in his flight from the avenging mob of Marseilles. Coketown is the essence of *Hard Times*, and it just is not there in depth; instead a number of journalist's happy phrases – for example, the description of the factory machines as mad elephants – have to do too much service. Since the novel cannot have the density Dickens so greatly relies on for his awakening of life, there is too often a sense that the bad writing is given us at too great length and the good is too circumscribed. Mr Bounderby, the self-made monster, comes to life in the sheer bullying repetition of his language; and the complicity of the old, dandy, aristocratic ruling class of England in Mr Bounderby's new brutal world is well suggested by his employment as a housekeeper of a soured old woman with aristocratic connections and no means to support them.

Around this uneasy alliance between wealth and birth the most suggestively absurd dialogue in *Hard Times* occurs – Mr Bounderby:

> 'At the time when to have been a tumbler in the mud of the streets, would have been a godsend to me, a prize in the lottery to me, you were at the Italian Opera. You were coming out of the Italian Opera, ma'am, in white satin and jewels, a blaze of splendour, when I hadn't a penny to buy a link to light you.' 'I, certainly, Sir,' returned Mrs Sparsit, with a dignity serenely mournful, 'was familiar with the Italian Opera at a very early age.' 'Egad, ma'am, so was I,' said Bounderby, 'with the wrong side of it. A hard bed the pavement of its Arcade used to make, I assure you. People like you, ma'am, accustomed from infancy to lie down on feathers, have no idea how hard a paving stone *is* without trying it.'

It is notable that this lively stuff, however, reverts to Mr Bounderby's and Mrs Sparsit's life in London – it is the world of *Bleak House* and *Little Dorrit* – not in the shadowy Coketown.

With industrial progress and the virtues of *laissez faire* and 'room at the top' added (at any rate temporarily) to his condemnation of Victorian society, Dickens's social charge sheet was nearly complete. In the mid-fifties, the years of *Hard Times* and *Little Dorrit*, his despair about England's condition reached its height; and it coincided, as we shall see later, with a gradually increasing despair about his domestic life that at last burst out into his separation from Catherine. To the cholera, the bad housing, the ignorance breeding crime about which the government was indifferent and did nothing, was now added the Crimean War, which was waged with inefficiency, muddle and a cruel indifference to the sufferings of the soldiers. It was during these years that Dickens was led for the only time in his life into some purely political activity, so certain had his feeling become that the total system needed change and needed change quickly.

The former excavator of Nineveh, Layard, a Radical member of Parliament, had seen some of the misconduct of the war at first hand. He now pressed for a reform of the whole English system of administration, and to back up his Parliamentary demands he organized a society to give voice to public opinion. Dickens took a leading part in the formation of the Administrative Reform Society, even speaking publicly on its platforms. A letter to Layard in April 1855 gives some picture of his grim analysis of the situation and his half-desperate hopes for its solution:

> There is nothing in the present age at once so galling and so alarming to me as the alienation of the people from their own public affairs . . . . They have had so little to do with the game through all these years of Parliamentary Reform, that they have sullenly laid down their cards, and taken to looking on. The players who are left at the table do not see beyond it, conceive that the gain and loss and all the interest of the play are in their hands, and will never be wiser until they and the table and the lights and the money are all overturned together. And I believe . . . that it is extremely like the general mind of France before the breaking out of the First Revolution, and is in danger of being turned by any one of a throng of accidents –

a bad harvest – the last strain of too much aristocratic insolence or incapacity . . . a defeat abroad . . . into such a devil of a conflagration as has never been beheld since. Meanwhile all our English tufthunting, toadeating, and other manifestations of accursed gentility . . .ARE expressing themselves every day . . . . It seems to me an absolute impossibility to direct the spirit of the people at this pass until it shows itself . . .you can no more help a people who do not help themselves, than you can help a man who does not help himself . . . . I know of nothing that can be done beyond keeping their wrongs continually before them.

And so in his magazine and in his next novel, *Little Dorrit*, he did. Not to much avail. Layard's motion was overwhelmingly defeated in the House. The Civil Service was not reformed until the year Dickens died. Almost a year after Sebastopol had fallen to the British and the war had ended in victory he wrote to Miss Coutts of:

The fearful mess they have made of the Peace. But I have never doubted Lord Palmerston to be . . . the emptiest impostor and the most dangerous delusion ever known. Within three months of the peace, here are its main conditions broken and the whole world laughing at us! I am as certain that these men will get us conquered at last, as I am that I shall die. We have been feared and hated a long time. To become a jest after that, is a very, very serious thing. Nobody knows what the English people will be when they wake up last and find it out.

And a year later, in 1857 after the Mutiny in India, his sense of England's weakness still uppermost:

I wish I were Commander in Chief of India. The first thing I would do to strike that

The charge of light Cavalry at Balaclava; Lord Palmerston caricatured in *Punch*.

Oriental race with amazement . . . should be to proclaim to them in their language, that I considered my holding that appointment by leave of God, to mean that I should do my utmost to exterminate the Race upon whom the stain of the late cruelties rested.

And in the same year he wrote a story, *The Perils of Certain English Prisoners*, which, though laid on the South American pirate coast, was intended to pay tribute to the bravery of English ladies during the Mutiny without mentioning India. A year later and private events had caught up with him. He was to remain the friend of the poor and a sceptic about Parliament, but he was never again, save for one provocative speech, to be publicly either so politically despairing or indeed so political as in the mid-fifties.

Little Dorrit

Little Dorrit, which was published as a monthly serial from the very end of 1855 to midsummer 1857, was the reflection of this social despair, but of quite another kind than *Bleak House*. Certainly the exploitation of the poor, the insolence and indifference of the rich, the snobbery and smugness of the middle class, are all there; but these count for far less than the general disease that holds every man and woman prisoner. And the accent is upon *every*. For never did Dickens portray so many characters who are grey rather than black and white – there are a few out-and-out villains, and one very striking embodiment of evil, but, for the most part, 'bad' humanity is seen to have its redeeming features, as 'good' humanity is seen to have its blemishes. The only wholly perfect character is the inventor, Doyce, a tribute, surely, by Dickens to the power of creation, the power of art to which he had given the core of his own life, and even Doyce can only market his inventions abroad, notably, with Dickens's scepticism about Parliament, in St Petersburg, in despotic realms – surely a bitter conclusion when England was at war with a Russian despot whom Dickens himself detested.

Even at the height of his attack on the social establishment, or the successful and the powerful, Dickens had never been kind to drop-outs or parasites (witness Harold Skimpole); but now in *Little Dorrit* the full force of his attack seems to be levelled against those whose cynicism, despair, hugged sense of injury, or nourished grievance of genteel poverty or of failure make them the silent, the withdrawn, the bitter or the amused participants in an unjust world. Never did Dickens so powerfully and with so much sophistication present such a gallery of neurotics – Mrs Clennam, chained to her chair by hysteric paralysis, coldly declaiming the thunderous curses of the Old Testament upon a sinning world outside her bedridden life, a world she knows that she has grievously wronged; Miss Wade, feeding her governess's sense of social insult, her seduced woman's hatred of domestic happiness, by her near lesbian encouragement of another orphan girl's fierce sense of injury; Fanny Dorrit, making a loveless, empty marriage in order to humiliate, in her hour of wealth, her handsome, proud mother-in-law who had patronized her in her youthful poverty; Henry Gowan, the failed, spoiled gentleman, playing at art

Hampton Court Palace by H. Ziegler.

to bring all artists into discredit, playing with life to bring all decent men of earnest good will down to his level; his wonderfully portrayed mother, the dowager, who hurts whenever she can so sweetly and genteelly to make up for being granted a grace and favour apartment at Hampton Court to live in; Edward Dorrit, arguably Dickens's most splendid dramatic presentation, the longest imprisoned debtor in the Marshalsea, 'its Father', who has made his shabby, foul-aired cell a throne room where the other prisoners pay him court, laugh behind his back, give him small tips which he regally accepts – all these are instruments in an extraordinary symphony of complicity in the world which they claim has outraged them. Even the only truly evil character of the book, the only Dickensian devil figure, Rigaud-Blandois, murderer-adventurer, chimes in with his 'gentleman's' demand that the world has a duty to him to offer itself to his criminal devices. It is a whole museum of insects – some dowdy, some ornate – impaled upon the little spikes of their own grievances.

Yet the sad, despairing note is not so pervasive as to mar Dickens's humorous powers, indeed there is a fusion of the horrible, the absurd and the plain farcical here which achieves a *grandeur* of pathos exceptional in his other work or elsewhere (for pathos, surely, has usually the fault of shrinking the human vision while it warms the human heart). We have seen how bitterly Dickens resented the better conditions of Newgate criminals than those of debtors' prisons. But now at last he returns to his father's old prison, the Marshalsea, to give up every pretence that imprisonment for debt is a martyrdom. Indeed the blemish left upon the gentle character of Little Dorrit through her prison associations is exactly the sort of resentment of her father's imprisonment that Dickens must have felt in youth: 'He is not to be blamed for being in need, poor love,' she says, 'who could be in prison a quarter of a century, and be prosperous?' But Little Dorrit, even in her devotion to her father, is never quite blind; as she says, 'Yes, I know I am wrong. Don't think any worse of me; it has grown up with me here.'

This horrible blight of genteel egotism that the air of the Marshalsea engenders is never so well satirized as in the scene where Mr Dorrit receives in his cell the honest old working man, Mr Nandy, who has been allowed out of the work-house for the day. In this shrimp tea, which the broken-down, imprisoned debtor provides for the honest pauper, as some Highland chieftain in a Scott novel would patronize a tenant from a remote, outlandish moor, Dickens blasts the gentility of the self-pitying sponger (the gentility of his family in youth) as he had once used the pampering of Newgate criminals to plead for the rights of his debtor father. And Dickens remorselessly reduces all the debtor prisoners' attempts at gentility and jollity and raffishness to nothing, as when they are holding a smoking concert at which Mr Dorrit in his capacity as Father presides:

> Occasionally, a vocal strain more sonorous than the generality informed the listener that some boastful bass was in blue water, or in the hunting field, or with the reindeer, or on the mountain, or among the heather; but the Marshall [i.e. the Governor] of the Marshalsea knew better, and had got him hard and fast.

Debtor prisoners' attempts at jollity and raffishness.

Mr Dorrit is a triumph of comedy – bitter, and in a certain moment when he shows us that he glimpses the truth about himself, terrible. His last speech at Mrs Merdle's fashionable banquet in Rome, when, forgetting that he is now a grand, rich, English milord, he reverts to the language of his debtor's cell, has all the power of those 'scandalous' scenes like the Governesses' Benefit Concert in *The Devils*, on which Dostoevsky's novels are pivoted.

But there is a wilder, more characteristically Dickensian humour in *Little Dorrit* in the person of Flora Finching, one of his free association speakers who can vie with Mrs Nickleby and Mrs Gamp. Flora comes out of Dickens's disappointment with his old love, Maria Beadnell, when she reappeared in his life as a stout, voluble, middle-aged, married woman in 1855, just before he began to write the novel. Flora, the former love of Arthur Clennam, is foolish, and her every word is a parody of the platitudes of the Romantic view of life. It is not for nothing that the book which Arthur had not returned to her, when their parents parted them twenty years before, was that Bible of the Romantics' view of the simple life, *Paul et Virginie*. But Flora's outpourings are not only a foolish flow of Romantic platitudes, they also embody, when she reports the views of her late commonsensical husband Mr F., many of Dickens's own comic prejudices about life. Every word of Flora's is quotable, but perhaps her view of Italy will suffice to give her essence, with its incorporation of Dickens's own distaste for classical sculpture contained in the last absurd sentence:

> 'In Italy is she really,' said Flora, 'with the grapes and figs growing everywhere and lava necklaces and bracelets too that land of poetry with burning mountains picturesque beyond belief though if the organ-boys come away from the neighbourhood not to be scorched nobody can wonder being so young and bringing their white mice with them most humane, and is she really in that favoured land with nothing but blue about her and dying gladiators and Belvederes though Mr F. himself did not believe for his objection when in spirits was that the images could not be true there being no medium between expensive quantities of linen badly got up and all in creases and none whatever, which certainly does not seem probable though perhaps in consequence of the extremes of rich and poor which may account for it.'

Maria Beadnell had seemed to the young Dickens beautiful, accomplished, gracious, desirable; but she had been cruel to him. Mrs Winter (as Maria Beadnell returned in 1855) is painted in Flora as fat, silly, clumsy, for ever offering herself where she is not wanted, but with the one virtue Maria had not – she has a heart of gold. Indeed she is one of Dickens's most likeable characters.

But so sombre was the colour of Dickens's mind at that time that Flora, the embodiment of romantic love that persists against all reason and propriety, is accompanied by another of the great comic figures of the world of Dickens, Mr F.'s aunt, the human legacy of her marriage; and Mr F.'s aunt, an old woman in a state of senile dementia, pursues Flora's old love, Arthur Clennam, with an inexplicable but ineradicable hostility as great as Flora's determined devotion. It is not necessary to resort to a Freudian view of personality to see in this strange pair a view of sick humanity that recognizes division and self-deception as almost incurable maladies.

Yet Dickens does offer a solution to this ill, neurotic world. From the moment that rich Mr Dorrit reverts to his old prison self and fraudulent Mr Merdle is revealed by his suicide to all the world for the sham that he is, some part, at least, of the truth is revealed; some of the characters, at least, attain to an admission of themselves – even Mrs Clennam escapes momentarily from the hysteric paralysis in which guilt and pride have held her for so many years. The analysis of this release from prison is complex and convincing; but unfortunately, despite recent defences of Dickens's technique, the culmination of the novel is to a great extent lost, swallowed up in an overcomplicated plot. We are left at last with the impression of the final paragraphs, as Dickens's resolution of the subtle ills he has diagnosed:

> Little Dorrit and her husband walked out of the church alone. They paused for a moment on the steps of the portico, looking at the fresh perspective of the street in the autumn morning sun's bright rays, and then went down. Went down into a modest life of usefulness and happiness. They went quietly down into the roaring streets, inseparable and blessed; and as they passed along in sunshine and shade, the noisy and the eager, and the arrogant and the froward and the vain, fretted, and chafed, and made their usual uproar.

It is a somewhat private, quietist proposal of the Sermon on the Mount; and it appears, for all its sincerity, too simple for the all-pervading grey evil of the world that the novel has described.

Theatricals

The private quality of so much of *Little Dorrit* reminds us that Dickens's life in the fifties had not been all politics or even social indignation and social good works; leaving aside his European jaunts and his long family sojourns in Paris and Boulogne, Dickens had been as energetic and active in pursuit of private pleasure as he had of public good. The two things, indeed, were never quite separate for him. His principal hobby of these years had been amateur acting and amateur stage management; but the theatricals were conducted for charities, in great degree on behalf of the arts. The proceeds of many of the performances went to writers who had fallen upon hard times, or to families that had been left unprovided for.

The large earnings of Dickens himself, George Eliot, or Bulwer Lytton, the considerable sufficiency left by Thackeray (all sums earned at the cost of driving hard work and extraordinary energy) make us forget what a high proportion of writers fell through the wide-meshed Victorian net into genteel poverty. There were vastly rich painters, like Millais, too, and some well-to-do actors; but, for the rest, the danger for all kinds of artists of disaster from ill health or bad luck was as great as it was for all the Victorian professional class who did not prosper. Dickens's associates lived in a journalistic world of writers depending upon placing articles, or of artists living by illustration – for them life was at once comfortable and very precarious. Both Dickens's principal illustrators, on whom, whether we like it or not, much of our vision

W. Telbin. Evans. Shirley Brook. Mark Lemon, Jun. W. Jones. E. Evans. Marcus Stone. F. Berger. Mark Lemon. A. Egg.

Albert Smith. Stanfield. Miss Evans. E. Pigott. Mrs Francis. Luard.

Keith. C. Dickens, Jun. Kate Dickens. Miss Hogarth. Mary Dickens. Wilkie Collins. Helen Hogarth.

Charles Dickens.

The Dickens Dramatic Company in 1854.

of Dickens's world depends – both Cruikshank and Phiz ended in receipt of Civil List pensions to keep them alive.

Dickens's energy in befriending and helping needy artists was extraordinary; theatricals were the self-indulgence which made his generosity possible. He was always awake to the need for some wider scheme to give decency to the closing years of members of his profession. It was to this end that he and Bulwer Lytton devised the Guild of Literature and Art by which a colony for writers in retirement was to be built upon the grounds of Lytton's estate at Knebworth. The first theatricals to raise money for the project were given in the Great Hall of Lytton's magnificent, sham-medieval castle at Knebworth in 1850. By this and other performances a large sum of money was raised. Lytton, an M.P., got a charter of incorporation through the Commons in 1854; but by law seven years had to pass before pensions could be granted. 'I do stoutly believe that this plan carried, will entirely change the status of the literary man in England,' Dickens wrote to Lytton. But when the time came, as so often happens where the organizing of the lives of artists is concerned, few writers of the desired kind were willing to take up the offer, and what could have been a remarkable scheme of welfare necessarily petered out. Nor, during this decade, was Dickens any more successful in his attacks upon the committee of the Royal Literary Fund, which he accused of spending more of their money upon administration than upon needy writers. 'I am determined to reform it or to ruin it,' he wrote to Macready in 1857; but he did neither.

The purposes of the theatricals, though sincere and no doubt a blessing to those who received the benefits, were really less important to Dickens than the sheer pleasure he got out of them – pleasure in acting, more pleasure still in management (particularly when, with Bulwer's play, *Not So Bad as We Seem*, laid in George II's reign, the company began provincial tours), and a great deal of pleasure in the sheer conviviality, for, as in his youth all his family had been involved in productions, now he involved all his friends. Not that, in the main, they needed to be involved. There were disappointments,

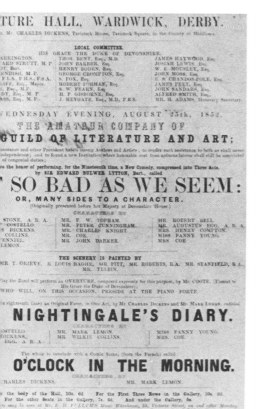

A playbill; a theatrical performance before Her Majesty.

let-downs, failures to learn parts, inconstancy in rehearsal, and as a result some minor quarrels; but in general Dickens succeeded in being a very strict manager, and there was extraordinarily little dissension – surely a remarkable tribute to his charm, his power of leadership and, perhaps less expected, his tact, but above all to his great power of liking and caring for his friends.

The theatricals fall into two main periods. From 1845 to 1851 came the playing of old plays: Ben Jonson's *Every Man in His Humour, The Merry Wives of Windsor*, and a new one, Lytton's costume play; each of these was usually accompanied by a short farce in which Dickens could let go in his old Mathews-Sam Weller vein. Ladies, including in small parts Catherine and Georgina, were in the private performances of these plays in the gracious settings of Rockingham Castle or Knebworth; professional actresses were substituted for the public tours. In the late fifties the theatrical activities were renewed when Dickens presented and acted in two melodramas, *The Lighthouse* (1855) and *The Frozen Deep* (1857), by Wilkie Collins, who as a new young friend had appeared some years before in Lytton's play. In these latter plays Dickens made a striking effect with two 'heavy' roles. Both Lytton's costume play and *The Frozen Deep* were presented before the Queen, the first at the Duke of Devonshire's London house, the second at a private performance in the Gallery of Illustration, Regent Street. Not the least of the pleasures Dickens had from the theatricals, I think – a very characteristic, easily mocked, but probably respectable pleasure – was the degree to which he met people of rank on his own terms. Such was the genuine friendship he formed with the Duke of Devonshire; such, too, was his polite refusal, twice repeated, to be presented to his sovereign when he was in theatrical costume. At the worst this was a complicated but harmless snobbery; at the best, and more probably, it was a further blow in his fight for the status of his profession.

Yet the theatrical activities, however absorbing, however frenetic, would hardly be of such interest today were it not that in the tour of *The Frozen Deep*, that Arctic melodrama, he met in July 1857 at Manchester Ellen Ternan, the young professional actress, whose captivation of him (albeit quite unintended) surely precipitated, if it did not cause, his separation from his wife.

'The failed middle class marriage.'

The complete truth about the break-up of Dickens's marriage (certainly not the truths as they were understood by the principals, or the truth as it was supposed by their immediate family) will never now be known. To some extent all judgments made about it are tinged with bias. Some critics, while admiring Dickens as a writer, do not care for his hearty, neurotic, often self-pitying character, and are secretly pleased to discover him acting, as they think, like a cad to his wife, or like a vulgarian in his public advertisement of his marital troubles. Other admirers of his work are equally attracted by his character – its vigour, sense of fun, generosity and magnetism; they are quick to believe that a woman who brought depression and frustration to such a man must have been

'The Awakened Conscience' by Holman Hunt, 1853. 'I had it from her own lips that she loathed the very thought of the intimacy.' A reported confession of Ellen Ternan, see page 276.

herself depressing or frustrating, phlegmatic or hypochondriac, or abnormally stupid, or all of these. The picture is not made more clear by the principals, since we have so much of Dickens's version of when and why things went wrong, and so little of Catherine's. That Georgina, Catherine's sister, so completely sided with her adored brother-in-law did not much help his cause then, and illogically, I think, tends even now to make one feel sympathy for the sister she did not support.

As for the children, or at any rate the elder ones, whom Dickens rather insistently put forward as witnesses to their mother's failure in the home, few of them made comments then or later – and those few comments are not without ambiguity. A short survey of the rather sad careers of most of these seven sons and two daughters is better reserved for the last chapter of Dickens's life. It can only be said here that, while they were dominated by him and naturally overawed by his greatness, only Mamey, the eldest girl, seems to have loved him adoringly. Katey, his second daughter, combined admiration with spirited opposition. Charley, his eldest son, probably loved him also but was dragged down by the sense that he had disappointed his father. As to their Aunt Georgina, whom Dickens so advertised as the real mother in the home, she was befriended throughout her long life by Henry, her most intelligent and successful nephew, and she had a close relationship with both her nieces. Yet events after Dickens's death suggest that Charley positively disliked his aunt, and that the other nephews were so indifferent to her as to ignore her. But Catherine's case, for all that she spoke of the attentions and love of her children, seems little better. One cannot help thinking that the tensions of the Dickens home ended by outweighing the benefits in the minds of most of their children.

Nor do the opinions of friends help us to discern the truth. Forster above all, in his mainly excellent biography, does little more than give a selection from Dickens's own case against his wife. He underplays Catherine's role in Dickens's life as much as he suppresses the importance of Collins's friendship. Biographers and writers, as a result, have tended to accept Dickens's hints or suggestions that his marriage had been a mistake from the first, and have tried to give this account substance by emphasizing or enlarging any sharp comments that the novelist made of or to his wife, any jealousies or incidents that can mark a line of disharmony from the early days of their marriage to its final breakdown.

I am not at all satisfied that this sad, fated view of the relationship is a true one. I have said in the second chapter of this book that there was a certain incompatibility in their ideas of management of the household, a certain doubt about the effect upon a wife of the sort of masterful assertion of what he required which Dickens announced from the days of their engagement. But against this must be set the fact that Victorian husbands did often expect this complete authority over their wives. I do not think that Dickens, given his temperament, was excessively severe; his tone is paternal rather than tyrannical, and he took care to commend his wife when he thought she had excelled

A Valentine card, 1865. 'Not to any young 'ooman, I hope, Sammy?' 'Why it's no use sayin' it 'aint. It's a walentine.' The Wellers in *Pickwick Papers*.

as much as he reproved her when she failed him. All this, however it may be accounted for as typical of his age, would still be repellent, if it were unrelieved.

But his remarks have to be read in context. Many biographers have quoted his postscript to her at Genoa: 'Keep things in their places. I can't bear to picture them otherwise,' and this is certainly characteristic of the dictatorial mania for orderliness of which he was very well aware. It would be unfair, however, not to point out that this minatory postscript is immediately followed by another, which greatly lightens its effect: 'I *think* I saw Roche [the courier] sleeping with his head on the lady's shoulder – in the coach. I couldn't swear to it, and the light was deceptive. But I think I did.' There are, from fairly early in their marriage onwards, many references to Catherine's absentmindedness, sometimes exasperated, more usually affectionate – for example in 1841: 'Kate wrote to thank you for it, but was guilty of the small omission (a very slight one) of forgetting to put it in the post,' or more riotously in 1854 telling of how Kate, overhearing someone at an exhibition of French pictures addressed as 'Mr Fairbairn from Manchester', secured his London address, and so led Dickens to invite the wrong Mr Fairbairn from Manchester to dinner. There are the much-quoted references to Catherine's accident-proneness on their American tour, which is often connected with her later failure to appear at an important social function in Glasgow in 1847 because of a miscarriage, and with her being forced to abandon a part in 1850 at Knebworth from spraining her ankle by stepping through the stage. All this can be made to appear both tiresome and ridiculous; and no doubt it was at the time – but almost any married life can be found to be strewn with exasperations. Dickens specifically expressed his gratitude for her competence, endurance and companionship on the American trip. And as for accident-proneness, it would be as easy to argue, remembering Wilkie Collins's broken leg on his trip with Dickens to the Lakes in 1857 – 'Mr Collins who never goes out with me on any expedition without receiving some damage or other' – that Dickens himself made his companions prone to accidents.

If there was one accident that he could not easily forgive his wife it was the bearing of his children. From early on he had found the domestic upset of childbirth a trial in his overpacked, carefully-planned working life. Later he saw each birth as another strain upon his money-earning energies: 'Mother and son blooming,' he wrote of the arrival of his last child, 'though I am not so clear that I wanted the latter.' He came to adore this son; indeed he certainly loved his children deeply, especially when they were small. But this treatment of fertility as though it were a purely feminine contribution to marriage is one of the most annoying features of his selfish masculinity – something, one would think, hard for Catherine to bear.

I believe that Catherine did not find it possible to live up to Dickens's meteoric career (but it would have been a rare wife who could); I suspect that his masterful management of her did not help her to shine (and the regular neatness inspections which he made of his children's rooms probably served them even less well); I think it unlikely that Georgina's exemplary behaviour (though not, of course, to be blamed) could have helped Catherine in her role as Dickens's wife. Certainly by 1851 she suffered from some giddiness, probably of nervous origin, which cannot have been improved by the sudden death in London of her infant daughter, Dora, when she was away being treated in Malvern. Yet Dickens's feeling and admiration for her then are quite clear:

> Kate is as well as I could hope. I do not yet know what the effect of such a shock may be upon her nervous condition, but she is quite resigned to what happened and can speak of it tranquilly. She is so good and amiable that I hope it may not hurt her.

The tone is not passionate. If that is what Mrs Dickens hoped when she gave to her daughter, Kate, her husband's letters to her, saying 'that the world may know he once loved me', then she was self-deceived. But until 1854 at least, the letters do show a warm and real affection; and what is more important, they show something that is not often present in his letters to anyone else. This is best illustrated by the group of letters he wrote to her as late as 1853, during his tour of Italy with Collins and Egg. Nowhere else does he provide such a lively, gossipy account of people as he does to her of the English residents of Genoa, Naples and Rome – slightly malicious, slightly censorious, but, above all, enjoying the fun of people. And in letters to Georgina he often adds pieces of such gossip specifically for Catherine. If I am right in my inference, then, considering how vital to Dickens's art his continuous sense of the absurdity of human behaviour is, we may think that he found some stimulation in his wife's company that was invaluable to him. It is some balance against the fact that his marriage did not waken in him a sufficient understanding of women to give reality to the central emotional relationships of most of his great novels.

In the fifties his general disillusionment with society, his distaste for England and London, his momentary depressive doubts about life's purpose, inevitably underlined whatever was lacking in his life with Catherine; indeed it would hardly be surprising if their depressions had not fed each other. His restlessness, their constant residences abroad, must have undermined what capacity for housekeeping Catherine possessed, as it surely must have damaged the continuity of his children's education. For this Dickens is not blamable – his temperament and his creative powers demanded this life; but neither are his wife and children blamable for not needing it. By 1855, I think, his marriage had become as irksome to him as much of the rest of life. In the long 1855–6 sojourn in Paris it is Georgina, not Catherine, who emerges as his happy, sightseeing companion. But the real augury of disaster, perhaps, was the arrival of his former sweetheart, Maria Beadnell, upon the scene.

That his loss of Maria in his youth had been traumatic, or that he thought it had been traumatic, I think we must accept. His inability to write about her in his autobiographical fragment, her appearance mixed up with Catherine as Dora in *David Copperfield*, suggest a confusion of his bitterness over Maria with his early disappointments with his wife. Such memories do not have to be constant to be traumatic, they have only to recur in times of stress. It is notable that it was in January 1855 that he wrote to Forster: 'Why is it, that as with poor David, a sense comes always crushing on me now, when I fall into low spirits, as of one happiness I have missed in life, and one friend and companion I have never made? . . .' But now here was Maria returned to fill this void. Any sensible man would have known that a quarter of a century had gone by since those wonderful, painful days. Yet perhaps this very fact explains Dickens's rapturous letters of welcome, his protestations, his anguished memories, for here was a young girl come out of the past; he, remembering those times, *felt* himself eternally young, perhaps Maria would prove to *be* eternally young. Poor Mrs Winter, of course, had warned him that she was stout and unromantic, but he would not believe it until he saw her. In fact, he found a voluble, arch, fat businessman's wife, whom he rather unkindly remarked to be addicted to secret brandy. He got out of the encounter not too well by emphasizing his grown-up affection for her little daughter. It would not be true to say that he could not forgive Maria for having changed – Flora Finching is a lovable character – though it is notable that she is ridiculous, plain and worthily kind, whereas Maria had seemed talented, beautiful and a little excitingly cruel. But the whole absurd, disappointing encounter cannot have helped Dickens to come to terms with his own domestic life, although it might have 'taught sense' to a more easily defeated man.

In April 1856 he is making a general complaint to Forster. Deploring the loneliness of Macready's life at Sherborne, he says that retirement is not for him: 'It is much better to go on and fret, than to stop and fret. As to repose, for some men there's no such thing in life.' His depression quickly changes to nostalgia. 'The old days! The old days! Shall I ever, I wonder, get the frame of mind back as it used to be?' And now his despairs are easily related only to his unhappiness at home, for he ends, 'I find the skeleton in my domestic cupboard becoming a pretty big one'.

His first open complaint to his friend Forster that his marriage was a failure came in September 1857, the month after he first met Ellen Ternan; yet it would be impossible to make the one a consequence of the other. Growing passion for Ellen, however, surely made discontent with Catherine turn to a determination to bring the marriage to an end. Forster urged his friend to remember the long years of marriage, the deep links, Catherine's services to him. Dickens in his reply still speaks of separation as an impossibility, but one devoutly to be hoped for: 'For her sake, as well as mine, the wish will force itself upon me that something might be done.'

> Poor Catherine and I [he next wrote], we are not made for each other, and there is no help for it . . . . She is exactly, what you know, in the way of being amiable and complying; but we are strangely ill-assorted for the bond there is between us . . . . I am often cut to the heart by thinking what a pity it is, for her own sake, that I ever fell in her way . . . . It mattered not so much when we had only ourselves to consider, but reasons have been growing since which make it all but hopeless that we should even struggle on. What is now befalling me I have seen steadily coming, ever since the days you remember when Mary [his eldest daughter b. 1838] was born; and I know too well that you cannot, and no one can, help me.

This letter does not suggest that Dickens yet considered separation; but it does first hint – 'reasons have been growing' – at that failure of Catherine as a mother that he was to emphasize so much when he justified the parting.

It is impossible now to say how true this charge was. He told Miss Coutts later, when she sided with Catherine, that all the appearance of love in public between his wife and the children was a little play and very bad for the children. 'She does not, and she never did care for the children, and the children do not – and they never did – care for her.' This is manifestly the cruelly exaggerated statement of a desperate man; it is not surprising that Miss Coutts cooled towards the man who wrote it. There may have been some public pretence of affection – families do act plays for public consumption – but his account suggests a falsity that does not emerge from the somewhat negative relationship of Catherine with her children after the break-up. It makes Miss Coutts, too, and many others very undiscerning observers. Georgina confirmed the statement, but she is too involved a party to be a reliable witness. Whatever the truth of the matter, Catherine's ways with the children were not what her husband wanted. The second point that Dickens now made, in tracing dissension back to the very early days of his marriage, was to be a central plank of his defence of the separation. I am much more sceptical about this. Dickens, as a novelist, saw his life as a series of patterns; but what is necessary artistic selection for a novelist is perhaps only an afterthought in a man seeking to explain his life to himself and to the world. Although he feels still that no help can be given him, he is perhaps already justifying any future action he may take. The action of the following month is of the essence of the failed middle-class marriage, at least until the First World War. He wrote to Anne Brown, that most trusted of servants, asking her to turn his dressing room into his bedroom, and to close it 'with a plain light deal door, painted white' – the door that communicated with Catherine's room.

By spring of the following year, 1858, he is writing to Forster: 'It is all despairingly over . . . a dismal failure has to be borne, and there is an end.' He had begun his new existence – part country gentleman at Gad's Hill, a house largely unconnected with Catherine, part strolling player with his public readings – which forms the core of the last chapter in his life. All that remained were squalid incidents which perhaps necessarily attended the end of a twenty-two-year-old marriage. The first, which we know from his second daughter Katey's revelations in her old age, is again typically Victorian bourgeois. It is the distress caused to Catherine by the delivery of a bracelet to her by a mistake of the jewellers – a bracelet intended by Dickens for Ellen Ternan. He had made presents previously to those who had acted for him, but Catherine no doubt sensed a difference. Her daughter found her weeping because (surely the most awful Victorian bourgeois note of all) Dickens had ordered her to visit Ellen. 'You shall not go,' Katey said angrily; but her mother obeyed her husband's instructions. There is little doubt that Ellen Ternan was not Dickens's mistress until several years after this; indeed it seems most likely that Dickens (as he passionately insisted by implications in his public utterances) was denying himself even the hope of making advances to her. But rumours spread.

Mrs Hogarth and her youngest daughter Helen urged Catherine to leave Dickens. It was part of Dickens's public case that Catherine had long been wishing to leave because she felt herself inadequate as a wife and mother. It may have been so; there is only Dickens's statement for this; it was certainly not the reason why she left now. She refused rather spiritedly a cover arrangement to disguise their parting, and chose their old Punch friend, Mark Lemon, as her negotiator. She was to have her own house and £600 a year. Charley, the eldest son, was to live with her, though he wrote to his father that the arrangement was not to imply any expressed preference on his part. All might have been well, at least publicly, when suddenly Dickens heard that Mrs Hogarth and her daughter, Helen, had been gossiping, although whether of Ellen or of Georgina as the guilty party, is not known – Georgina's name, not unnaturally in view of her declared intention to stay with her brother-in-law, was on many gossips' lips. This behaviour of his in-laws threw Dickens into a rage. 'My father was like a madman,' Katey said years later. In his rage he decided to make a statement to his public, the readers who were so vital to his hold on life. All his good friends advised him against the action, but he was supported by Delaney of *The Times*. He also refused to make provision for his wife until his mother-in-law and sister-in-law had signed a retraction of their statements.

On the front page of *Household Words* for 12 June 1858 appeared his explanation to the public of his separation from his wife. He also sent to his American agent a much fuller statement, praising all that Georgina had done for his children, talking of 'two wicked persons' and of a young lady: 'I know her to be as innocent and pure, and as good as my own dear daughters'. His accompanying note almost encouraged the publication of this letter, yet he was furious when it appeared in the *Tribune* of New York. He always called it 'the violated letter' and apologized through his lawyers to Catherine for its publication. There were a number of adverse newspaper statements about all this public confession of private affairs. Certainly, as one newspaper pointed out, the public charging of Catherine as a bad mother is most distasteful, and a veiled suggestion that she was mentally abnormal is even more disgraceful. There is, too, a horridly vulgar ring about his account of his settlements upon Catherine: 'Of the pecuniary part of them, I will only say that I believe that they are as generous as if Mrs Dickens were a lady of distinction and I a man of fortune'. It is clear that he felt trapped by life and was prepared to tear anyone to pieces in order to free himself. The sad thing is that it seems to have been so unnecessary. He was so admired, such an institution, that, contrary to what is sometimes said, even this unseemly public washing seems to have done little harm to his reputation, although there was one resulting coolness and one resulting quarrel that helped to change the shape of his life in the next decade.

Chapter VI

In Harness 1858–70

he pattern of Charles Dickens's life after his separation from Catherine, in the decade before his death, changed greatly. The centre of his home life became the country, not London. His published novels were fewer, and his style of writing, always volatile and inventive, now changed radically. His amateur philanthropy and his amateur theatrical hobby indulged for charitable purposes gave way to a new professional activity – readings of his own works to public audiences for his own financial benefit. Only his constant link with his readers by means of a magazine remained of the external shape of his old life – and even here the magazine was a new one and his own property.

To take these changes in turn, we must first consider Dickens as the squire of Gad's Hill. What this house meant to him we can see most clearly in his description of it in his letter to his Swiss friend, Cerjat, in January 1857:

Down at Gad's Hill, near Rochester, in Kent – Shakespeare's Gads Hill where Falstaff engaged in the robbery – is a quaint little country house of Queen Ann's time. I happened to be walking past, a year or a half or so ago with my sub-editor of *Household Words* [Wills], when I said to him: 'You see that house? It has always a curious interest for me, because when I was a small boy down in these parts I thought it the most beautiful house (I suppose because of its famous old cedar trees) ever seen. And my poor father used to bring me to look at it, and used to say that if ever I grew up to be a clever man perhaps I might own that house, or another such house. In remembrance of which, I have always, in passing, looked to see if it was to be sold or let, and it has never been to me like any other house, and it has never changed at all.' We came back to town and my friend went out to dinner. Next morning he came in great excitement, and said: 'It is written that you were to have that house at Gad's Hill Place. The lady [Mrs Lynn Linton, a regular contributor to *Household Words*] I had allotted to me to take down to dinner yesterday began to speak of that neighbourhood. "You know it?" I said, "I have been there today." "Oh yes," she said, "I know it very well. I was a child there, in the house they call Gad's Hill Place. My father was the rector, and lived there many years. He has just died, has left it to me, and I want to sell it." ' 'So,' says the sub-editor, 'you must buy it. Now or never!'

I did, and hope to pass next summer there, though I may, perhaps, let it afterwards furnished from time to time.

Such may have been his original intention, but after his separation he came to decide otherwise. In 1860 he sold his large London house in Tavistock Square. In the last ten years of his life he rented from time to time houses in London so that his daughter, Mamey, who loved society, could indulge her tastes; but for the most part his London stays were now to be at the rooms he had furnished above his magazine office. As his health failed him and he refused to admit it, he occasionally cried off social occasions. Yet his social zest remained strong; only his distaste for contemporary English high society had grown.

London, as his novels show, had become increasingly repellent to him during the fifties. He had written from Lausanne to Forster in 1846, saying how much he missed London: 'the toil and labour of writing day after day, without that magic lantern, is *immense!*' But by 1851 he was writing to Bulwer Lytton:

London is a vile place, I sincerely believe. I have never taken kindly to it, since I lived abroad. Whenever I come back from the country now, and see the great heavy canopy lowering over the house-tops, I wonder what I'd do there except on obligation.

Throughout the 1860s Dickens not only wrote novels at Gad's Hill but, helped by Georgina and Mamey, acted host there to innumerable visitors, and squire to the locals. He would never, I am sure, have found such a life sufficient – but then his life with Ellen Ternan, his visits to France, above all his readings,

Gad's Hill.

satisfied his vagrant need enough to allow him to play the host at Gad's Hill with pleasure in the intervals.

A description by his young journalist friend, Edmund Yates, perhaps best gives the atmosphere of Gad's Hill as the many guests found it:

> Life at Gad's Hill for visitors, I speak from experience, was delightful. You breakfasted at nine, smoked your cigar, read the paper, pottered about the garden [the shrubbery of which was cut off by a main road under which Dickens had a tunnel made] until luncheon at one. All the morning Dickens was at work, either in the study . . . or in the chalet [a Swiss chalet given to him in 1865 by his actor protégé, Fechter] . . . . After luncheon (a substantial meal, though Dickens took little but bread and cheese and a glass of ale) the party would assemble in the hall, which was hung round with a capital set of Hogarth prints, now in my possession, and settled their plans. Some walked, some drove, some pottered . . . I, of course, elected to walk with Dickens; and off we set, with such of the other guests as chose to face the ordeal. There were not many and they seldom came twice; for the distance traversed was seldom less than 12 miles, and the pace was good throughout . . . . It was during one of these walks that Dickens showed me, in Cobham Park, the stile close by which, after a fearful struggle, Mr Dadd had been murdered by his lunatic son in 1843 . . . .

Gad's Hill was never, and is not today, more than a pleasant if somewhat inconveniently situated gentleman's house, but Dickens changed it from a modest country rectory to a place of modern comfort and fine appointment. Mrs Lynn Linton, from whom he had bought it, visited it after his death, and comments a little acidly on the somewhat suburban improvement of the old garden; but she was looking back nostalgically to her own childhood. Among

John Forster; Dickens with his two daughters, Kate and Mamey.

the vast burden of expenditure of his last years certainly the improvement of his country home was a considerable item.

The Readings

In 1857 he gave this expenditure as an explicit reason for undertaking public readings to Forster, who wholly disapproved of the idea. It was a question of some importance, for it involved one of Dickens's primary concerns – his dignity as a writer. Years before, almost in jest, Dickens had written to Forster from Lausanne in 1846:

> I was thinking the other day that in these days of lecturings and readings, a great deal of money might possibly be made (if it were not *infra dig.)* by one's having Readings of one's own books. It would be an *odd* thing. I think it would take immediately . . . I don't think you have exercised your usual judgment in taking Covent Garden for me. I doubt it is too large for my purpose.

Thackeray, pressed to provide sufficient fortunes for his two daughters after his death, had read aloud in the United States; but Dickens's ambiguous feelings towards Thackeray, soon to break out in an open quarrel, would hardly make this a satisfactory precedent for his own behaviour. Forster, taking an old-fashioned view, saw only the vulgarity of public appearance. Dickens, whose appetite had been whetted by his successful readings for charity, was ardent to continue. Since his whole foundation for independence was his mass readership, his instinct for what added to his status was probably correct. Luckily Miss Burdett Coutts, an even more important critic of social behaviour than Forster, saw nothing against such readings, and the first organized tour was planned before Dickens's separation from his wife.

The first readings took place in June 1858, almost immediately after the publicity over his broken marriage. Despite the misgivings of some friends, their reception was overwhelmingly favourable. Large audiences acclaimed them everywhere. Men as well as women were moved to tears at the pathos as well as the farce. It is perhaps a pointer to how popular Dickens was in his own day as a writer of short stories as well as of novels, that the first readings included selections from *A Christmas Carol, The Cricket on the Hearth, The Chimes,* the Boots' story from *The Holly Tree,* and *The Poor Travellers,* as well as the perennially loved scenes from *Pickwick* – the trial scene and Bob Sawyer's party. Mrs Gamp was an early favourite. Only a selection called 'The Story of Little Dorrit' belonged to the middle and later novels, now so much admired. The tour, which took in Scotland and Ireland as well as innumerable towns in England, lasted on and off for six months. For weeks at a time, now as in the later tours, Dickens was travelling from place to place performing 'one night stands'. 'I cannot deny that I shall be heartily glad when it is all over . . . . But perhaps it is best for me . . . to wear and toss my storm away – or as much of it as will ever calm down while the water rolls – in this restless manner,' and again, 'Sometimes before I go down to read . . . I feel so oppressed by having to do it that I feel perfectly unequal to the task. But the people lift me out of this directly; I find that I have quite forgotten everything but them and the book in a quarter of an hour.' After this triumphant progress of 1858, only a doctor's explicit command could eventually wean Dickens, eleven years later, from what had become a sort of orgy of warm personal communication with his great mass of readers.

But for the moment the readings were partially interrupted by another change brought about by his separation. His relations with Miss Coutts merely cooled. Though this coolness meant an end of his management of her vast philanthropic concerns, they sent friendly New Year messages to each other in 1865. But his rupture with his publishers, Bradbury and Evans, was complete. They were also the proprietors of *Punch* and, with his old friend, Mark Lemon, who was editor of that paper, they had refused to publish Dickens's public explanation of his differences with Catherine. He was reconciled with Lemon some years later at the death-bed of their old artist friend, Clarkson Stanfield. From Bradbury and Evans he was irrevocably estranged. To Evans, whom he particularly disliked, he wrote:

> I have had stern occasion to impress upon my children that their father's name is their best possession and that it would indeed be trifled with and wasted by him if, either through himself or through them, he held any terms with those who have been false to it, in the only great need and under the only great wrong I have ever known. You know very well, why (with hard distress of mind and bitter disappointment) I have been forced to include you in this class. I have no more to say.

Nevertheless, two years later in 1860 his eldest son, Charley, married Evans's daughter. Dickens did not attend the wedding. The incident is an example of the pressures that the separation laid upon the Dickens children.

For the publication of his books he went back to Chapman & Hall, but, more important, he ended absolutely his editorship of *Household Words* and, since he owned three quarters of it, he forced a public sale at which he bought it up and then incorporated it into his own new magazine, *All the Year Round*. It is a ludicrous mark of his stubborn refusal to face the possible public image of his separation that he seriously proposed to Forster that he should call his new paper *Household Harmony*: 'Don't you think this is a good name? . . . I have been quite delighted to get hold of it.' However, under the title *All the Year Round*, and with the continued sub-editorship of Wills, it proved a resounding success, indeed it lasted on for many years after Dickens's death, until 1895.

A Tale of Two Cities

To secure the initial success for his periodical Dickens returned to that weekly serialization of a novel which he found so irksome. *A Tale of Two Cities* made an immediate appeal to readers, and it was followed by Wilkie Collins's first real best-seller, *The Woman in White*.

Oliver Twist has proved to be Dickens's 'pop' novel; *A Tale of Two Cities* has been his great middlebrow success. For theatre-goers of the early twentieth century it was a beloved favourite as *The Only Way*, with Sir John Martin Harvey as Sidney Carton; at the moment of writing it has reappeared as a musical, which seems likely to take a place in the somewhat old-fashioned repertoires of local amateur operatic societies. I should have liked, simply in order to avoid the charge of artistic snobbery, to number it among his great books; but I cannot do so. It is an important novel in Dickens's canon for two reasons, but neither of them do more than lend it interest irrelevant to artistic success.

The first peculiarity about it is its odd treatment of renunciation and redemption. In his previous novel Dickens had shown how Arthur Clennam had to accept life actively, and even Little Dorrit, the very embodiment of 'blessed are the meek', had to assert herself in order to find herself. Only when they had both accepted happiness and life could they seek salvation away from the world and its noisy, crooked ways. In *A Tale of Two Cities*, however much the nominal hero is Charles Darnay, the real hero is Sydney Carton, the drunken, idling, old-Salopian barrister, and he finds salvation by dying for the happiness of others on the guillotine. The theme of renunciation and redemption continues in the two complete novels Dickens was still to write – Pip must give up the world's goods in *Great Expectations* to redeem his snobbery; so must Bella Wilfer be tried and tried again in *Our Mutual Friend*; and in the same novel idle, cynical Eugene Wrayburn (also a barrister) must come near to death to purify himself for marriage with the heroine, Lizzie Hexam.

Renunciation, redemption, resurrection – we are in these last novels of Dickens well into the world of Tolstoy in his late works, or in that of Dostoevsky's *Crime and Punishment*, or of Dmitri and Ivan Karamazov. It is essentially a Christian New Testament world, with transcendental overtones. Sydney Carton, who actually gives his life, should surely preach the most Christian of all sermons. And to a degree he does so. As he rides in the tumbril beside the little sempstress she tells him: 'But for you, dear stranger, I should not be so composed . . . nor should I have been able to raise my thoughts to Him who was put to death, that we might have hope and comfort here today;' and as the little girl is guillotined and the knitting women count 'Twenty-two', an unembodied voice (is it Sydney Carton or is it the author?) recites: 'I am the Resurrection and the Life, saith the Lord: he that believeth in me, though he were dead, yet he shall live: and whosoever liveth and believeth in me shall never die.' And this Christian note has relevance to the general theme of the book where the two regimes of France – the old order of the Marquis St Evremonde and the new of the revolutionary Defarges – exalt their class, their abstract principles, above the personal ethics of Christianity.

At one point, when the revolutionaries urge Dr Manette to testify against his own son-in-law as an *aristo* and an *emigré*, Dickens directly points out how the old pagan heroism of sacrificing one's nearest of kin to the good of the republic has been brought hideously alive in French revolutionary zeal. To this extent the book's exaltation of private relationships, private loves (of father for daughter, daughter for father, or of lovers for one another) over

'Trafalgar Square at Night' by Henry Pether, 1861–7. 'The Great steps of St Martin's Church as the clock was striking Three. Suddenly a thing . . . rose up at my feet with a cry of loneliness.' 'Night Walks' in *The Uncommercial Traveller*.

Overleaf. 'A Chelsea Interior' by Robert Tait, 1858. (Carlyle's drawing room.) 'No one can hope to add anything to the philosophy of Mr Carlyle's wonderful book.' Preface to *A Tale of Two Cities*.

abstract principles seems to work with the Christian scheme that Carton's self-sacrifice suggests. And yet, as John Gross has acutely pointed out, in this most seemingly Christian of novels, Dickens's Christian sense seems strangely lacking. Carton's sacrifice is so much a matter of human love that it comes full wheel round to another sort of pagan heroism, not that of the hero who dies for his country, but that of a hero who dies for the sake of love. Christ's death seems only accidental in such a setting; for a Christian reader perhaps the references to Him may seem a little blasphemous. And on the same page, describing Carton's death from which I have quoted the passages about the Crucifixion, Carton and the little sempstress are suddenly called 'these two children of the Universal Mother'. Nevertheless, the novel marks clearly the emphasis on personal relationships as the salvation from the world's evils that was already to be seen in *Little Dorrit* and was to continue in his novels. This in itself makes nonsense of the book's form; for it is intentionally the tale of two cities and above all the tale of a cruel whirlwind that arose and swept through one of them – Paris – in the shape of the Terror.

Dickens, aware by now of the limitations and needs of weekly serialization, searching (and searching successfully) for a book that would quickly grip his readers' interest, had decided to pare down all in the novel that took away from the action, the events, the rush of the story. To a large extent he was successful. *A Tale of Two Cities* has a minimum of dialogue, subplot, humorous or even melodramatic ornament. It was a sacrifice of all his greatest gifts; and in my opinion it shows that those gifts – of fantastic speech, of animistic description, of deeply absorbed symbolic overtones – are essential to the success of his action. There are splendid scenes, notably Mr Lorry sitting in the quiet, old-fashioned order of Tellson's countinghouse in Paris while the horrors of the September Massacre outside are only suggested in the noises he hears. But the picture of the French Revolution in action (or indeed the cruelties of the nobility that preceded it) seem to me no more than efficient. It is Dickens's revered Carlyle in story form; and Carlyle's *French Revolution* is a good enough story anyway, without fictionalization. Yet it is all there on the pages – Dickens's understanding of the causes of the Revolution, his sympathy with the revolutionaries, his abhorrence of their excesses; but because of its over-simple, active form it becomes a statement and not an evocation. If this were Dickens, he could be counted a proficient master of literature of action to which detail is added without much conviction to give a sense of history. The scenes are greatly inferior to those in *Barnaby Rudge* because the madness which should inform them, which indeed is Dickens's charge against both the *ancien régime* and the Terror, is quite absent – absent because there is none of the black humour, the wild dialogue, the horrible absurdities of Dennis the hangman, Hugh, Simon Tappertit and Barnaby.

The most telling scenes in *A Tale of Two Cities* are the extremely retired, private scenes in Dr Manette's house in Soho, a house remarkable for its seclusion. The noise of distant feet heard there is used rather heavily by Dickens to warn us of the Revolution to come; but when it comes, it has not

Charles Dickens by Spy, 1870. 'The cost in health was prodigious.' See page 284.

'The Royal Family of France in Prison' by Edward Ward, 1851.

the reality of the Soho garden's privacy. Maybe this is a triumph in a book intended to exalt family love, but I doubt if Dickens intended such a kind of triumph – purposefully to fail to bring alive a whole revolution in order to preserve the life of one or two scenes of domestic calm is a modern sort of complexity alien from his genius. The truth is, I think, that for all the two cartloads of reference books from the London Library, which Carlyle sent round to him to help him prepare the novel, the French Revolution remained unrealized in Dickens's book. Private renunciation and private love are the real themes of a novel which ostensibly treats of the greatest public event of his era. It is a sort of Brecht in reverse; but to see it as such is badly to mistake the century in which it was written.

Despite the irony of this failure, his paring down of his usual way of writing had great importance for his next, and what is very likely his most perfect novel, *Great Expectations*.

Great Expectations

After the completion of *A Tale of Two Cities* Dickens no doubt felt that he had made his necessary contribution to the initial success of *All the Year Round*, apart from his constant editorial attention. *The Woman in White* was delighting readers. Charles Lever's *A Day's Ride* was chosen to follow it in the summer of 1860. After a few issues the sales of *All the Year Round* began to fall off badly; it was clear that the public did not like Lever's novel. Dickens's action is illustrative of his ruthless promptitude where business matters were involved, and of his extraordinary patient kindness and sensitivity towards friends or brother artists. He immediately decided that he must contribute to his paper the new novel which he was designing for his usual monthly serialization; he knew that this would be a terrible blow to Lever's pride, but he tempered his action with a series of the most feeling, tactful and genuinely friendly letters to the disappointed author, and he tried hard to secure the best terms for Lever for the publication of *A Day's Ride* in book form. The whole episode is characteristic of what made Dickens both frightening and lovable. Yet more astonishing is his certainty that he could make a work of a certain length out of a novel he was designing for quite another length.

Miraculously, *Great Expectations* is the most completely unified work of art that Dickens ever produced; formally concentrated, related in its parts at every depth of reading. It was perhaps not only Dickens's final mastery of the close, tightened form needed for weekly serialization which accounts for this artistic unity; he mentions in a letter, 'for a little piece I have been writing, or am writing, for I hope to finish it today, such a very fine, new and grotesque idea has opened upon me that I begin to doubt whether I had better not cancel the little paper, and rescue the notion for a new book' – in short the great book, although later designed for a leisurely monthly form, was conceived at first in little and never lost that tightness. The exactitude is typified in the title – for *Great Expectations* describes with irony exactly the triviality of the silly, idle life, that Pip aspires to when he inherits his mysterious fortune; that Magwitch, the escaped transported convict, designs for Pip when he decides to make him a gentleman; the triviality, indeed the death in life, which Miss Havisham prepares for Estella when she plans to make her a beautiful, richly-endowed instrument of revenge upon the hearts of men; its irony even extends to the seemingly all-powerful manipulator figure, Jaggers, the lawyer, before whom the criminals cringe, for what does his profession of an amoral superior-

Hobart Town chain gang, Van Diemans Land.

ity to the feelings of humanity come to but a mechanical, empty, lonely life in which he is forever hopelessly washing his hands to free himself from the guilt common to humankind, a guilt from which he claims the false freedom of a puppet master?

The trivial, genteel aspirations also stand, but not obtrusively – since this is never a broadly panoramic social novel like *Bleak House* or *Little Dorrit* – for the pursuit of gentility in England which Dickens had declared so often in the fifties to be the curse of the country, the enslavement of its people to a loveless system. But these false gentilities that Pip pursues are only half the pseudo-great expectations, for just as Magwitch has tried to create him, and Miss Havisham has tried to mould Estella, so Pip, in his painful, consuming passion for Estella tries to impose upon her the shape of a love object, of great romantic expectations to which she, in her anaesthetized coldness of heart, cannot respond. Romantic love is seen as the private sin parallel to the social sin of snobbery, and the sentimental by-product of a money-centred society. And, since the social in the novel is thus kept subordinate to the private and personal, since every character and incident is seen only as a facet of the wonderfully rounded, complex, yet simple-seeming character of Pip himself, it is possible, as seldom in Dickens's work, to be conscious all the time of the metaphysical overtones – the trivialities of expectation are not merely what Pip makes of his fortune, or England of her riches, or man of his civilization, or even Pip of Estella upon whom he imposes his romantic dreams.

When Pip, the boy, first meets with Estella's coldness, and says, 'I looked at the stars and considered how awful it would be for man to turn his face up to them as he froze to death, and see no help or pity in all the glittering multitude,' we are led on inevitably to think upon the spiritual death which mankind creates for itself by preventing or suppressing true love and feeling. Yet once again, because the story is so unified, so enveloping, this allegorical element is never overstressed nor overplayed, it just is always there at a deep level as the tale develops.

The social and the metaphysical can look after themselves to such good effect because the novel is essentially the successor to *David Copperfield*, a novel of the education of a young man in the lesson of life; and, like *David Copperfield*, it is closely related to Dickens himself. Indeed, like *David Copperfield* its events are laid in the years of Dickens's own childhood and youth. Dickens was quite aware of this, for he wrote to Forster that he had been re-reading the earlier novel to make sure there was no repetition. He need not have feared. The direct autobiography that went into *David Copperfield*, making it, for all its poetry of memory, a loose, voluminous, picaresque novel, had been used up. The self in *Great Expectations* came from a much deeper, more bitter, and yet finally more secure, level of his review of his own life.

Socially the later novel does penance for the large element of the genteel, the cosy, in the second half of *David Copperfield* – as Bernard Shaw in his preface to *Great Expectations* wrote: 'The adult David Copperfield fades into what stage managers call a walking gentleman; the reappearance of Mr Dickens in the character of a blacksmith's boy may be regarded as an apology to Mealy Potatoes.' Certainly Trabb's boy's splendid mockery of Pip dressed up as a 'toff' is a perfect send-up of all that went with David Copperfield's establishment 'in fame and fortune'. *Great Expectations* has no direct connection in story with Dickens's own life. It is only in the character of Estella that critics have seen, perhaps justly, some reference to Ellen Ternan's coldness towards Dickens's passion. The speech of Pip's I have just quoted about the stars and the frozen man must be an echo of *The Frozen Deep* – a story of Arctic heroism and endurance – in which he had first met Ellen. I am not very impressed by the argument frequently used of relating the letters of fictitious names to those of real people – E. T. being prominent letters in both these. But Estella does represent a real advance in Dickens's perception of women. It is not that we know her from inside, the form of the book precludes this; but we do see, in her resistance to others' management, a recognition of a woman as an individual having her own demands on life (demands that neither Pip nor Dickens quite wish to recognize). Since Bella Wilfer in his next novel, *Our Mutual Friend*, was to be an even more living development of the same qualities, we may attribute to Ellen Ternan the only directly autobiographical aspect of *Great Expectations*, and, more importantly, a real examination of romantic love that shows up the creating of Dora, the killing of her, and the replacing of her by ministering Agnes, for the masculine self-gratification it is.

False expectations are the mark of the lives of all the dominating characters – and as a comic parallel we have Mr Wopsle's absurd ambition to play Hamlet. But powerful though the forces of snobbery and gentility are shown to be, corrupting not bad people but good ones – for Pip, Estella, Magwitch, Jaggers and even Miss Havisham are not the black villains of many of Dickens's works, but in varying degrees spoiled, likable people – Dickens is triumphant also in the creation of the good characters to offset them. Joe is perhaps, with Mr Toots, Dickens's most successful divine idiot – he has indeed that curious power we find in Dostoevsky's Myshkin; we are convinced at once that he is simple and that he is wise. Dickens, when he first wrote to Forster about the book, seems to have designed Joe as a comic clown; and so, in a sense, he remains, but with all the implications of seriousness, of criticism of the shallowness and emptiness of sophistication and worldly wisdom, that the figure of the clown at its fullest implies. I know of no more convincing statement of the possibility of simple happiness, simple pleasure, than Joe's 'Wot larks, eh, Pip, old chap?' Biddie, perhaps, is more shadowy, but she expresses simple goodness and dignity without mawkishness. And Herbert Pocket allows Dickens to show that it is not intended solely as the property of the working class.

Paradoxically this remarkable novel, born out of a time of Dickens's disillusions, grey and realistic as no other of his works; only very moderately successful in its comic effects; ending (in its original and its substituted final scenes) on a very muted note, is nevertheless one of Dickens's warmest novels because of the compassion extended by the author to almost all his characters, because of the love of Joe for Pip, because of the love that Pip learns to feel for the 'warmint' Magwitch. There is more heart and less parade of heart than in the early novels; more of acceptance and less parade of humility than in the virtues of Little Dorrit or Esther Summerson. Not the less so because in this more sober, compassionate mood for humanity Dickens does not give up his sense of absolute evil. Only one grey note seems to me to mar the scene: there is in Joe's moral condemnation of Pip's childish fancies as lies a certain undertone of Tolstoyan puritan condemnation of art (especially of Dickens's own art – fiction).

Dependants and family

In the sixties Dickens's compassion was constantly called upon. In the first place his old circle of friends, so very important to him, was dying off. Of his contemporary intimates only Forster, Lytton and old Macready survived him. It was easier to write, as he did to a mourning friend, 'Close up the Ranks and March On', than to banish thoughts of mortality with spurred-on energies. In many cases these old friends left unprovided families behind them – for the strain of competitive literary and artistic life in Victorian England killed people off before they could lay enough by. The future of his many dependants increasingly haunted Dickens in this last decade, as his daughters' future made Thackeray's last years anxious.

As to Dickens's family – his brothers and sisters – their dependence upon him had increased to frightening proportions. His brother, Alfred, though hardworking and honest, died in 1860 at thirty-eight, leaving his wife, Helen, and his children on Dickens's hands. His favourite, comic and lovable brother Fred, after a runaway marriage of which Dickens disapproved, had left his wife and become a hopeless sponger. Many years before his death Dickens had had to refuse him further loans. 'I have already done more for you than the most dispassionate person would consider right or reasonable in itself. But, considered with any fair reference to the great expenses I have sustained for other relations, it becomes little else than monstrous. The possibility of your having any further expenses from me is absolutely past.' When finally Fred died in 1868 among strangers in Yorkshire Dickens was greatly distressed. He wrote to those who had befriended him: 'How tenderly I write these words you can scarcely imagine, unless you know that he was my favourite when he was a child, and that I was his tutor when he was a boy.' And to Forster he wrote, 'It was a wasted life, but God forbid that one should be hard upon it, or upon anything in this world that is not deliberately and coldly wrong.'

For his youngest brother, Augustus, who also inherited their father's feck-lessness, he had less strong affection. To his sister, Letitia, when she urged him to recommend Augustus to his American friends, he wrote, 'I have no hope of him. If I had any suitable employment in my own gift, in America, I would give it him; but I can *not* recommend another man to do it, and least of all a stranger, who doing it at all, would only do it in his confidence in me . . . .' Nevertheless he had to help support the wife Augustus abandoned in England, and in 1868, when he lectured in America, he was attacked in the press for not supporting the mistress and illegitimate children that Augustus had left in Chicago. On the premature death of his good friend and brother-in-law, Henry

Austin, in 1861 his sister, Letitia, also fell mainly upon his charge. She lived with their mother until the old lady died senile in 1863. But after Dickens's death Georgina had to find provision for her. There is an element of hysteric distaste with which Dickens speaks of all these dependants; a distaste that frequently obliged him to refer interviews with them to Georgina or to Wills, but he never ceased his generosity to them or to take infinite pains on their behalf, as he also did for friends in need. It is not surprising that Miss Havisham's relatives are portrayed as so vulture-like a flock as they gather round her crazy sick room.

But more important in this last decade than friends, or sisters and brothers, were his own children, although the two subjects were connected. Having seen the fecklessness of his parents repeated disastrously in the lives of two of his brothers, Dickens was early determined that the upbringing of his own children (especially of his seven sons) should avoid this inherited snare. It is easy to criticize him for his failure; much of his method must seem repulsive to us as it would not to a Victorian. Some of the more pettifogging aspects of his paternalism came from the naturally masterful qualities of his own character, particularly his obsession with order. 'It is so remarkable (being almost a *dis*-order),' he once himself remarked. Inspection of the children's rooms, of the pegs upon which their coats were to be hung, and so on and so on, was a daily feature of childhood and of school holidays. The two girls were not spared this; and Katey, the impulsive, lively, second daughter frequently received a severe note of reprimand fixed to her pincushion.

More harmful than any direct discipline, probably, was the darker side of their father's temperament, at its worst in the years before his separation from Catherine. But the continuous arrival of fresh babies upon the scene brought no relief from the nervous exacerbation that children impose at times upon all adults, and especially upon adults whose creative work must be done at home. When Catherine and Dickens were separated their youngest child, the beloved 'Plorn', was only six; when Dickens died at the age of fifty-eight, Plorn, not yet seventeen, had already joined his elder brother, Alfred, in Australia, but Harry, his immediate senior, an undergraduate at Cambridge, was still at home. Dickens was never without dependent children. And as late as 1862 he is still writing: 'The house is pervaded by boys; and every boy has (as usual) an unaccountable and awful power of producing himself in every part of the house at every moment, apparently in fourteen pairs of creaking boots.' There was probably, throughout his writing years, child-tension that he felt Catherine no help in allaying, that he loved Georgina for moderating.

He was strict but he was far from a fierce, or a gloomy, or an ungenerous father. He always kept the New Testament before his children as their guide; he wrote a special *Life of Our Lord* for them; he gave to each son a copy of the gospels with a letter of simple Christian advice when he went out into the world; but, hating always the Old Testament, joyless, Calvinistic gloom he portrays in the Murdstones' treatment of David or in the childhood of Arthur Clennam, he prided himself on not introducing the name of religion or the words even of the Saviour into the affairs of everyday life.

Dickens's children: Charles Culliford Boz; Kate and Mamey; Walter Landor.

His affection for his children was strong, despite all occasional resentments. He had his favourites – Plorn the youngest, little Sidney who became a sailor, both the girls in different ways. When they were young he entered into all their games with fervour, particularly the elaborate parties of Christmas and Twelfth Night – perhaps even in his enjoyment being a little too masterful, a little too bossy. As his sons grew older, Dickens, like many emotionally immature men, found them harder to get on with, as though he feared their rivalry when they grew to maturity. (It is typical, perhaps, of this determined youthfulness that Charley's children, his only grandchildren, 'are instructed from their tenderest months to know me as "Wenerables" which they sincerely believe to be my name and a kind of title which I have received from a grateful country'.) Yet even with his adolescent sons he could break through barriers, as his delighted and delightful account of a river trip with Charley, his eldest boy, and two other Etonians, shows. He recalled with distaste Macready's over-strict treatment of his children – how they 'used to come in at dessert and have each a biscuit and a glass of water, which last refreshment I was always convinced that they drank with the gloomiest malignity, "Destruction to the gourmandizing grown-up company!"' A lively and a firm regime of life at home – such was his scheme to avoid both the many painful, overdisciplined childhoods he describes in his novels or the disastrous results of indulgence he had seen in his brothers.

But what was their *education* (particularly that of the boys) to be? 'I am strongly impressed with the conviction that the sons of a father whose capital can never be the inheritance of his children must – perhaps above all other

Sydney Smith Haldimand; Henry Fielding and Francis Jeffrey; Edward Bulwer Lytton.

young men – hew out their own paths through the world by sheer hard work. And my boys are well accustomed to the admonition that so only, can they hope to sustain their name.' When he wrote this in 1865 his son Walter had already died in India, leaving large debts; his eldest son, Charley, had been through the bankruptcy courts; little Sidney was soon to be forbidden his home because of the debts he had incurred at sea; and beloved Plorn was clearly not making a go of it in Australia. Nor was Dickens quite consistent about expectation, for he left something to each of his sons, not enough to maintain them (how could he, poor man, with a wife, a sister-in-law and a daughter to provide for absolutely?) yet enough to make his clever son, Frank, at least, a wastrel.

In part the failure was that of a self-made man who was genuinely bewildered by what education meant. He revered it above all social forces; yet he mistrusted its too long prolongation. Only Charley (paid for by Miss Coutts) went to a public school (to Eton), and he was taken away early to learn German for a business career. All the others combined many shifts of school with private tutors abroad; they were all expected to show preferences for careers early on; to make their way with manly independence as their father had. But save for one they had no such clear inclinations. It was the age of the dawning Empire, and so with not much confidence, or with assumed confidence (and with their father's assurance that they and he were meeting squarely a new world of overseas responsibility) they set off for India or Australia – or the Navy – and failed. Only Harry, proving himself a scholar, went up to Cambridge and there won bursaries to delight his father's last years. Only he, after his father's death, was to go on to win, like David Copperfield, 'fame and fortune' (ironically in the law). As to the girls, Katey secured herself an education in art, and despite a rather sad first marriage to Wilkie Collins's invalid artist brother, for which Dickens blamed himself ('But for me, Katey would not have left home'), grew up to be a distinguished, very individual figure in Edwardian artistic circles. But Mamey, the passionate worshipper of her father, the natural socialite and conservative, went on into an eccentric, erratic, lonely spinster-hood. In John Lehmann's *Ancestors and Friends*, he quotes his grandfather, Frederick Lehmann, an intimate of the Dickens circle, as writing to his wife of the two Dickens girls in 1866, 'My dear, those two girls are going to the devil as fast as can be . . . society is beginning to fight very shy of them.' Dickens certainly guessed enough of all this before he died to feel deep disappointment; yet it is in his last three novels, and especially in *Edwin Drood*, that he brings alive the nature of young people (not children) as never before. But finally he was too much for his children, as he had been for his wife.

Ellen Ternan

And as he probably was for Ellen .Ternan, the young woman who formed the centre of his life in his last years. So little is known about their relationship, and so much has been written about that little, that my inclination is to play it down. But it would be wrong to do so; the extreme precautions Dickens took to hide their relationship, the degree to which Ellen herself felt the need for this, surely mark a very close intimacy. Certain facts must be remembered, however: she could, in age, so well have been his daughter; her family, though a theatrical one and slightly bohemian, was eminently respectable. Some years after Dickens's death she eventually married a private schoolmaster. From a disputed source, Thomas Wright, we have a report that a canon of Canterbury claimed to have received the story of her illicit relationship from her in later life – 'I had it from her own lips that she loathed the very thought of the intimacy'. Most biographers seem to report this with a certain relish, but, unless we are strongly puritanical moralists, we must surely hope, however much we may deplore some aspects of Dickens's treatment of his wife, that Ellen Ternan was looking back with repentant but false hindsight.

Whether happy or not, their intimacy from 1863 or so was probably complete. He paid the rates for her houses, first at Slough and then at Peckham, under an assumed name; he rented lodgings nearby in New Cross. He took her to France in 1865 (but, it must be remarked, with her mother) and in returning they were involved in a terrible railway accident near Staplehurst in Kent, where many around them lay dying. One of the few letters preserved in which she is referred to is written to Dickens's servant, John Thompson, a few days later: 'Take Miss Ellen tomorrow morning, a little basket of fresh fruit, a jar of clotted cream from Tucker's, and a chicken, a pair of pigeons, or some nice little bird. Also on Wednesday morning, and on Friday morning, take her some other things of the same sort – making a little variety each day.' He was clearly glad of the chance to spoil her a little. With his usual optimism he hoped that she might join him on his American lecture tour in 1867, and arranged a code with Wills to facilitate her arrival; but once in New York he saw that it would not do. Most of their relationship will probably never be known, but subsequent research has tended to support the claim that they were intimate, first made by Thomas Wright and then suggested by the revelations made to Miss Story by Dickens's daughter, Katey, in her old age. Some of what is known remains mysterious: we know from Katey that from the mid-sixties Ellen was received at Gad's Hill as a frequent guest; the family sent for her as Dickens lay dying, although she arrived too late to see him conscious; Georgina and Mamey continued to see her after Dickens's death. Even more curious, Dickens's will begins with a bequest of £1,000 to Ellen Ternan, too little to make a real provision for her, enough surely to excite remark. All that can be said – and it is, after all, the most important thing – is that if biographical inference is ever permissible in literary criticism, something of the greater realism of his young women in his last novels, the firmness, even hardness, of their wills, their liveliness, the greater sexual reality of Estella, and Bella Wilfer, and perhaps of Rosebud and of Helen Landless, must surely be Ellen Ternan's very valuable contribution to the English novel. From Ellen Ternan, I think, Charles Dickens acquired late in his career some sense of what it was like to be a woman. In his association with her he finally entered the large company of Victorian respectable men with secret lives. Out of that dark secrecy all that we can be sure of are two of his finest fictional creations – Bradley Headstone, the respectable schoolmaster, with murderously jealous passions, and Jasper, the cathedral choirmaster, who in disguise haunts an East End opium den.

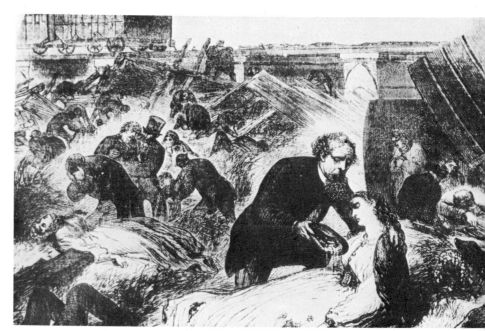

Ellen Ternan; the Staplehurst railway disaster.

Our Mutual Friend

It was not long after the publication of *Great Expectations* that Dickens began to compose his next novel. The first mention of some of the characters – the Lammles, the Veneerings and the Hexam father and son – occurs in a letter to Forster in 1861; yet the first number did not appear until the latter part of 1865. No other novel (save *Barnaby Rudge*, delayed by the writing of other books) took him so long. Although there were other reasons – a lengthy and successful reading tour under a new and less competent manager: 'I am not sorry to see land and a little rest before me; albeit, these are great experiences of the public heart,' a trip to Paris with Georgina to help her recover from some heart disorder, a further visit to Paris in January 1863 to give two triumphant readings at the British Embassy – the principal cause of Dickens's delay in constructing and indeed in writing the new novel was his failing health.

Dickens had subjected himself all his life to the most demanding of regimes, physical, mental and nervous. He had played as hard as he had worked; and although he grew up in the middle class before that class became devoted to the cult of athletic sports he had in his young manhood ridden strenuously, in later years he often rowed (probably the worst thing possible for a man later to suffer from heart degeneration), and throughout his whole life he walked enormous distances at a fast pace. His temperament, his ambitions, his sense of his own dignity, would never allow him the indulgence of a thought of exhaustion, let alone of ill-health. Yet as a boy his spasms had been a serious handicap at times. Just before he left for America in 1846 he had a painful and weakening operation for fistula. The origin of his childish illnesses is now said by some medical writers to have been a congenital kidney disorder, a forerunner of the condition from which he eventually died. Certainly from the early fifties (when he had passed forty years of age) he knew repeated bouts of ill-health which he boisterously suppressed, and by 1858 the strain of his life told so upon him that he looked a much older man than he was. But he scouted such suggestions. During his readings in Ireland he wrote, 'One gentleman comes out with a letter at Cork, wherein he says that although only forty-six I look like an old man. *He* is a rum customer, I think.' But in the summer of that year he had to admit to feeling ill.

How cavalierly he treated himself may be seen from the following sequence of quotations from letters: To G. H. Lewes on 6 August he wrote: 'I have not been quite well since we had the great summer heat – a circumstance so unusual with me, that I have been lost in indignant surprise.' To Wilkie Collins on 16 August he wrote: 'I should have written to you this week from Gad's Hill, but that I was tempted out on the Medway for two summer days (rowed 20 miles at a stretch one afternoon).' To Collins again on 25 August he wrote: 'I am not quite well – can't get quite well, have an instinctive feeling that nothing but sea air and sea water will set me right.' From that time on he was hardly quite well again, although his sanguine spirits refused to accept the hints of mortality. Luckily for his immediate health the outbreak of the American Civil War made an American lecture tour impossible; and even his indomitable

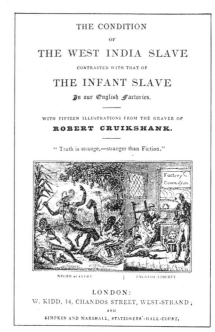

The American Civil War: Richmond burning; 'That platform sympathy with the black afar off, and indifference to our own countrymen.'

self-discipline wilted before the prospect of an Australian tour and the long distance and absence from Ellen and his family that it would entail.

It is lucky that both schemes failed, for his energies could hardly have sustained them and the writing of *Our Mutual Friend*. Nor was the painful, sometimes delayed writing of this novel to proceed without a worsening of his health; in 1864, after a long winter walk, he complained of persistent lameness from a frostbitten foot (though it was probably a more serious circulatory disorder), and the shock to his nerves from the Staplehurst railway accident persisted for the rest of his life, making all rail travel, which had once been his joy, a severe nervous strain.

Our Mutual Friend is undoubtedly a triumph for an ailing man. In recent years with the admiration given to Dickens's use of symbols and the emphasis on the power of his pessimism, this novel has been put among his greatest. I cannot agree with this judgment, although I think the novel to be as near a miss of greatness as, say, *Dombey and Son*, which for most novelists would mean a masterpiece. The difficulty is that, if one thinks in retrospect of *Our Mutual Friend*, especially in distant retrospect, it has all the qualities that we demand and find in his great social novels: its picture of society is all-encompassing; each part is held together by the common concept of money as the false measure of human worth in a corrupt society; the symbol for money in the dust mounds of old John Harmon is striking; the corruption of nearly all the individual characters by money in some form or another is convincing, and variously and appropriately conveyed; the symbol of the river for life in its ebb and flow seems to me too general to contribute powerfully to the effect of the novel, but it is better worked out than the sea image in *Dombey and Son*, or the river image in *Little Dorrit*; the renewal of life in the four principal young characters – Bella, Eugene, John Harmon junior, and Lizzie – by means of suffering, physical or mental, or of purgation, is convincingly told and not at all mawkish. In short, *Our Mutual Friend* passes with flying colours the sort of abstracting trial that modern criticism tends to make of a novel, and this abstraction can certainly be supported by telling quotations of lines or scenes.

Yet criticism must test a work not only in retrospect but in the reading. I have, throughout the preparation of this study of Dickens, re-read each novel immediately before describing it. Long familiarity, of course, is a necessary and perhaps the most important prerequisite for criticism – a novel must live and shape itself in the memory after a number of readings. Nevertheless the immediate reading has its claims on our attention, and here, I think, *Our Mutual Friend* falls short of *Bleak House*, *Little Dorrit* or *Great Expectations*. It is hardly longer than the first two, yet it seems much more so, for there are many dead passages: Mr Boffin's pretences are legitimate but they are over-worked (we should be as outraged by his 'Mew, bow-wow, quack-quack,' as Bella is, but we are not); Wegg is a most complex character and yet somehow his complexity comes out as a smudge rather than as an intricacy; we do not feel Mr Twemlow's shame as Fledgeby taunts him, for Riah the good Jew is upon the scene, and Riah is a dead figure wherever he appears. Yet there are such deadnesses even in Dickens's greatest works. The difficulty with *Our Mutual Friend* goes a little deeper.

It is an entirely modern novel – the only novel he wrote of society as it was in the mid-Victorian world. It is ironic that the young Henry James attacked it, for it is a novel that prophetically explores into James's Late Victorian world, into the world of sophisticated, empty vulgarity, into the world where money values are no longer solid but simply a feverish way of getting through life. Mr Merdle's bogus financial empire fell in *Little Dorrit*, and its fall entailed the financial ruin of almost everyone in the novel; but in *Our Mutual Friend* Veneering goes bankrupt, Lammle turns out to be a fraud, and no one is the worse; for all Mr Podsnap's reiterations of 'Rule Britannia', and with all his assertions of Britain's commercial might, everyone knows that it's all a fraud, simply a joke of Lady Tippins about the vulgar people one must call on today, my dear, and then cut tomorrow. We are in the world of Vanderbank and Mrs Brookenham, of Aggie and the Duchess, in short, of Henry James's own *The Awkward Age* (the English novel that best incorporates the hollowness of the turn of the century). Indeed Georgiana Podsnap, used as a bait by the Lammles to repair their fortunes, is a Jamesian heroine; she is Nanda. We are also in the world of Lady Bracknell, and it is appropriate that Eugene Wrayburn and Mortimer Lightwood should speak, as Dickens makes them, in the world-weary *Yellow Book* tones of *The Importance of Being Earnest*. What is so extraordinary is that the tired Dickens should so nearly capture this world of the future, this world only glimpsed by a few beneath the seeming-solid surface of the sixties.

He employs a completely new style to write about it, for as I have said, he had begun to throw off his old style, especially his old ironic style, with that determined essay in action writing, *A Tale of Two Cities*. That old ironic style which pervades his books from *Nickleby* to *Little Dorrit*, becoming ever more refined and brilliant, is a sort of pastiche, a mocking yet loving parody of the grand Gibbonian language of the previous century. This, as Alice Meynell points out in a brilliant essay, had by Victoria's reign become the small change of journalism or public speech.

But as though weary with the joke, weary with his own perfection, in his last novels Dickens devised a new and brilliant shorthand to level his fierce attack at a rotten society. It is to be seen first in *Little Dorrit* in the reduction of the grand social circle of Merdle to 'Bishop', 'Bar' and so on; impressionism is carried further in the attack on Miss Havisham's greedy relatives where Mrs Camilla, Sarah Pocket and so on are reduced to a mere abbreviation of the sort of elaborate irony that showed the Chuzzlewit clan gathered at Mr Pecksniff's. Now, in the Veneering and the Podsnap scenes of *Our Mutual Friend*, he brings this new shorthand to perfection.

Yet somehow the abbreviated form – with its repeated 'Brewer' and 'Boots', its turning of metaphor into direct use as when Veneering's butler from being compared to a chemical analyst becomes 'The Analytical' – is more tiring, less fresh than the old, more splendid mock verbosity. In part this is because there is no room for the old verbal farce and dramatization in this new tight form. More importantly, this new form fails somewhat because its very brilliance, inclining always to the high comedy of, say, Oscar Wilde, suppresses the delicate psychological nuances of relationship which are new to Dickens, yet which he rightly saw were the only sudden illuminating realities in such a sham world. They do occur, and when they do we must marvel that the great master of the old form could pull off things so modern, so Jamesian – they are there between Mr and Mrs Lammle, in all Mrs Lammle's dialogue with Georgiana Podsnap, in the more sombre moments of Eugene's friendship with Mortimer, in much that goes almost unspoken between Mrs Boffin and John Harmon, and, incredibly (seeing how much we fear the mawkish in such an encounter) when the Boffins talk with old Betty Higden. Save for the scene at Greenwich (and nothing, for a modern reader, can quite exonerate such a coy father-daughter flirtation), Bella wonderfully satisfies the demands of this modern, new world.

This, I think, is the triumph of *Our Mutual Friend*, but it is a triumph that doesn't come off. This, and the magnificent macabrerie, the criminal psychology of Bradley Headstone and all that melodrama, which really touches depths of human feeling, that goes with the scenes at the lock house, or in the painful rejection in the City churchyard. But this brilliant analysis of jealousy, and of what Dickens thought to be the criminal mind, is best reserved for praise when we reach his last and unfinished novel, *Edwin Drood* and the evil of John Jasper. Such successes, such new uses of the familiar are enough to make *Our Mutual Friend* an important, exciting work in Dickens's canon.

But the dirt-money symbol, by virtue of which it has crept to the top of the

The George Inn, Greenwich.

chart in some modern critics' estimation is, I believe, too much emphasized
by critics, perhaps because it helps the reader to forget the weariness of some
of the chapters, because it appears to unite parts of the work that, during our
reading, in fact never completely fuse. Nor do I believe that the presence of
human sewage in Victorian dustheaps, emphasized by Edmund Wilson and
Humphrey House, added any of the same disgust for Victorian readers that it
does for us. It is true that human excrement was an even less mentionable
subject to the Victorians than to us, but this does not mean that they were
not a great deal more familiar with the *idea* of night soil carts and all that
went with them. The Victorian critic or reader would not have pointed out
that Dickens was making a connection between money and human faeces, but,
as part of his general conception of dustheaps, he probably took it for granted.
Our Mutual Friend, indeed, would be a triumph of that large-scale realistic-
symbolic depiction of a whole society in which Dickens already excelled, if it
were not also something more – a book of strangely subtle, psychological
nuances, of moments, glances, asides that mean more than the whole, in short
a novel before its time; but since the two kinds of novels remain even with
Dickens's extraordinary mastery, different worlds, it ends as something less,
even though only a little less, than the best of its predecessors.

Its difference from its predecessors was, by chance, marked in another way,
for a new young illustrator appeared in its pages – Marcus Stone, the son of
an old friend of Dickens, now dead. After his father's death Marcus Stone had
written to Dickens, showing him a sketch of Jo, the crossing sweeper, which

he had made at the age of thirteen. This so pleased Dickens that, glad to help the son of his old friend, he engaged him to illustrate *Our Mutual Friend*. Stone's drawings are altogether more 'realistic' – curiously unsatisfactory, I think, where, as with the Boffins or Sloppy or Wegg, the grotesque is suggested, but more consonant than those of Phiz with mid-Victorian domesticity and drama in the pictures of the heroes and heroines, Eugene or Bella or Lizzie. Indeed Stone, who did not die until 1921, became a famous painter of the late Victorian age, especially of those narratives of dramatic domestic events, eighteenth-century in costume, irrevocably Victorian in everything else, that until recently decorated the flyblown walls of sea-side lodgings or boarding houses. Even more successful in giving a dramatic high-Victorian realism to Dickens's late work was the young Luke Fildes, later a distinguished Academician, in *The Mystery of Edwin Drood* (particularly in the picture of Jasper forcing his love upon Rosebud).

The disappearance of Hablot Browne (Phiz) from Dickens's world should not pass unchronicled here. His last drawings had been for *A Tale of Two Cities*, where he was clearly not at home. But from those first drawings he had made for *Pickwick Papers* and for 'Sunday Under Three Heads' in 1836, as the depictor of Dickens's characters, whether we like it or not, he had bitten deeply into the readers' vision of Dickens's world. He is at his best from Mrs Gamp and Mr Pecksniff onward, through Mrs Skewton and the Major, the Micawbers and Mr Dick, Mr Skimpole, to Mrs Merdle entertaining Mrs Gowan, or, greatest triumph, Mr Dorrit entertaining Mr Nandy. Many of Dickens's illustrators were finer craftsmen – Cruickshank, Samuel Palmer, perhaps Leech and Cattermole – but none did more for Dickens that this shy man, who seems to have fallen out of Dickens's life almost by accident, as indeed he did out of literary life generally.

The American Tour

For the next four years of his life, after the publication of *Our Mutual Friend*, Dickens, increasingly ailing, gave himself up to an even more intense life of public readings, the frenzy, exhaustion and excitement of which undoubtedly made him more gravely ill.

In February 1866 his doctor, Frank Beard, brother of his oldest friend, Thomas Beard, insisted on giving him a full physical examination. The results Dickens softened down a little in writing to Georgina:

> There seems to be degeneration of some functions of the heart. It does not contract as it should. So I have got a prescription of iron, quinine, and digitalis, to set it going, and send the blood more quickly through the system. If it should not succeed on a reasonable trial, I will then propose a consultation with someone else. Of course I am not so foolish as to suppose that all my work can have been achieved without *some* penalty, and I have noticed for some time a decided change in my buoyancy and hopefulness – in other words, in my usual 'tone'.

A second opinion proved necessary, but in no way lessened the gravity of

Beard's diagnosis. Yet on 10 April Dickens gave the first of thirty readings
arranged through Chappell's, who were henceforth to organize his tours. The
only mitigating feature of the enterprise was that Chappell's provided him
with a manager, Alfred Dolby, whose effective care and liveliness were to make
Dickens's life much happier in those last hectic years; this, and the fact that
though the readings were damaging him, he so greatly enjoyed the performances and their tumultuous receptions, save when he was in physical pain.
There were also incidents – women fainting, old friends in tears, Dickens himself preventing a panic stampede – that marked particular performances.

'Au Revoir!' from *Judy, or The London Serio-Comic Journal*, 1867.

Such occasional dramas were necessary, perhaps, to break the tension of
those month-long tours – the railway journeys, the hotels (for he would accept
no private invitations), the long morning walks, the afternoon and/or evening
recitals, the excitement and triumph, the few old friends received in the
dressing room, the suppers ever more light (champagne and oysters only at the
last) as his health grew worse, the hotels, the railway journeys, and so on – all
over the British Isles and all over again. The cost in health was prodigious, the
gain in money equally so. To gain more meant an earlier possibility of rest and
retirement from writing out of a tired imagination (but did he ever believe in

that retirement?); at the worst it meant more money to leave his beloved Georgy and Mamey independent, to provide honourably for Catherine, to spoil Ellen, to help the sons out of their increasing jams when he was no longer there. An extract from a letter of 1867 gives some idea of the painful routine:

> It is but a week since I came back from Ireland in the worst of hard weather, after a very tiring week there; since then I have read in London and Cambridge and Norwich; tomorrow I shall get to Colchester just in time for an early dinner; next morning betimes I am away to Swansea to read there at Night; next morning away to Cheltenham to read there at night, and again next day; and on Monday I read again in London, and start immediately afterwards for Hereford.

And all this time there was the temptation of the greater profits from an American tour. The Civil War, during which he had felt an almost equal dislike for both sides, had allowed him to postpone the decision. But at last there was no retreat. Dolby advised him that his profit would be £15,500. In the event he returned with £20,000 gain. Forster and Wills were both earnest in begging him not to go, but the lure was too great. He brought his English and Irish tours temporarily to an end in the spring of 1867; and in November of that year he left for the United States, after a great farewell dinner at the Freemason's Hall with Lytton in the chair.

His first 1846 Atlantic crossing had been made in January. He did not choose his months well. However, on this occasion the auguries proved wrong as far as his reception in America was concerned; and for his part he had the strongest impression of a country infinitely more agreeable and civilized than twenty years before. But nothing could really do more than palliate the effect of the vigorous programme upon a very sick man. Dolby and his assistants were devoted to Dickens and did everything to keep up his spirits, including a comic walking match in bitter winter weather. Fields, who was the American initiator of his tour, soon became a close friend, and Mrs Fields, a lively, sympathetic American woman, gave him just the understanding and slightly flirtatious companionship that he needed. The American crowds respected his wish to be alone. He saw the congenial and the great – Longfellow, Dana, Emerson, Wendell Holmes. He took his long walks. His first fortnight was without readings. When they began they were a triumph. Yet he met his schedule with difficulty, commuting each week for the first month or so from Boston to New York. Two days after Christmas he wrote: 'Today I am so very unwell that I have sent for a doctor; he has just been and is in doubt whether I shall not have to stop reading for a while.' But he kept going, with a New England tour, visits to Baltimore, Washington, Philadelphia, a series of one night stands in New York state, and the last, triumphal readings in New York city: 'They are a wonderfully fine audience, even better than Edinburgh, and almost, if not quite as good as Paris.' At the final banquet given to him at Delmonico's he was lame and in very great pain, and with permission of the company left after he had made his speech. On 20 April 1868 he gave his last New York reading and, exhausted, returned home. The strain upon Dickens of this American tour must have been greatly heightened by his absence from Ellen.

Immediately he arranged with Chappell's a farewell British tour of one hundred readings. The first was given in October at St Martin's Hall, London. He introduced for the first time Sikes's murder of Nancy, a token of the culmination of his life-long concern with murder and violence as the expression of human evil, which was soon to find imaginative shape in John Jasper. The 'Nancy Scene' was an immediate triumph of horror with the public; and very nearly his own death warrant from the nervous effect it produced on him. However he continued his tour, electrifying Macready in his retirement at Cheltenham, visiting Ireland again, almost collapsing at Edinburgh. At last, at Preston in Lancashire, Frank Beard, his doctor in attendance, forbade any further public appearance, so serious was the condition of his pulse and heart, so regular now after the readings were the near paralyses of left foot and hand. But Preston was not to be the end of this great theatrical triumph, for in January 1870, six months before he died, he gave a last tremendous performance at St James's Hall, London.

When he died he left £93,000, of which nearly half came from the profits of these readings.

They had taken up most of his energies, his interests and his time in the last years, yet there is one general aspect of his attitude to public affairs at this time which must be mentioned, for it ties in with the concern of his last unfinished novel.

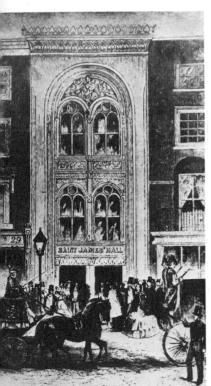

St James's Hall; *Edwin Drood:* 'Jasper's sacrifices' by Fildes.

Edwin Drood

In a sense this curious last decade of Dickens's life, though more than half of it was lived behind the gas flares of the stages of theatres and public halls and institutes, was very much more private and secret than had been the forties and the fifties with their public speeches, charitable works and occasional forays into public affairs. This private note, as we shall see, was reflected in his last novel, *The Mystery of Edwin Drood*, where the broad social canvases of his novels almost from their start in 1836, certainly increasingly from *Martin Chuzzlewit*, shrink almost to the dimensions of the professional classes of one cathedral town; but behind the private façade of Edwin Drood the problem of evil in man and therefore in human society presses more closely than ever before. This conflict of evil, always so powerful in Dickens's view of life, limiting his optimism, curbing his humanitarianism, shattering much of his Christian humanism, had always attached closely to violence. Some reasons for this I shall shortly suggest. But, as we have seen, it was manifested in a horror of public disorder almost as much as in a terror and disgust at private disordered passions. In the public sphere political mobs, artistic or moral bohemians, vagrants, rowdies, tramps, gipsies, hermits, the loose world of the racecourse, all were equally disturbing and objectionable to him.

This concern for public order seems to have grown upon him in the last decade of his life. We should hardly judge the 1860s permissive, nor, looking back from our viewpoint of a hundred years later, should we see Britain's loss of power and authority as the mark of that time. Yet Dickens (like many naturally neat, authority-loving people today, coming originally from that neat and authority-loving class, the petty bourgeoisie) undoubtedly felt himself in a world of collapsing standards. Many of his *All the Year Round* essays are directed against the increase of public ruffianism. In 1861 he wrote against tramps, shortly before his savage article against the choice of disorder and filth by a wealthy hermit in *Tom Tiddler's Ground*. And in an article entitled 'Ruffians' he wrote:

> A proved notorious thief, he is always consignable to prison for 3 months. When he comes out, he is surely as notorious a thief as when he went in. 'Then send him back again.' 'Just Heavens!' cries the society for the protection of remonstrant Ruffians, 'This is equivalent to a sentence of perpetual imprisonment.' Precisely for that reason it has my advocacy ... when he infamously molests women coming out of chapel on Sunday evenings for which I would have his back scarified often and deep ....

His admiration for the police (and especially for the detective forces in London, Liverpool, etc.) had grown steadily from the fifties; now all he felt was that police powers were insufficient or insufficiently backed up by the public. The thoughts were not new (witness his disgust at the lawlessness of the prairies in America in 1846): 'otherwise we have the Far West and the bowie knife'. Nor was he unwilling to practise what he preached. In 1853 he had limited himself to remonstrating with the baker's man who 'used the corner just outside our gates into the Square, for his private purposes'. But the result of such remonstrance was only that the man proved 'very impertinent'. In the 1860s he went further. He passed in the street a group of young Irish, merry from some celebration (a wake?), who shouted obscene and abusive language. Keeping up with them until a policeman came on the scene, he persisted in giving in charge a young girl, who was all that was left of the disorderly band, for her male companions had made a fast getaway. Despite all the unco-operativeness of the policeman and of the magistrate, who clearly regarded him as a thundering nuisance, he persisted, law-regulation book in hand, with following up the charge. He even appeared next morning at court, where the Irish girl was now dressed demurely in a white bonnet. He tells the story with a certain humour, but there is no doubt of his conviction of righteousness. I find the whole incident most distasteful; others will not. Certainly it connects with his general attitude to public affairs in those years.

In 1865 a rebellion in Jamaica was put down with severity by Governor Eyre. Some liberal intellectuals like Mill and Herbert Spencer attacked his actions. Others, Carlyle, Ruskin, Tennyson, then replied defending him. Dickens joined their ranks. His advocacy of this cause of stern authority has usually been charged to his admiration for Carlyle. Yet a letter to Cerjat of 30 November 1865 gives two definite reasons for his support of the Governor's harsh actions – his own dislike of missionary concern for blacks when our own people were in need, and his alarm that government in England was inefficient:

> The Jamaica insurrection is another hopeful piece of business. That platform sympathy with the black – or the Native or the Devil – afar off, and that platform indifference to our own countrymen at enormous odds in the midst of bloodshed and savagery, makes me stark wild. Only the other day, there was a meeting of jawbones of asses at Manchester, to censure the Jamaica Governor for his manner of putting down the insurrection! So we are badgered about New Zealanders and Hottentots, as if they were identical with men in clean shirts at Camberwell, and were to be bound by pen and ink accordingly . . . . But for the blacks in Jamaica being over-impatient and before their time, the whites might have been exterminated, without a previous hint or suspicion that there was anything amiss. *Laissez aller,* and Britons never, never, never!

It is all so familiar and muddleheaded and understandable and depressing.

It is not therefore surprising that the only public figure in *Edwin Drood* should be Mr Honeythunder, a reforming philanthropist, who is savagely lampooned for his tyrannical imposition of his humanitarian, reforming views upon private citizens who think otherwise: and the private citizen who quietly puts this public-reforming blusterer into his place is Canon Crisparkle, that rowing, boxing, classic-loving, eminently likable bachelor clergyman, who with manly modesty and conviction holds to the decent, right view of life in his own private, unassuming way.

The course of Dickens's political views did not change, though there were those who occasionally thought it had. In 1869 in a speech at Birmingham he said: 'My faith in the people governing is, on the whole, infinitesimal; my faith

'The bull's eye'; 'The lascar's room in *Edwin Drood*' from *London* by Doré.

in the People governed is, on the whole, illimitable.' The sentence was reproduced with two small ps and taken by many to declare his rejection of democracy.
He was quick at once to assert his general faith unaltered; he had no belief in
the rulers of England, every belief in the People.

Yet there was always, I think, a sharp limit to this liberalism. For all his
celebration of eccentricity, groups that did not 'fit in' did not easily gain
Dickens's charity. He was never wicked in prejudice. It was certainly not that
he was anything so uncharitable or crudely defined as a racist. He carefully
put Riah, the good orthodox Jew, into *Our Mutual Friend* because the Jewish
purchaser of Tavistock House, Mrs Davis, told him that Fagin had made the
Jewish community think him hostile to it. Yet, horrified though he was by the
charge, he had professed himself surprised by the financial honesty of the
Davises when they purchased his house – considering that they were Jews.
And so with Negroes: 'but it is indubitably the fact that exhalations not the
most agreeable arise from a number of coloured people got together, and I was
obliged to beat a quick retreat from their dormitory. I strongly believe that
they will die out of this country [U.S.A.] fast. It seems, looking at them, so
manifestly absurd to suppose it possible that they can ever hold their own
against a restless, shifty, striving, stronger race.'

And among the foolish, prejudiced rumours that assaulted poor, persecuted Neville Landless after Edwin Drood's disappearance was that before coming to England, he had caused to be whipped to death sundry 'natives . . . vaguely supposed in Cloisterham to be always black, always of great virtue, always calling themselves Me, and everybody else Massa or Missie'. The common prejudices of the class he came from died hard in him; but then so did private illusion. In April 1869 he wrote to an enquirer: 'I beg to inform you that I have never used any other armorial bearings than my father's crest; a lion couchant, bearing in his dexter paw a Maltese cross. I have never adopted any motto, being quite indifferent to such ceremonies.' But this private snobbery was more harmless than public prejudice. Evil in public life easily attached for him to what was difficult to absorb into his scheme of things. Perhaps this accounts for the real strengthening of private virtues that is to be found in his last, unfinished novel.

But his temperament did not easily let him leave hold of a public life. Even in the last year he was busy in London until the summer with a round of dinner-parties and social gatherings – his spirits improved by the cessation of the readings, even though his physical health was not really improvable. In March 1870 he had an interview of an hour and a half with the Queen, she graciously standing as court etiquette did not allow him to sit. He was surely her most world-famous citizen, though, as he said of his idol, Shakespeare, 'a commoner . . . who nevertheless did the State some service'. It was thirty years before that, at the time of her marriage, he had written to Forster half in jest:

> I am utterly lost in misery, can do nothing. I have been reading *Oliver*, *Pickwick* and *Nickleby* to get my thoughts together for the new effort, but all in vain:
>> My heart is at Windsor,
>> My heart isn't here;
>> My heart is at Windsor
>> A-following my dear.

Now the Queen had lost her beloved Albert, the cause of Dickens's parodied jealousy; and Dickens had lost the wild, facetious high spirits of that letter. It was a curious meeting. He followed it up by attending a royal levee of the Prince of Wales. His leg was too painful for him to take Mamey to the Royal Ball; however, he wrote to a court official:

> En attendant, I send for Her Majesty the first number of my new story which will not be published till next Thursday, the 31st. Will you kindly give it to the Queen with my loyal duty and devotion? If Her Majesty should ever be sufficiently interested in the tale to desire to know a little more of it in advance of her subjects, you know how proud I shall be to anticipate the publication . . . .

Alas, she was not.

The Mystery of Edwin Drood, of which Dickens had finished six instalments out of twelve when he died, appears as the greatest departure from his usual course to be found in any of his novels. Here is neither a broad social panorama like *Chuzzlewit* or *Dorrit*, nor a parable of man's private and social growth like

Copperfield or *Great Expectations*. Most of the energy of commentators has been spent upon trying to guess the mystery – has Edwin Drood been murdered and if so, who did it? The general consensus of opinion is that Jasper was the murderer. But if this is all that the novel involves (and its title, *The Mystery of Edwin Drood*, could be used to back up such a limited view) it is an almost incredible shrinkage from his other work. It may have been that he had set himself to master a relatively new, limited genre, to rival Wilkie Collins; but it seems more likely that the murder (or the mystery) is incidental, as is that of Mr Tulkinghorn or of Montague Tigg. If so, what is the theme of the book? To ask this is immediately to see what a composer, a long-term artist Dickens was, for all his serial methods of publication and occasional outrageous extemporisations. Not very much that is meaningful can be said about the totality of *Edwin Drood*, because Dickens was the sort of artist whose parts (whatever the contrary appearance) are so interrelated that only the whole gives the key to the whole. We can, however, notice certain new aspects of this work that are unknown in his previous novels; and we can relate Jasper, the probable murderer (certainly the criminal mind) to the whole theme of evil and murder as it runs through his novels – in this the novel is a convenient culmination.

The oddest aspect of *The Mystery of Edwin Drood* as we have it is the degree to which England has shrunk to a cathedral town and its classes to the upper-middle, professional class. I write 'as we have it' because the later chapters branch off into London and into the London of early Dickens – Billickin, the Cockney landlady, is David Copperfield's landlady writ large. Indeed, the dating of the novel (unlike *Our Mutual Friend)* specifically returns to the past of Dickens's youth, but the important characters are, on the whole, quite modern. Edwin Drood himself, likable, spoilt, charming, loving life but taking it too much for granted, comes out of early Imperialism, with his assumption that he will set Egypt to rights as soon as he gets there. Neville and Helena Landless with their Ceylon background also seem products of mid-Victorian England with its far-flung burden of duty and privilege. That they should all be brought together under Canon Crisparkle's decent patronage seems a eulogy of the public school as the mentor of youth to whom the Empire belongs. And noticeably everyone 'on the good side', including even Rosebud, who at first seems a coquettish version of Dora, is much tougher, much more positively embattled against evil. Meekness, humility, self doubt – the world of Esther, Little Dorrit – have been replaced by a more positive, manly, strenuous, though private, army of the good.

To them, this public school cathedral group, is added as ally – of all things! – a lawyer, Mr Grewgious. Dry he may be as his law books, and a bachelor early crossed in love, but there is none of the ambiguity of Mr Jaggers about him (let alone the scoundrelly qualities of early lawyers). Mr Grewgious brings to the side of the angels a tenacious, stonewalling bat, and a steady bowling that will wear down the evil opponents. If, as I think most likely, Mr Datchery should turn out to be a professional detective (that profession whose tenacity, wiliness and knowledge of the ways of the evil Dickens so admired) we should have, as never before in Dickens's novels, the forces of the law, both in the advisory and in the executive branches – arrayed against Evil. It is a small world, but a compact one, this world of professional men, and young men and women connected with our Imperial role (add to them that honourable and adroit young retired Naval officer, Lieutenant Tartar). And in these suggestions of a new Imperial role it has, for all its limited class, geographical boundaries far beyond even the social range of *Bleak House* or *Little Dorrit*.

It is possible that Dickens had shrunk his world because like many ageing novelists he could not encompass the new one; but I don't think so – there are other figures from other classes – I think he arrayed what he felt to be the dependable, good, manly (or womanly) and above all, healthy part of English society against Jasper's evil. Not authority as constituted, or the louder voices: Mr Honeythunder, reformer and philanthropist, is a bullying fraud; the Dean is a time-server; the Mayor is a pompous fool. No, the forces that must meet the evil in contemporary society are private ones; and, despite the dating of the book in earlier time, they are essentially modern, of 1870.

What about the evil forces? Here too there is a modern element, for Mr Jasper with his music and his opium looks forward as did Wrayburn and Light-wood to the nineties – if we did not know that the nineties were already begun by the middle of the century. And for all Jasper's insane passion for Rosebud there is no doubt, I think, that Dickens reflects a more equivocal passion in Jasper's attitude to his 'dear boy', to Edwin himself, whom perhaps he murders. Here we move into the more hidden side of *Tom Brown's Schooldays*, the more hidden side of Victorian life. Jasper is not entirely modern, he is also a crude Gothic figure (going back to Monks in *Oliver Twist* with his fits). But the general picture is clear: manly, gentle courage confronts self-tormented, violent energy, an energy that is wasted as is all criminal energy.

Death

Jasper is by accident of Dickens's death the last of the long line of violent, murdering men, that typify the criminal mind in Dickens's novels. If we could understand this obsession, we should perhaps reach the central core of Dickens's personality – but no personality is finally open to such invasion. Nevertheless we can probe and search for patterns.

Dickens's obsession with murder is from the start closely connected with his obsession with capital punishment, and both are united in his belief that the criminal is a special kind of person set apart from all others – Cain wandering the face of the earth. As early as *Sketches by Boz* he attacked Byron for (among other things) romanticizing murderers. Murderers are not the superhuman Cains of Byron's imagination, but cowardly bullies and vain brutes. Yet in the same book in 'A Visit to Newgate' his voice becomes deep with awe, horror and mystery when he approaches the condemned cell:

> How much more awful is it to reflect on this near vicinity to the dying – to men in full health and vigour, in the flower of youth or the prime of life, with all their facul-

ties and perceptions as acute and perfect as your own; but dying nevertheless – dying as surely – with the hand of death imprinted upon them as indelibly as if mortal disease had wasted their frames to shadows, and corruption had already begun.

Then:

> An overwhelming sense of his helpless, hopeless state rushes upon him [the condemned man], he is lost and stupefied, and has neither thoughts to turn to, nor power to call upon the Almighty Being, from whom alone he can seek mercy and forgiveness, and before whom his repentance can alone avail . . . .

As the hours strike, the condemned man's 'thoughts will wander back to childhood'. Then:

> No matter; he will escape. The night is dark and cold, the gates have been left open, and in an instant he is in the street, flying from the scene of his imprisonment like the wind . . . the open fields are gained . . . . At length he pauses; he must be safe from pursuit now; he will stretch himself on that bank and sleep till sunrise. A period of unconsciousness succeeds. He wakes, cold and wretched. The dull grey light of morning is steady in the cell, and falls upon the form of the attendant turnkey. Confused by his dreams, he starts from his uneasy bed in momentary uncertainty. It is but momentary. Every object in the narrow cell is too frightfully real to admit of doubt or mistake. He is the condemned felon again, guilty and despairing; and in two more hours he will be dead.

This is crude, early stuff, but in its detailed imagination of the terror, hopes, deceptions and sensations of a condemned murderer, it is only the first of many such passages – Fagin, the Gordon rioters, Jonas Chuzzlewit, Mr Carker (whose crime against Mr Dombey makes him like a pursued murderer), Hortense, Rigaud, Headstone, Jasper, all are anatomized, but with the greatest possible tension, drama, and sensational psychology.

All this is in his novels, yet it seems exactly counter to the purposes he expresses in his many journalistic campaigns – first in his *Daily News* letters of 1846 against capital punishment; then after he had been so horrified by the hanging of Mr and Mrs Manning in 1849, which he witnessed, not against execution but only against *public* execution; and in 1856 he is still urging the public not to romanticize murderers, not to play into the hands of vain exhibitionists like the notorious Palmer the Poisoner, but to treat criminals as the dangerous but contemptible scum they truly were. His objection to capital punishment was, as he most roundly asserted, not out of any sympathy for criminals, especially murderers, but because the death penalty (and especially public execution) fed the warped, romantic dreams of the criminal mind, as well as feeding the unhealthy interests of the mob. In his 1846 letters he speaks of a young murderer, Thomas Hocker:

> Here is an insolent, flippant, dissolute youth; aping the man of intrigue and levity; over-dressed, over-confident, inordinately vain of his personal appearance; distin-

guished as to his hair, his cane, snuffbox and singing voice; and unhappily the son of a working shoemaker . . . . How can he distinguish himself? . . . The stage? No, not feasible . . . . A murder, now, would make a noise in the papers! There is the gallows to be sure; but, without that, it would be nothing. Short of that, it wouldn't be fame. Well! We must all die at one time or another . . . . They always die game at the Minor Theatres and the saloons . . . . Come, Tom, get your name up! . . . You are the boy to go through with it and interest the town.

All true enough, possibly, as criminal psychology; but as the article proceeds he seems to have too teasing an interest in the state of Hocker's mind, even the bodily effects of his vain hopes and final terrors. And the same is true in his article ten years later on Palmer, 'On the Demeanour of Murderers'. And it is there in the novels – Jonas Chuzzlewit is a mean brute, but his dreams and terrors after he murders Tiggs are built into Gothic visions, and there is a little too much interest in his body's failure when he is arrested, as there is in the physical reactions of Hortense, the French maid, when Bucket arrests her. In fiction even a prurient interest in condemned men and women may serve art's purpose, but the note is at times distasteful.

More important, there is confusion. A paragraph in his famous *Daily News* letters about judges may serve to explain his feelings more than he realized. In contesting the support of the judges for capital punishment he writes:

There is another and stronger reason still, why a criminal judge is a bad witness in favour of the Punishment of Death. He is a chief actor in the terrible drama of a trial, where the life or death of a fellow creature is at issue. No one who has seen such a trial can fail to know, or can ever forget, its intense interest. I care not how painful this interest to the good, wise judge upon the bench. I admit its painful nature . . . I know the thrall . . . how awfully the prisoner and he confront each other; two mere men, destined one day, however far removed from one another at this time, to stand alike as suppliants at the bar of God. I know all this, I can imagine what the office of the judge costs in the execution of it; but I say that in these strong sensations he is lost, and is unable to abstract the penalty as preventive or example from an experience of it . . . which can be only his, and his alone.

This seems to me well said; but it is also surely clear that the good judge with his mixed emotions is Dickens himself.

He is right, given his view of the criminal mind as special, self-concerned, unrelenting, mean and vain, to urge that all publicity should be removed from it; that if it must be obliterated, then the obliteration should be carried out privately and speedily. But if this evil is so trivial, so coarse and brutish, what is the meaning of this life-long obsession with its workings, especially its working upon the threshold of death? There is sadism here, clearly; and not far from the surface there is self-punishment, a pursuit in every terror, physical and mental, of those violent and lustful elements his strong will so deeply suppressed in himself. But these are surely the usual hidden reverse sides of an implacable pursuit of justice. There is perhaps reflected too deep a horror of his own suppressed self — so that it is elevated into some transcendent evil in a

The grave of Charles Dickens in Poet's Corner, Westminster Abbey.

view of life which, though Christian, was otherwise primarily rational and humanistic. But above all I think there is a preoccupation with the horror of death – death that is to come irrevocably and consciously to a man in his full vigour. I do not doubt that Dickens had a full trust in an after life (though its form may have been shadowy), his positive statements support it, more still his complete rejection of what he thought the impious commercial frauds of the fashionable spiritualist mediums of the sixties. But I think that, even when he seems most weary and worn out in the last decade of his life, his humorous engagement with life never let go of him, nor did his energetic need to act out every moment of his living (and these two powers, after all, are the real foundations of his imaginative genius).

It is not, surely, the New Testament message of the ending of *Little Dorrit* that finally sustained Charles Dickens in his late and pessimistic novels. The nineteenth century, after all, was not the first century A.D., and only a mystic or a divine fool could have believed that the gospels alone could answer the complex contemporary questions of man's role in the world of Chancery and Coketown, Merdledom or the city of Jaggers. Dickens sincerely hoped that the divine fool existed, but he was certainly not one himself. As to mysticism, he did not, like Dostoevsky, have the Tsar for Little Father; nor, much though he respected the English common people, did they have the semi-mystic aura of Dostoevsky's narod, the Russian People. A simple gospel faith was precious to Dickens, but it is hard to believe that it finally preserved him in his stupendous labours. It is not the combination of New Testament truth and Victorian wedding bells with which his great novels end that truly give them their life; that life comes from his intense enjoyment of human activity – not least when it is absurd and devilish. This joy in watching human behaviour is the key to his greatness; and perhaps also a measure of his limitation. For though no George Eliot or Thomas Hardy, what he enjoys is finally, though richly various, human predictability – his power to predict the goodness, the wickedness and the absurdity of his own characters. But then what novelists have not been so limited? Tolstoy perhaps; Stendhal in the first three quarters of *The Charterhouse of Parma*. For the rest, the quirks, the apparent unexpectedness of some fictional life, are no more than a brilliant technical trick (often delightful as well as admirable as in, say, Sterne or Diderot, but still a trick). Within this almost universal limit Dickens had extraordinary powers of playing with human speech, human manners and above all human environment, and making works of art out of them. Such a man, whatever his spiritual convictions, must be both fearful of giving up life (especially of doing so knowingly) and morbidly curious about the feelings of those who have to die.

In the last five years or so of his life he must have known many moments of horrible certainty that the end was coming soon; perhaps most of all when he appears to be singing to keep his spirits up. To Katey, his daughter, on her last visit to Gad's Hill, he said that he hoped for great things from *Edwin Drood*, 'if, please God, I live to finish it . . . . I say if, because, you know, my dear child, I have not been strong lately'. Perhaps it was a sense of the shortness of time left to him that made him abandon his usual routine on 8 June and work all day in the chalet on his novel. At dinner he admitted to Georgina that for an hour he had been very ill. Some moments later he rose from the table, saying he must go to London, and collapsed. He lay on a sofa in the dining room breathing heavily all that night and the next day. At six o'clock in the evening of 9 June 1870 he died.

So much has been written about the unhappiness of his last years and the suicidal nature of his readings, that his death has been made to seem for us (and for him) an inevitable, almost consoling curtain to a play that was over. With our preference for disregarding death, for letting men and women be shuffled off the scene, such a version is satisfactory, but it is against all that the Dickens world stands for. Dickens 'died in harness' because it was the nature of his eager, vital personality to explore and fight to the end, not because it is comforting for us to think that he had a fitting end to his life. Our response to his death should be entirely a sense of loss for the riches he still had to give us and could not. In this sense the Victorians understood better. They mourned his death all over the world as a diminution of the richness of their lives. Luke Fildes's 'Empty Chair' was not, as we have come to think, a sentimentalism, but a fitting tribute to the void left by this untimely parting. The teasing possibility of a whole new extension to his world in *Edwin Drood* remains as a permanent reminder of it. But the lasting legacy of Dickens is the wonderful, shaped vitality of his novels: a life so strong and so individual that it could feed writers following him as diverse and idiosyncratic as Dostoevsky and Daudet, Gissing and Shaw, Proust and Kafka, Conrad and Evelyn Waugh; and yet be accounted, as he rightly called himself, 'Inimitable'.

'The Empty Chair', from *Judy*, 1870.

Acknowledgments for Illustrations

Colour

Frontispiece reverse by courtesy of Gordon Beckwith, Esq.
Frontispiece by courtesy of Mrs. Roger Field. 'A Sunny Day' by Mulready, 1874.
Page 25 from the Opie Collection. Photo: Phototeale, Hampshire, England.
Page 26 by courtesy of Mrs Linda Hannas. Photo: Scott Lauder Photography, Kent, England.
Page 39 from the Mansell Collection, London.
Pages 40 and 41 from the George Speaight Collection.
Page 42 by courtesy of the Victoria & Albert Museum, London. Photo: Michael Holford, London.
Page 69 detail, by courtesy of the Bury Public Library and Art Gallery, Lancashire, England.
Page 72 detail, by courtesy of the Rutland Gallery, London.
Pages 85 and 142 details, both by courtesy of the Royal Holloway College, Egham, England.
Page 86 detail, from the Raymond Mander and Joe Mitchenson Theatre Collection, London.
Page 111 detail, by courtesy of the Harrogate Art Gallery, Yorkshire, England.
Page 125 detail, by courtesy of John Rickett, Esq.
Pages 126 and 127 by courtesy of the Borough Library, Richmond upon Thames, England.
Page 128 by courtesy of the Guildhall Art Gallery, London.
Page 141 detail, from the Tate Gallery, London.
Page 155 detail, by courtesy of the Birmingham City Museum and Art Gallery, Birmingham, England.
Pages 156 and 157 by courtesy of Mrs B. Fane.

Page 158 detail, copyright reserved.
Page 172 detail, by courtesy of Alfred Dunhill Ltd., London. Photo: by courtesy of Sir Isaac Pitman & Sons, Ltd., London.
Page 197 detail, from the Tate Gallery, London.
Page 198 by courtesy of Sir William Cooper, Bt.
Page 223 by courtesy of the Tunbridge Wells Museum, Kent, England.
Page 249 by courtesy of the trustees of Sir Colin and Lady Anderson.
Page 250 by courtesy of the Victoria & Albert Museum, London.
Pages 264 and 265 by courtesy of the Marquess of Northampton.
Page 266 by courtesy of the University of London.

The illustrations on pages 55 (detail), 56 (detail), 70 and 71, 112 (detail), 171, 224 (detail), 263 (detail) are shown by courtesy of the trustees of the London Museum.

The photographs on the frontispiece reverse and pages 39, 40 and 41, 85, 86, 126 and 127, 141, 142, 156 and 157, 197, 198, 250, 264 and 265 are by John Freeman Ltd, London.

The photographs on the frontispiece and pages 69, 111, 125, 128, 155, 223, 249 are by permission of the Royal Academy of Arts, London.

In many cases the illustrations of paintings reproduced in this book do not comprise the entire canvas area. Where only a detail has been reproduced, this is specifically mentioned.

Monochrome

The Trustees of the Dickens House gave permission to reproduce the illustrations on the following pages, which were photographed by Alexandra Lawrence, London: 16, 108 (both), 183 (both), 174, 219, 246, 258, 259 (both), 274 and 275 (all), 277 (both).

The Mansell Collection, London, supplied the originals of the illustrations on the following pages: 10, 11 (both), 23, 48, 66, 92, 95, 97 (left), 117, 130, 151, 167, 168 (top), 184, 187, 190, 192 (both), 193 (both), 195, 200 (both), 203 (both), 214 (right), 227, 229, 243, 269, 279 (left), 297.

The Mary Evans Picture Library, London, supplied the originals of the illustrations on the following pages: 12, 14, 33, 33 (right), 47, 65, 80, 97 (right), 118, 122, 123, 163, 166, 169, 202, 214 (left), 221, 232 (right), 279 (right), 284.

John Freeman Ltd, London, photographed the illustrations on the following pages: 17, 19, 36 (both), 46 (both), 53, 75, 76, 83, 89, 106, 115, 131 (both), 133 (both), 137, 139, 161 (both), 176 (both), 191, 201, 204, 208, 230 (both), 232 (left), 240 (left), 247 (right), 286 (right), 295.

Page 13 drawn by George Cruikshank.
Page 17 from *Life in London* by Pierce Egan.
Page 19 from *The Life and Adventures of Michael Armstrong, the factory boy!* by Frances Trollope, illustrated by A. Hervieu.
Page 23 Little Red Riding Hood by Doré.
Page 31 Irvingites – 'The Sinner on the Cutty Stool'.
Page 33 from *The Life and Exploits of Don Quixote*, abridged, 1778, from the Opie Collection. Photo: Phototeale, Hampshire, England; and right, from *The Citizen of the World*, 1797.
Page 34 by courtesy of the trustees of the London Museum.
Page 35 from *Young Troublesome or Master Jacky's Holidays*, designed and etched by John Leech, from the George Speaight Collection.
Page 36 Chatham by G. Shepherd; and below, Gravesend by H. Harris.
Page 37 from the Rochester Museum. Photo: M. Harris, Kent.
Page 46 top, Potter Bequest, by courtesy of the trustees of the British Museum.
Page 46 bottom, Building the Stationary Engine house, Camden Town, 1837, by courtesy of the trustees of the British Museum.
Page 47 drawn by George Cruikshank.
Page 48 'Inside' by Phiz.
Page 53 Crace Collection, by courtesy of the trustees of the British Museum.
Page 62 both drawn by George Cruikshank, from the Raymond Mander and Joe Mitchenson Theatre Collection, London.
Page 65 the prerogative office.
Page 66 from *Pickwick Papers*.
Page 75 and Page 76 by courtesy of the trustees of the British Museum.
Page 77 from the Rochester Museum. Photo: M. Harris, Kent.
Page 88 from *London* by Doré and Jerrold. Photo: Alexandra Lawrence, London.
Page 89 drawing by T. H. Shepherd from the Crace Collection, by courtesy of the trustees of the British Museum.
Page 91 from *The Mysteries of London* by G. W. M. Reynolds, illustrated by G. Stiff, from the George Speaight Collection. Photo: Alexandra Lawrence, London.
Page 95 'Tremendous Sacrifice' by George Cruikshank.
Page 97 Mary Magdalen by C. Staal; and right, 'Day's Doings II: a pretty little supper party interrupted'.
Page 104 from the Raymond Mander and Joe Mitchenson Theatre Collection, London.
Page 106 Abbotsford by T. H. Shepherd, from 'Views of Edinburgh', by courtesy of the trustees of the British Museum.

Page 109 by courtesy of the trustees of the National Portrait Gallery, London.
Page 121 from *London*, by Doré and Jerrold. Photo: Alexandra Lawrence, London.
Page 130 'Homes of the London Poor' by C. W. Skeeres, view of Wild Court.
Page 135 'The Manager's Daughter' by C. K. Lancaster, 1837, from original by Pierce Egan, from the Raymond Mander and Joe Mitchenson Theatre Collection, London.
Page 136 Enthoven Collection, Victoria & Albert Museum, London. Photo: Alexandra Lawrence.
Page 139 from the *Illustrated London News*, 1867.
Page 153 Broadstairs by R. Brandard. Photo: Courtauld Institute, London.
Page 161 A skin lodge of an Assiniboin chief, and Indians hunting bison.
Page 165 drawn and etched by T. Horner, 1836, from the New York Public Library.
Page 166 from *The Graphic*, 1870.
Page 167 Slaves for sale in New Orleans.
Page 168 top 'A race for the buck horns' (on centre ship, *Queen of the West*).
Page 168 bottom 'The Mississippi delta, with hunter' anon. By courtesy of Christie, Manson & Woods Ltd. Photo: A. C. Cooper, London.
Page 169 Horse-shoe falls, Niagara, by T. Allom, 1839.
Page 175 by courtesy of the University of London Library.
Page 184 Genoa, from The Heights.
Page 186 from the Tate Gallery, London.
Page 189 both by courtesy of Christie, Manson & Woods Ltd. Photo: A. C. Cooper, London.
Page 190 drawn by Pisan.
Page 193 top, Alfred submitting his law to the Witan by Bridges, and below, Cromwell refusing the crown, after Maguire.
Page 195 'Midnight, the sub-editor's room'.
Page 201 'Conflict at Lucerne' from the *Illustrated London News*, 1845.
Page 202 from the *Illustrated London News*, 1846.
Page 204 from the *Illustrated London News*, 1848.
Page 213 by courtesy of the Earl of Shelburne. Photo: Courtauld Institute, London.
Page 215 from *Curiosities of Street Literature*, from the George Speaight Collection. Photo: Alexandra Lawrence, London.
Page 225 a series of eight plates by George Cruikshank.
Page 230 both from *The Life and Adventures of Michael Armstrong, the factory boy!* by Frances Trollope, illustrated by A. Hervieu.
Page 232 right, 'The Bank Nun', an actual Chancery victim.
Page 237 from the *Illustrated Times*, 1862.
Page 240 from the *Illustrated London News*, 1854; and right, 'The judicious bottleholder or Downing Street pet'. Photo: Courtauld Institute, London.
Page 242 photo: Courtauld Institute, London.
Page 243 'Supper scene in Kings Bench prison' by Phillips.
Page 247 from the Rochester Museum. Photo: M. Harris, Kent; and right, from the *Illustrated London News*, 1849.
Page 268 by courtesy of the Harris Museum and Art Gallery, Preston, England. Photo: by permission of the Royal Academy of Arts, London.
Pages 274 and 275 all Dickens's children except Alfred Tennyson, the sixth child, of whom there is no picture as a child, and Dora Annie, the ninth child, who died in infancy.
Page 279 right, title page of a pamphlet by Robert Cruikshank.
Page 282 by courtesy of the trustees of the London Museum.
Page 286 left, by courtesy of the trustees of the London Museum.
Page 288 both from *London* by Doré and Jerrold. Photo: Alexandra Lawrence, London.
Page 295 from *The Graphic*, 1870.

Index

Titles of works are in *italics*.
Names of characters are followed by an abbreviated title of the work they appear in (see below).
'Mr', etc., is added only where necessary.
Page-references: the more important references are sometimes quoted first.
Illustrations: *numbers in italics* indicate pages on which text illustrations occur, or page-numbers of colour plates.

Abbreviations

D	Charles Dickens
D.'s	Charles Dickens's
(BH)	Bleak House
(BR)	Barnaby Rudge
(CC)	A Christmas Carol
(Ch)	The Chimes
(DC)	David Copperfield
(DS)	Dombey & Son

(ED)	Edwin Drood
(GE)	Great Expectations
(HM)	The Haunted Man
(HT)	Hard Times
(HW)	Household Words
(LD)	Little Dorrit
(MC)	Martin Chuzzlewit
(MH)	Master Humphrey's Clock

(NN)	Nicholas Nickleby
(OC)	The Old Curiosity Shop
(OM)	Our Mutual Friend
(OT)	Oliver Twist
(PP)	Pickwick Papers
(SB)	Sketches by Boz
(T2)	A Tale of Two Cities
(UT)	The Uncommercial Traveller

These are placed immediately after the surname where there are several persons.
Artists: illustration-references include their portraits and their works.

PR4581 .W52   CU-Main
c.1
Wilson, Angus./World of Charles Dickens.

3 9371 00022 8403